essential
VEGETARIAN

essential
VEGETARIAN

bay books

This edition published in 2012 by Bay Books, an imprint of Murdoch Books Pty Limited
First published in 2011 by Murdoch Books Pty Limited

Murdoch Books Australia
Pier 8/9
23 Hickson Road
Millers Point NSW 2000
Phone: +61 (0) 2 8220 2000
Fax: +61 (0) 2 8220 2558
www.murdochbooks.com.au

Publisher: Kylie Walker
Project Editor: Melody Lord
Food Editor: Anneka Manning
Editor: Katri Hilden
Concept Design: Vivien Sung
Designer: Susanne Geppert

Photographers: Jared Fowler, Julie Renouf
Stylist: Cherise Koch
Food preparation: Alan Wilson

Text copyright © Murdoch Books Pty Limited
Based on The essential Vegetarian cookbook, first published by Murdoch Books in 1996
Recipes developed in the Murdoch Books Test Kitchen
Design copyright © Murdoch Books Pty Limited

ISBN: 978-1-74266-703-4

Printed by 1010 Printing International Limited, China

IMPORTANT: Those who might be at risk from the effects of salmonella poisoning (the elderly, pregnant women, young children and those suffering from immune deficiency diseases) should consult their doctor with any concerns about eating raw eggs.

CONVERSION GUIDE: Cooking times may vary depending on the oven you are using. For fan-forced ovens, as a general rule, set the oven temperature to 20oC (35oF) lower than indicated in the recipe. We have used 20 ml (4 teaspoon) tablespoon measures. If you are using a 15 ml (3 teaspoon) tablespoon add an extra teaspoon for each tablespoon specified. We have used 60 g (Grade 3) eggs in all recipes.

a world of flavours

Vegetarian fare is no longer a poor relation on the restaurant menu, no longer regarded as the province of the brown-rice-and-lentils brigade. Our eating habits have evolved to such a point that many of us live on a virtually meat-free diet without considering ourselves strict vegetarians — and not simply because of a particular philosophy, or for reasons of health or economy. Today's widespread interest in food and cooking, our discovery of the extensive range of appetising non-meat dishes from other countries, and the sheer abundance of all kinds of vegetables, grains, nuts and pulses now available have combined to make vegetarian cooking exciting and innovative, and extended our appreciation of good food.

contents

fettuccine with creamy mushroom and bean sauce (page 98)

the vegetarian choice

A good vegetarian diet meets all today's requirements: it's nutritionally sound, easy to follow, and gastronomically sensational. With the days of overcooked vegetables and a-hundred-ways-with-soya-beans long gone, a vegetarian menu is now first choice for a growing number of people of all ages and lifestyles.

People can be drawn to a vegetarian diet for a variety of reasons. Some have ethical or health concerns, while for others it is a matter of religious belief.

However, the decision to eat in this way could just as easily be an aesthetic or gastronomic one. The variety of ingredients, abundance of possible dishes and the sheer scope that vegetarian cuisine offers for creative cooking and eating are often dismissed or not recognised by confirmed meat-eaters.

For many in the developed world, meat — and less often chicken or fish — has always been the 'easy' option. Certainly, flesh foods have formed the centrepiece of most meals. This tradition has led to a diet that is often lacking in variety. Consequently, it lacks a beneficial balance of nutrients, as well as leading to the health consequences from eating too many saturated fats. A diet that relies heavily on meat is generally a product of affluence, and not necessarily a good one.

Many people have recognised an imbalance in their way of eating and are modifying the amount of flesh foods included in their diets. The discovery of vegetarian food often begins in this way. As people gain confidence, experiment more and discover the pleasures of cooking vegetarian foods — the wealth of colours, flavours, textures and aromas — they often welcome increased vitality and say goodbye to weight problems. Other benefits people report include clearer skin and less constipation — so much so that many choose to abandon eating meat and fish altogether.

The term 'vegetarian' is often used quite loosely. Some people call themselves vegetarian (or semi-vegetarian) while still eating a little fish or chicken on occasion but no red meat. Many just exclude all meat and fish from their diets. Vegans, on the other hand, exclude all other animal products such as milk, cheese, eggs and honey. Most vegetarians, however, are lacto-ovo vegetarians, who still eat eggs and dairy products.

Meatless meals need never be bland or boring. They offer enormous variety, stimulating the imagination and even offering the opportunity to learn new cooking skills. Vegetarian cuisine offers the cook much scope to be inventive.

some basic principles

Many people who have discovered the joys of vegetarian eating are unaware of a few dietary pitfalls that can easily be avoided with a little knowledge. With the increasing popularity of vegetarian food, and despite a high level of awareness of basic facts about nutrition, there are still gaps in many people's knowledge about how to get the most out of their diet. Filling in these nutritional gaps can enhance the vegetarian experience and make it beneficial as well as enjoyable.

If you were raised as a vegetarian, you are probably already in the habit of making sure all your nutritional needs are met, but for those making the transition from eating flesh foods — or even to eating substantially less of them — there are a few important issues to bear in mind.

■ It is perfectly possible, and not at all difficult, to live a healthy life eating only vegetarian foods. The key is to ensure variety in the diet: eat as many different kinds of food as possible and all the essential nutrients that the body requires will be available.

■ It is a common mistake to think in terms of 'substituting' the nutrients provided by meat, fish or poultry. A little knowledge, awareness and enthusiasm for trying new things, plus a willingness to broaden your culinary repertoire to include delicious vegetarian dishes from all over the world, is more important than any specialised scientific knowledge about nutrition.

■ Make sure you include grains, pulses, vegetables, fruit — and, if you are not a vegan, eggs and dairy food — in your diet and you can't go wrong.

■ Many studies have shown that populations with a diet that is high in unrefined foods and fibre and low in salt and sugar have a lower incidence of blood pressure problems, heart disease, bowel disease (including cancer), diabetes and gallstones. Unrefined whole foods are best. (The term 'unprocessed' is misleading, since many valuable foods must undergo change of some sort before we eat them: think of pasta and rice, many other grains, and bread.)

■ It is important that any produce you buy is as fresh as possible so that the nutrients have not had time to deteriorate. For this reason, as well as for economy, it is a good idea to get into the habit of shopping and eating seasonally, when fruit and vegetables are at their freshest, most flavoursome and cheapest.

■ Similarly, it is wise to freeze some fruits and vegetables when they are in season and abundant. Also, if you get into the habit of preparing sauces from tomatoes and red capsicums (peppers), and purées from berries and stone fruits, you can enjoy the taste of summer throughout the year.

is a vegetarian diet safe for children?

Children thrive on a vegetarian diet — and in fact many make the choice for themselves at quite an early age.

When planning meals for vegetarian children, the principle of maximising the number of different kinds of food in the diet is even more vital. Most of the nutritional needs of children will be met this way, but there are a few important things to remember.

Pulses such as beans and lentils, eaten at the same meal with grains, nuts or seeds, provide complete protein, which is an absolute necessity for children. This is not as daunting or difficult as it may sound: the possibilities can be as simple as serving baked beans on toast; lentils with rice; a felafel sandwich; or serving a red kidney bean chilli with tortillas or tacos.

Growing children need concentrated foods rich in the many nutrients their bodies require, and they also need more fat in their diets than adults. There are lots of healthy ways for children to obtain healthy fats: convenient sources include peanut butter, avocado, cheese, yoghurt and nuts. Most children enjoy all these foods anyway, which means there is no excuse for resorting to nutritionally bankrupt sources such as cakes, biscuits, chocolate, or fried take-away foods.

Also, make sure your children eat a good breakfast, being sure to avoid sugary, processed cereals. If you start them off eating home-made muesli and wholemeal (whole-wheat) toast, you'll set up an eating pattern that will benefit them all their life.

about this book

This book features recipes using no flesh foods, but occasionally an option such as fish sauce is included as a flavouring to keep a recipe more authentic to its original cuisine. It is not specifically a vegan cookbook, in that eggs, butter, milk and cream are used liberally. However, there are plenty of recipes suitable for vegans, particularly recipes using grains.

Nor is this a book of vegetarian substitutes for a meat-centred diet, offering recipes for pale imitations of meatloaf or burgers. The recipes are for anyone who loves preparing, serving and eating good food.

All the delights of richer foods are available for vegetarians — for example, there are plenty of luscious desserts to be sampled here. This is neither a diet book nor a health food book, but is designed to expand the menu of possibilities, to show that one can simultaneously be a connoisseur of good food, a fine cook *and* a vegetarian.

For those of us who have a busy lifestyle (and who hasn't, these days?) we've included a selection of fast recipes that can be made from beginning to end within 30 minutes. They're all listed in the index under Fast recipes for easy reference.

Our star rating:

When we test recipes, we rate them for ease of preparation. The following cookery ratings are used in this book:

✹   A single star indicates a recipe that is simple and generally quick to make, perfect for beginners.

✹✹   Two stars indicate the need for a little more care or a little more time.

✹✹✹   Three stars indicate special dishes that need more investment in time, care and patience, but the results are worth it. Even beginners can make these dishes as long as the recipe is followed carefully.

nutritious and delicious

the healthy food pyramid

It is just as possible to have a poor diet eating exclusively vegetarian foods as it is eating excessive amounts of animal products. The 'vegetarian food pyramid' is a good starting point if you want to check whether your diet is adequate. Its principles are simple:

eat most
- grains: wheat, rice, barley, corn, oats, rye, millet, buckwheat
- foods made from grains: pasta, bread, wholegrain breakfast cereals
- fruit and vegetables

eat moderately
- dairy: milk, yoghurt, cheese
- pulses: peas, beans of all kinds, and lentils
- nuts
- eggs

eat least
- sugar, honey
- butter, cream
- margarine, oils
- alcohol, tea, coffee

Meal planning becomes easier if you make a habit of using the food pyramid as a guide. There should be in each day's diet a preponderance of foods from the 'Eat Most' group: fruit, cereals and toast for breakfast, bread or bread rolls, salads or cooked vegetable dishes and fruit for lunch; pasta or a rice-based main course for dinner with fresh bread or rolls, and more fruit for dessert or snacks.

Small amounts of dairy foods from the 'Eat Moderately' group can be part of the day's meals (unless you are a vegan): for example yoghurt with breakfast or lunch, a little cheese with lunch or dinner. Dinner or lunch can include filling dishes and hearty soups made from dried beans or lentils, as well as tasty egg dishes. Nuts are great for snacking.

The 'Eat Least' category means exactly that — a small amount of butter or margarine on your breakfast toast, a little extra virgin olive oil with your salad or to stir-fry vegetables for the evening meal, and the occasional glass of wine with dinner. A sugary treat is fine if it isn't a regular occurrence, and tea and coffee can be enjoyed in moderation.

You can balance the nutritional content of the day's meals so that the overall pattern easily satisfies the food pyramid guidelines. Compensate for an unavoidably fatty lunch, for example, with an evening meal made up of vegetables, grains and fruit.

Eating out can be a nutritional trap, but it is easy to keep the food pyramid in mind when ordering food (salads, soups and bread for first courses, plus fruit and cheese instead of dessert), and to compensate for any imbalances when preparing food for yourself at home.

Changing the habits of a lifetime is not something we can do overnight. If your usual diet doesn't bear much resemblance to the food pyramid, you can move gradually towards a healthier way of eating. Don't worry to begin with if every meal is not perfectly balanced. You can correct the proportions over the course of each week as you adjust to buying and cooking healthier foods, and experiment with new dishes.

Replace refined foods with whole foods, and high-fat dairy products with reduced-fat versions. Check food labels for salt, sugar and fat content, and for food additives. Have fun making your own versions of soups, sauces and even breakfast cereals, rather than always buying the ready-made product. This way it is easy to control what goes into your body.

Children generally enjoy healthy eating options: pastas, fruit, yoghurt, peanut butter, cheese, milk and nuts are usually popular. The difficulties only arise if you are trying to change bad habits, so remember that doing it gradually is best.

menu planning

Aim to shop and eat for good health, using the food pyramid as a guide. Stock up on several different kinds of rice, couscous, a variety of pastas, lots of breads (freeze loaves and flatbreads if you have room), breakfast cereals and interesting flours.

Get into the habit of replenishing your store of fresh produce regularly, but do it systematically. To avoid wastage, shop with some idea of your meal plans from week to week. Taking advantage of enticing seasonal produce by buying up big is pointless if fruit and vegetables languish at the bottom of your refrigerator while you think of a way to use them. Vary your choices as much as possible to keep your diet interesting and to maximise the nutritional benefits.

Buy cheeses, milk, yoghurt and eggs regularly, but plan how much you are likely to need to avoid introducing too much fat into your diet.

Tinned foods are an essential pantry item: tinned beans of every variety are great time-savers if you don't want to soak and cook your own. Tomato pastes (concentrated purées) and tinned tomatoes are invaluable as they can be used to flavour so many different kinds of meals. Bottled sauces such as pesto, basic pasta sauces and chilli sauce are other invaluable flavour enhancers. Also keep a selection of oils on hand — extra virgin olive oil for flavour, and lighter grades and vegetable oils for cooking.

carbohydrates

The critical importance of complex carbohydrates in a good diet cannot be overstated. Carbohydrates are vital for energy. They occur in the form of starches and sugars from grains and their products — flour, bread and pasta; in potatoes, pulses and to a lesser degree nuts; and in fruits and sugars.

There are probably still people who think potatoes are fattening, but fortunately we now have a far greater awareness of the benefits of loading our diet with pasta, rice, breads, cereals — and yes, potatoes. It is difficult to eat too much carbohydrate — usually excess flab comes from eating too much fat, rather than too much carbohydrate.

There is a whole range of delicious grain foods that has only recently come into its own in the Western diet. They include: couscous, buckwheat, quinoa and hybrid grains such as triticale, which has been bred from wheat and rye and has a deliciously nutty flavour — try it instead of, or as well as, rolled (porridge) oats in home-made muesli. Take advantage of these grains to add variety to your menus.

Many different rices are now readily available: fragrant basmati and jasmine rice; pearly arborio, essential for the perfect risotto; and wild rice (actually an aquatic grass), which, although expensive, is available in more economical mixtures and makes a delicious change.

The fibre component of carbohydrate foods is a bonus, and the less processing the food has undergone the more of it there will be. The presence of fibre in complex carbohydrates allows the energy from sugars to be used by the body at an even rate, whereas refined sugars hit the bloodstream rapidly and are quickly used, leaving energy levels depleted. This is why you may feel elated and then lethargic in quick succession after eating sugary foods. Complex carbohydrates, with a sustained release of energy, provide more stamina.

foods rich in complex carbohydrates

- breads
- potatoes
- rices
- wheat
- barley
- corn
- buckwheat
- rye
- dried beans
- bananas
- pasta

tea and coffee substitutes

If you wish to reduce your intake of caffeine, there are several tasty alternatives to coffee and tea available from supermarkets and health food stores. Decaffeinated coffees that have been processed using water extraction rather than chemicals are best. Cereal-based coffee substitutes, made from roasted grains, can be an acquired taste, but many are quite palatable. Various brands of low-tannin teas are also available, and it's worth remembering that Chinese tea is low in caffeine and very refreshing. Many different fragrant herbal teas are delicious by themselves or with a little honey or lemon juice added. Carob powder makes a warming drink to replace caffeine-rich cocoa — prepare it using skim milk and add a cinnamon stick.

Instead of cola drinks, try unsweetened fruit juice mixed with mineral water, or plain mineral water with a squeeze of lime juice — heavenly on a hot day. Many refreshing fruit juice and yoghurt drinks can be whipped up in the blender with some crushed ice. Make a deliciously filling and healthy smoothie with skim milk, yoghurt, a ripe banana and a sprinkling of nutmeg. Or try a frappé — crushed ice and fresh fruit whipped together in a blender. A mango frappé is one of life's little joys.

ABOVE: Pasta is one of the best sources of carbohydrates. Combined with fresh vegetables and nuts — such as Tagliatelle with tomato and walnut sauce (page 102) — it is a quick and delicious source of energy.

fibre

The term 'fibre' includes the cellulose and gums found in fruit and vegetables. Animal products do not contain any fibre at all — there is none in dairy foods, fish, poultry or meat, despite their sometimes chewy texture. A well-balanced vegetarian diet, on the other hand, will be naturally rich in fibre.

Among other things, fibre acts as a broom in the bowel by moving food along at such a rate that the potential for problems is minimised. It prevents constipation and lowers the risk of bowel cancer and other intestinal malfunctions.

Because different types of dietary fibre have different functions, again it is important to vary the diet as much as possible. Some types of fibre (mainly from fruit and vegetables) help lower blood cholesterol. It is not enough — as was the fad at one time — to simply heap spoonfuls of unprocessed bran onto your breakfast cereal. Apart from some uncomfortable consequences while the body adjusts to the unfamiliar onslaught of fibre, unprocessed bran contains large amounts of phytic acid, which inhibits the uptake of iron. Since non-meat eaters need to maximise their intake of iron from sources other than meat, this fad is to be avoided.

For overall balance, it is a good idea to try to include some fibre-rich foods in every meal.

foods rich in fibre

- dried beans and peas
- fresh green beans and peas
- cabbages
- carrots
- potatoes (especially in their jackets)
- spinach
- corn
- cereals such as oats and wheat (if wholegrain, germ and husk included)
- products made from whole grains, such as wholemeal (whole-wheat) bread

ABOVE: There is more fibre in wholemeal (whole-wheat) bread than white bread, but even white bread contains some fibre (you can now also buy white flour boosted with added fibre). Lemon pepper bread (page 196) is an example of a quick-to-make, yeast-free bread. It has a chewy crust, a delicious cheesy taste and plenty of fibre.

smart shopping

- Never shop for food when you are hungry. Foods high in sugar and fat never look quite so inviting as when you're desperate for a quick snack.
- Resist sweet and fat-laden food at the supermarket and you won't have to resist it again, while you're watching TV and feel the urge for a chocolate treat.
- Keeping unhealthy food out of your kitchen means that your children will naturally grow up healthier. If there are no chips in the house, they'll eat fruit.
- Read food labels. When you are at the supermarket, take the time to read the labels of any tinned, bottled or frozen food. You'll be surprised at how much salt, sugar, oil and additives some foods contain. For example, you might think that all brands of tomato pasta sauce are the same, but some contain sugar and some do not.

- dried fruits (apricots are good)
- fresh fruit, especially apples, bananas and oranges — it is important to eat the whole fruit and not just drink the juice.

a word about sugar

Excessive amounts of sugar in the diet interfere with the body's ability to metabolise fat. If you eat lots of sugar, the fat you eat will be stored more readily as body fat, instead of being 'burned off' with physical activity.

Few people, however, are happy to eliminate sugar entirely from their diets as they simply enjoy the taste too much.

Like all good things, sugar is fine in moderation. A delicious pudding or sweet treat enjoyed on a special occasion does no harm; it is when these foods displace other foods of more nutritional value that problems arise.

Do remember, however, that cane sugar is valueless in terms of vitamins and minerals. Those with a sweet tooth can always indulge in the many delicious fruits available in season, for the sugars they contain come accompanied by fibre and other nutrients. Fruits are also more filling than other forms of sweet foods, so there is less danger of overeating.

complex carbohydrates

Complex carbohydrates fill you up while adding valuable vitamins and minerals to your diet, with little fat. They are economical, tasty, and should make up about 50 per cent of your daily energy intake.

Baked beans
Carbohydrate per 100 g: 11.2 g
Fat per 100 g: 0.5 g

Bread
Carbohydrate per 100 g: 47.3 g
Fat per 100 g: 2.5 g

Butterbeans (lima beans), cooked
Carbohydrate per 100 g: 10.2 g
Fat per 100 g: 0.3 g

Burghul (bulgur), soaked
Carbohydrate per 100 g: 30 g
Fat per 100 g: 0.9 g

Chickpeas, cooked
Carbohydrate per 100 g: 13 g
Fat per 100 g: 2 g

Corn, cooked
Carbohydrate per 100 g: 20 g
Fat per 100 g: 1 g

Lentils, cooked
Carbohydrate per 100 g: 9.5 g
Fat per 100 g: 0.4 g

Oats, raw
Carbohydrate per 100 g: 61 g
Fat per 100 g: 8.5 g

Pasta, cooked
Carbohydrate per 100 g: 24.6 g
Fat per 100 g: 0.3 g

Pearl barley, cooked
Carbohydrate per 100 g: 21 g
Fat per 100 g: 0.9 g

Polenta, cooked
Carbohydrate per 100 g: 40 g
Fat per 100 g: 1 g

Potato, cooked
Carbohydrate per 100 g: 10 g
Fat per 100 g: 0.1 g

Puffed millet
Carbohydrate per 100 g: 77 g
Fat per 100 g: 2.9 g

Quinoa, dry
Carbohydrate per 100 g: 70 g
Fat per 100 g: 3 g

Red kidney beans, cooked
Carbohydrate per 100 g: 9 g
Fat per 100 g: 0.5 g

Rice, cooked
Carbohydrate per 100 g: 28 g
Fat per 100 g: 0.2 g

Sweet potato, cooked
Carbohydrate per 100 g 16.7 g
Fat per 100 g: 0.1 g

finding fibre

The value of fibre in our diet has been widely
recognised in recent years as an aid to digestion
and even a protection against disease. The
recommended daily intake is 25–30 grams.

Apricots, dried
Fibre per 100 g: 10 g
Fat per 100 g: 0 g

Bran cereal
Fibre per 100 g: 28 g
Fat per 100 g: 4 g

Brussels sprouts, cooked
Fibre per 100 g: 3.5 g
Fat per 100 g: 0 g

Coconut, fresh
Fibre per 100 g: 8 g
Fat per 100 g: 29 g

Corn, tinned
Fibre per 100 g: 3.2 g
Fat per 100 g: 1.2 g

Dates, dried
Fibre per 100 g: 10 g
Fat per 100 g: 0 g

Figs, dried
Fibre per 100 g: 14 g
Fat per 100 g: 1 g

Haricot beans, cooked
Fibre per 100 g: 8.0 g
Fat per 100 g: 2.2 g

Hazelnuts
Fibre per 100 g: 10 g
Fat per 100 g: 61 g

Lentils, cooked
Fibre per 100 g: 3.5 g
Fat per 100 g: 0.7 g

Peanuts
Fibre per 100 g: 8 g
Fat per 100 g: 52 g

Pine nuts
Fibre per 100 g: 15 g
Fat per 100 g: 70 g

Pistachio nuts
Fibre per 100 g: 10 g
Fat per 100 g: 50 g

Prunes, tinned
Fibre per 100 g: 8.0 g
Fat per 100 g: 0 g

Pumpkin seeds
Fibre per 100 g: 25 g
Fat per 100 g: 15 g

Raisins
Fibre per 100 g: 5 g
Fat per 100 g: 1 g

Red kidney beans, cooked
Fibre per 100 g: 11 g
Fat per 100 g: 0.3 g

Rice, brown/wild, cooked
Fibre per 100 g: 2 g
Fat per 100 g: 0.9 g

Rolled (porridge) oats, cooked
Fibre per 100 g: 1.0 g
Fat per 100 g: 2.2 g

Sesame seeds
Fibre per 100 g: 10 g
Fat per 100 g: 55 g

Soya beans, cooked
Fibre per 100 g: 7 g
Fat per 100 g: 7 g

Split peas, cooked
Fibre per 100 g: 4 g
Fat per 100 g: 0.3 g

Sultanas
Fibre per 100 g: 5 g
Fat per 100 g: 0 g

Sunflower seeds
Fibre per 100 g: 3.3 g
Fat per 100 g: 47 g

Walnuts
Fibre per 100 g: 6 g
Fat per 100 g: 70 g

Tamarillo
Fibre per 100 g: 4.6 g
Fat per 100 g: 0 g

Strawberries
Fibre per 100 g: 2.4 g
Fat per 100 g: 0 g

Peas, fresh
Fibre per 100 g: 7 g
Fat per 100 g: 0.6 g

Broad beans
Fibre per 100 g: 4.2 g
Fat per 100 g: 0 g

Silverbeet, cooked
Fibre per 100 g: 3.3 g
Fat per 100 g: 0 g

Pumpkin, cooked
Fibre per 100 g: 1.8 g
Fat per 100 g: 0.5 g

Tomatoes
Fibre per 100 g: 1 g
Fat per 100 g: 0 g

Parsley
Fibre per 100 g: 5 g
Fat per 100 g: 0 g

protein

Nobody actually needs huge amounts of protein from any source, but everybody needs some protein. Growing children and pregnant women need a little more than other people.

Protein is essential for cell growth, for tissue repair and reproduction, and to manufacture the substances that protect us against infection. Our daily requirements, however, are quite small.

It is easy to get too concerned about obtaining protein — this is probably a legacy of the meat-rich diets of the past. The truth is that most people in Western societies eat far more protein than they need, and if there is too much protein in the diet it is simply converted to body fat. Affluent communities very rarely produce a case of protein deficiency, even when its members are otherwise careless of their nutritional needs and live on too much take-away food, for example. The real nutritional problem is likely to be too much fat, sugar and salt in the diet.

Deriving protein from vegetable sources has a distinct advantage: the high fibre content of food such as legumes and grains puts the brake on overeating.

Tofu and other soya bean products as well as wheatgerm and oatmeal come pretty close to being complete proteins, and are the only non-animal products to do so. This is why they are so highly valued by vegetarians.

Vegans can obtain all the protein they need by eating a wide range of foods of purely vegetable origin.

sources of protein
Good sources include the following:

- dairy: cheese, milk, yoghurt
- nuts and seeds: sunflower, sesame, pumpkin, pecans, brazil nuts, hazelnuts, almonds, walnuts, cashews, pine nuts
- pulses: peanuts, peas, beans, lentils, soya beans and soya bean products like tempeh and tofu
- grains: rice, oats, corn, wheat/flour products and pasta couscous, rye, barley.

Eating foods from at least two of the above groups together will make more protein available to the body. There is no need for mathematical calculations — making sure you eat a varied diet will ensure you get enough protein.

vegans
Vegans — people who eat only foods of plant origin and no animal products — can obtain all their nutritional needs with just a little planning. Some extra care is needed with vegan children, as their needs are slightly different.

Again, variety is the key. Vegans need to be especially vigilant about eating a variety of foods from the four plant food groups every day:

- grains in the form of bread, cereals, pasta and rice
- pulses, nuts and seeds including peanut butter and tahini, beans of all kinds (including baked beans), chickpeas, soy products (tofu, tempeh, soy milk — fortified with calcium and vitamin B12), especially for children
- vegetables
- fresh fruit and juices

Vegans need to ensure they do not miss out on vitamin B12, as the usual sources

ABOVE: Dairy foods are a good source of complete protein. Combining them with grains and vegetables, as in our delicious Brown rice tart with fresh tomato filling (page 124), also provides valuable vitamins and carbohydrates in one tasty dish.

in a lacto-ovo vegetarian diet are eggs and dairy products. Supplements may be necessary, although fortified soy milk is a good source. Mushrooms and tofu also contain vitamin B12.

Soy milk also supplies calcium, as do some green vegetables, almonds, sesame seeds and tahini, and breads and cereals fortified with calcium.

The iron that is found in meat, and which lacto-ovo vegetarians can obtain from eggs, can also be obtained from pulses, soy products, green vegetables, breakfast cereals, dried fruits, nuts and seeds — provided that a wide variety are eaten. The amount of iron available from these foods can be maximised by eating these in conjunction with foods that are rich in vitamin C, such as oranges or blackcurrants.

Remember that children need more fat in their diets than adults to provide them with energy for growth. Vegan children can thrive if they obtain fat from healthy foods such as peanut butter and nuts, vegetable oils, tahini and avocados.

Snack foods can include dried fruit, nuts, seeds and fresh fruit juice.

sample day's menu for vegans

- Breakfast: porridge or muesli with fruit and soy milk; wholemeal (whole-wheat) toast with jam or peanut butter
- Lunch: wholemeal salad sandwich, or chickpea or rice salad
- Dinner: pulse and grain dish with vegetables, or a vegetable dish with wholemeal bread, or a rice or pasta dish with salad
- Dessert: fruit
- Snacks: fresh or dried fruit, crispbreads, nuts, vegetable sticks

ABOVE: Chickpea curry (page 112) is a great example of vegan food. When served with chapatti or naan, it is perfectly balanced — the combination of a pulse and grain making it a complete protein meal.

combining for protein

Combining pulses with grains or with nuts or seeds will provide all the amino acids necessary to make the complete proteins your body needs.

Protein is made up of 23 different amino acids — substances that combine to make what is termed a 'complete' protein. Digestion breaks down complex proteins from food into these simpler units so that they can be used by the body to build up proteins of its own. For this to occur, 'complete' protein is needed by the human body.

Amino acids occur in different combinations and proportions in various foods. The body can make most of them itself if the diet is adequate. However, eight essential amino acids can't be made by the body and can only be obtained directly from food. Some foods have these in almost the right proportions for the body to use immediately.

Protein from animal sources — meat, eggs, cheese, fish, poultry, milk, cheese and yoghurt — provides all the essential amino acids and is therefore considered 'complete'.

Although cheese and eggs are complete proteins, overloading on these will introduce too much fat into the diet; vegans do not even have this option. Vegetarians and vegans need to look beyond cheese: hence 'food combining'.

Pulses and cereals contain some but not all of the essential amino acids, but if they are eaten with other foods that contain the missing amino acids — for example, a grain with a pulse (such as rice and beans) — the body combines the amino acids to form a complete protein. These foods don't even have to be eaten at the same time — within a few hours of each other will do.

Most vegetarians are aware of the importance of getting their protein from a range of sources. Food combining needn't be a complicated business. By following a few simple principles you can invent a delicious way of eating. The proteins in dairy products, nuts and seeds, pulses and grains are complementary, so eating foods from two or more of these groups together makes plenty of protein available to the body.

In most societies, ways of combining complementary proteins have evolved in the indigenous diet. Think of dal and rice, beans and corn, hummus and pitta bread — all are combinations of a pulse and a grain. Other common combinations might include:

- peanut butter sandwiches on wholemeal (whole-wheat) bread
- baked beans on wholemeal toast
- split pea soup and a bread roll
- brown rice and chickpeas
- rice and tofu
- corn tacos with red kidney beans
- lentil patty on a bun
- hummus and lavash bread
- red beans and rice
- pasta and cheese
- muesli with milk
- beans and vegetables
- tabouleh and bean salad
- vegetable pies: potato, spinach
- muesli with nuts and seeds
- chickpeas and couscous
- falafel and pitta bread (pictured)

vitamins and minerals

Vegetarians who combine food to get enough protein can still miss out on some essential nutrients that meat-eaters obtain easily. The most important of these are the minerals iron, zinc and calcium, and vitamin B12.

Including dairy foods and eggs in the diet will generally ensure enough protein, riboflavin, calcium, iron, vitamins and minerals are present. Vegans, however, need to take particular care.

Freshness is important when buying fruit and vegetables. Although most nutrients are retained quite well in snap-frozen products, the flavour may not be as good.

Taking vitamin and mineral supplements is a waste of time if your diet is inadequate, as they are unable to be used effectively by the body in the absence of the right kinds of foods.

vitamins

The body needs vitamins from the B group to metabolise food and to allow proper functioning of the nervous system. These vitamins are found in wholegrain cereals, bread and pasta, nuts and seeds, peas, beans, leafy green vegetables, potatoes, fruits, avocado and yeast extract.

- Vitamin B12, found in dairy foods, eggs, yeast extract, alfalfa, seaweeds and fortified soy milk, is essential for red blood cells and nerve cells. If there is one vitamin vegetarians are deficient in, it will be this one.
- Vitamin B1 (thiamine) is found in soya beans, wheatgerm, sunflower seeds, brazil nuts, peas and beans.
- Vitamin B2 (riboflavin) is obtained from milk products, mushrooms, soya beans, leafy green vegetables, almonds, prunes and dates.
- Vitamin B3 (nicotinic acid) is contained in mushrooms, sesame and sunflower seeds.
- Vitamin B6 (pyridoxine) is found in currants, sultanas (golden raisins), raisins, bananas, sunflower seeds and soya beans.
- Folic acid is found in lettuce, endive, oranges, walnuts, almonds and avocado.
- Vitamin C is essential to protect against infection, for healing, and to help absorb iron from foods. It is found in leafy green vegetables, tomatoes, peppers (capsicums), blackcurrants, oranges, strawberries, kiwifruit and papaya.
- Vitamins A, D, E and K are fat-soluble vitamins found in foods such as milk, butter, cheese, margarine, vegetable oils, nuts and seeds. Deficiencies in these vitamins are rare.

When exposed to sunlight, the body makes vitamin D, which is needed to allow the absorption of calcium into the bones. Vitamin A is needed for good eyesight, healthy skin, hair, nails and mucous membranes, and for resisting infection. It is found in dairy foods, green and yellow vegetables (especially carrots), apricots, red capsicums (peppers), parsley and spinach, so it would be difficult to develop a deficiency in a normal vegetarian diet. Vitamin E is an important antioxidant, guarding against cell damage, while vitamin K helps the blood to clot.

preparing and cooking vegetables for nutrition

To retain the vitamins and minerals in fresh vegetables, wash them quickly (don't soak them), then dry and store in the crisper compartment of the refrigerator. As far as possible, use them unpeeled — brush root vegetables rather than scrape them. Sprinkle cut surfaces with lemon juice to prevent browning. Save peelings and bits such as carrot tops to make stock. Cook vegetables in stainless steel pans. Vegetables taste better when they are undercooked rather than overcooked.

Many vitamins are destroyed by cooking. To minimise this loss, steam rather than boil them — or, even better, use the microwave, which cooks vegetables quickly and in very little water, retaining their colour and nutritional value. Save the cooking liquid for use in other dishes such as soups, stocks and sauces.

ABOVE: Vegetable and bean mixtures such as Creamy corn and tomato soup (page 39) are packed with vitamins and minerals — and adding a dollop of yoghurt supplies some extra protein too.

Vegetarians should not need to take vitamin supplements, except on medical advice. The key once again is variety: a well-balanced vegetarian diet will supply all the vitamins you need.

minerals

Iron is needed for the formation of red blood cells. One of the biggest problems for non-meat eaters can be the spectre of iron-deficiency anaemia. For women, this is even more of a possibility.

A varied vegetarian diet provides enough iron if it includes pulses (most especially lentils and soya beans); whole grains and products made from them, and nuts and seeds (pistachio nuts, pumpkin seeds, sesame seeds). Dark, leafy green vegetables, brewer's yeast, wheatgerm, egg yolks, dried fruits (especially apricots and prunes) and seaweeds are also good sources of iron.

Signs that you may not be getting enough iron include tiredness and lethargy, paleness and shortness of breath.

Calcium is needed for good teeth and bones, and for healthy functioning of the muscles (including the heart) and nerves. Cheese is rich in calcium, as are milk, yoghurt and cream. It's worth remembering, if you are concerned about the amount of fat in your diet, that low-fat and skim versions of dairy products have the same amount of calcium as the full-fat variety. Eggs contain calcium as well.

For vegans, there are many non-animal sources of calcium. One of the richest is sesame seeds, which can be sprinkled on cereal or salads, or used in the form of the ground paste tahini, an essential ingredient in hommus. Soya beans contain calcium, as do flour, figs and other dried fruits, almonds, sunflower seeds, dark green vegetables, broccoli, brewer's yeast, carob, molasses and seaweeds. Vegans need to eat these foods to avoid becoming deficient in calcium.

Women have a greater need for calcium and should be aware of this from early adulthood. Obtaining regular supplies of calcium fortifes the store of dense bone for after menopause, when osteoporosis —

ABOVE: Eating a balanced diet from a wide variety of foods will almost certainly provide you with enough vitamins and minerals every day. Lentil and chickpea burgers with coriander garlic cream (page 121) are a delicious way to serve lentils.

alternatives to salt

Most people consume more salt than the body needs. Eating too much salt contributes to high blood pressure and has been implicated in increased susceptibility to strokes. Salt should be used sparingly, and the good news is that taste dependency on it can be reduced. Instead of salt, sprinkle chopped fresh herbs, spices, or lemon or lime juice over cooked or salad vegetables, or replace it with *gomasio*, a mixture of one part toasted, crushed sesame seeds to one part salt.

a painful and sometimes crippling deterioration of the bones — is a very real possibility if dietary calcium has been inadequate in earlier years. Osteoporosis can be prevented but not cured.

Zinc is needed for growth, healing, and metabolising carbohydrates and protein. Signs of a zinc deficiency include white flecks on the nails and skin problems.

Sources of zinc include wheatgerm, oatmeal, cheese, skim milk, brewer's yeast, dried figs, peanuts, nuts, sesame and pumpkin seeds, corn and peas, as well as mangoes, spinach and asparagus.

Magnesium is also necessary for metabolising carbohydrates. It is not damaged by heat, but is water soluble, so it's a good idea to save vegetable cooking water for stock or sauces. Magnesium deficiencies are rare. Fresh fruit and vegetables, nuts and seeds, brewer's yeast, whole grains, dried fruits, pulses and soya beans all contain some magnesium.

Iodine, needed for the thyroid gland, is required in tiny amounts and is present in iodised salt and seaweeds.

sea vegetables

There are many species of edible seaweeds that are excellent sources of protein, vitamins (including vitamin B12) and the minerals calcium, sodium, potassium, iron and iodine. Nori, used to make sushi, can be cooked and used in salads. Wakame can be served as a green vegetable. Kombu sweetens the flavour of stocks and soups. These are sold in health food shops in dried form.

the fat trap

Meat-lovers face one pitfall a vegetarian largely avoids: eating a lot of animal products, including cheese and full-fat dairy, means eating a lot of fat, and of the kind that has been implicated in some serious health problems if eaten in excess.

Vegetarians tend not to suffer weight problems, as the perils of a diet high in saturated fats are more easily avoided by eating in this way. But there are plenty of non-meat sources of saturated fat, and these are best eaten in moderation. One example is coconut oil, which is used in a lot of commercial baked goods. Coconut cream or tinned coconut milk used in many curries is another.

Children need more fat than adults to help them grow, but they can obtain this from a range of nutritious vegetarian foods, such as milk, avocado, peanut butter, yoghurt and cheese.

Everyone needs some fat in their diet, as fatty acids are essential to the formation of cells in the body, especially those of the nervous system. It would be harmful to try to eliminate all fat from the diet, but eating a variety of foods will supply plenty without any special effort.

healthy fats

Dietary fat comes from two sources: animals and plants. Sources of animal fats that vegetarians (excluding vegans) can use include butter, cheese, cream, yoghurt and egg yolks. Plants provide oils and margarine, and the hard vegetable fats made from them.

Fats containing essential fatty acids and occurring in foods that have other nutrients (olive and other vegetable oils, nuts, seeds, avocado, grains) are a better source of fat than fried take-away food, cakes, biscuits (cookies), chocolates or ice cream.

kinds of fat

Saturated fats solidify at room temperature. Most animal fats are saturated; some examples are lard, butter and dripping.

Saturated fats are thought to raise the level of the harmful type of cholesterol in the blood and lower the amount of the beneficial type. They are also thought to be implicated in some cancers.

Polyunsaturated fats include vegetable oils such as safflower, sunflower, corn and soya bean oil. These lower the overall amount of cholesterol in the blood. They are liquid at room temperature, but can be chemically processed into margarines.

The effects on the body of eating a lot of polyunsaturated fats are still being investigated. It used to be thought that they had a beneficial effect on the amount of cholesterol in the blood, but it is now known that this effect is indiscriminate and reduces 'good cholesterol' as well as 'bad cholesterol'.

Margarine in the diet in large amounts is thought to contribute a kind of fatty acid implicated in heart disease. Large quantities of polyunsaturated fats can also oxidise to form free radicals in the blood. These are responsible for tissue damage and contribute to the formation of plaques on the artery walls. Eating plenty of fruits and vegetables reduces this effect, as these foods are rich in antioxidants.

Monounsaturated fats have recently come into favour, for several of reasons. When it began to be noticed that people in Mediterranean countries such as Spain and Italy had a lower incidence of heart disease than those in other cultures, it was realised that the so-called 'Mediterranean diet' was high in olive oil and low in dairy fats.

Large amounts of monounsaturated fats occur in olive and canola oils. These kinds of fats reduce the levels of 'bad' cholesterol and increase 'good' cholesterol, protecting against heart disease. In addition, populations that

ABOVE: To reduce the amount of fat in your diet, don't simply give up fat, but eat more pulses, grains and vegetables, which provide bulk and therefore sustain you. Borlotti bean moussaka (page 126) contains yoghurt, eggs and cheese, but each serving is so full of nutrients that you'd be unlikely to eat any more fat at that meal.

use olive oil as the main fat in their diets have been shown to have lower rates of breast and bowel cancer, although the exact reason why this should be so is still disputed.

dieting

The different kinds of fat usually occur in combination in foods. More important than worrying about which kind of fat you are eating is being aware of the overall amount of fat in your diet. This means being conscious of hidden fats in items such as pies, crisps, chocolate (and carob) bars, cakes, biscuits (cookies) and other commercially produced, ready-to-eat foods. Many people worry about the sugar in these foods and forget about the fats.

Eating out a lot and eating take-away foods and commercially produced snacks can easily lead to an excess of fat in the diet. A good guide is to aim at getting only a quarter of your total daily kilojoules from fat, or to eat 30–40 g (1–1½ oz) of fat per day if you are a woman or a child, and 40–60 g (1½–2¼ oz) for a man. Very active adults and teenagers need about 70 g (2½ oz) a day, and athletes and those engaged in heavy physical work need 70–80 g (2½–2¾ oz).

There also hidden fats in many innocuous-looking so-called 'health foods', for example toasted muesli, which contains a lot of vegetable oil. Avocado and nuts are also high in fat and should be eaten in moderation. Remember, also, that foods labelled 'low cholesterol' are not necessarily low in fat!

The body only needs small amounts of fat, and nobody eating a Western diet is ever in danger of suffering a fat deficiency. It is very important — just as much for someone on a non-meat diet as for meat-eaters — to be aware of how much fat they are eating. The pitfalls for vegetarians are just different.

Vegetarians can sometimes be under the illusion that they are eating a healthy diet simply because they have eliminated meat with its hidden and not-so-hidden fats. But unthinkingly loading up on cheese, cream, sour cream or even vegetable oils is just as hazardous.

Excessive amounts of fried food will lead to weight gain, whether they're fried in animal or vegetable fats. The only difference is a that a vegetarian eating lots of food fried in, say, olive oil — and not burning up kilojoules with increased physical activity — will gain weight, but without increasing their blood cholesterol levels in the way a meat-eater on a high-fat diet will.

If you are concerned about your weight, it is more important to be aware of the amount of fat in foods you eat on a daily basis than to try counting kilojoules from all sources, as was done in the past. Excess kilojoules from fat are readily stored as body fat, whereas those from carbohydrates, for example, are made available to the body as energy.

hero foods

Some foods have been called the 'heroes' of a vegetarian diet because they are rich sources of certain essential nutrients that meat-eaters obtain in abundance. Including these in your diet will help to ensure that you don't run into any deficiency problems.

- Lentils contain protein, fibre, complex carbohydrate and B vitamins, as well as potassium, magnesium and zinc.
- Soya beans have the best-quality protein of all pulses, some B vitamins, polyunsaturated fat and fibre.
- Rolled (porridge) oats are a good source of protein, thiamin, niacin, iron, fibre and carbohydrate.
- Wheat bran is an excellent source of soluble fibre, iron, thiamine and niacin.
- Eggs supply iron, phosphorus, vitamin B12, vitamins A and D, and protein.

- Dried apricots contain beta carotene (vitamin A), fibre and vitamin C.
- Almonds offer monounsaturated oil, dietary fibre and vitamin E.
- Milk, yoghurt and cheese provide calcium, phosphorus, protein and vitamin A. Milk and yoghurt also retain the B vitamins that are removed in the processing of cheese.
- Spinach contains fibre and most of the vitamins and minerals found in meats.
- Unhulled sesame seeds are rich in calcium and contain vitamin E, magnesium, phosphate and zinc.
- Tofu and tempeh provide magnesium, calcium, phosphorus, iron and protein.
- Yeast extract is a source of B vitamins.

recommended daily intakes

- Iron: 8 mg for men, 8–18 mg for women
- Vitamin B12: 2.4 mcg
- Folate: 400 mcg
- Protein: 64 g for men, 46 g for women
- Calcium: 1000 mg
- Zinc: 14 mg for men, 8 g for women.

Women who are pregnant, breast-feeding, or aged over 70 years require different amounts of these nutrients.

hero foods

The foods listed here contain significant amounts of
the nutrients which, without care, may be lacking in
a vegetarian diet. See the recommended daily intakes
of these nutrients on the previous page.

Almonds
Protein per 100 g: 20 g
Calcium per 100 g: 250 mg
Iron per 100 g: 3.9 mg
Zinc per 100 g: 3.8 mg
Folate per 100 g: 96 mcg

Apricots, dried
Calcium per 100 g: 67 mg
Iron per 100 g: 3.1 mg
Zinc per 100 g: 0.8 mg

Bran, wheat
Iron per 100 g: 12 mg
Zinc per 100 g: 4.7 mg
Folate per 100 g: 260 mcg

Cheddar cheese
Protein per 100 g: 26 g
Vitamin B12 per 100 g: 1.5 mcg
Folate per 100 g: 60 mcg

Egg
Protein per 100 g: 13.2 g
Calcium per 100 g: 43 mg
Iron per 100 g: 1.8 mg
Vitamin B12 per 100 g: 1.7 mcg

Endive
Folate per 100 g: 330 mcg

Lentils, cooked
Protein per 100 g: 6.8 g
Calcium per 100 g: 17 mg
Iron per 100 g: 2 mg

Milk
Protein per 100 g: 3.3 g
Calcium per 100 g: 120 mg

Parsley
Calcium per 100 g: 200 mg
Iron per 100 g: 9.4 mg

Tempeh
Protein per 100 g: 19 g

Tofu
Protein per 100 g: 10 g

Rolled (porridge) oats, raw
Protein per 100 g: 10.7 g
Iron per 100 g: 3.7 mg
Zinc per 100 g: 1.9 mg

Sesame seeds
Protein per 100 g: 22.2 g
Calcium per 100 g: 62 mg
Iron per 100 g: 5.2 mg
Zinc per 100 g: 5.5 mg

Soya beans, cooked
Protein per 100 g: 13.5 g
Calcium per 100 g: 76 mg
Iron per 100 g: 2.2 mg
Zinc per 100 g: 1.6 mg

Spinach
Calcium per 100 g: 53 mg
Iron per 100 g: 3.2 mg
Zinc per 100 g: 0.6 mg
Folate per 100 g: 120 mcg

Sunflower seeds
Protein per 100 g: 22.7 g
Calcium per 100 g: 100 mg
Iron per 100 g: 4.6 mg
Zinc per 100 g: 6.4 mg

Yeast extract
Protein per 100 g: 24.4 g
Zinc per 100 g: 5.1 mg
Vitamin B12 per 100 g: 5 mcg

Yoghurt
Protein per 100 g: 5.0 g
Calcium per 100 g: 195 mg

a world of flavours

One of the great joys of vegetarian eating lies in its versatility. There are many exotic detours available through the world's cuisines, which can broaden your options and expand your cooking skills. The limitations of the Western diet of the past will soon become very obvious.

Many cultures feature a strong vegetarian component and some are exclusively vegetarian, having evolved this way of eating for economic as well as religious reasons. These cuisines are the source of delicious, nutritious dishes that any cook can easily master.

Some dishes are classic examples of efficient and tasty food combining. From Mexico, for example, we get tortillas and beans; from the Orient, silken tofu, tempeh and rice; from the Middle East, hummus with lavash or pitta bread; from North Africa and the Mediterranean, couscous and chickpeas.

Asian cooking is another great source of inspirational vegetarian food, so if you're new to being a vegetarian, Asian cuisines are an ideal place to start.

Many exotic vegetarian dishes can be served as either a side dish, main course, light meal or snack. All you need is a little knowledge, a few interesting ingredients, and some thought about complementary flavours and textures. You will then discover perhaps the biggest advantage of vegetarian eating: the opportunity to cook and eat a whole glorious palette of flavours, colours and textures. Once you become aware of all the possibilities it is impossible to be bored by vegetarian food.

ABOVE: Trying new foods and different combinations of food is one of the joys of vegetarian eating. It's hard to get into a rut when there's so much fresh produce to be sampled. If you've only ever tasted pumpkin (winter squash) baked or mashed, try this lovely Asian-inspired dish, Pumpkin with chilli and avocado (page 169).

wake up your tastebuds

The incomparable flavours of fresh whole foods can be enhanced with spices and condiments: harissa, chermoula, chilli pastes and curry spice mixtures. Herbs are indispensable, and pickles, chutneys, sauces, mustards and relishes can be used to dress up any number of dishes.

Certain herbs and spices go particularly well with certain foods:
- basil with tomatoes and cheeses
- cloves with oranges
- cinnamon, cardamom and cloves with yoghurt, cream and milk dishes
- chives in soups, dips, salads, sandwiches and sauces; and with eggs, potatoes and cheese
- dill in salads, with potatoes, and in egg dishes
- chopped herbs with pasta and rice
- ginger with carrots
- lemongrass in rice dishes and Asian-style sauces
- lemon thyme in salads and with cooked vegetables
- oregano and marjoram with eggs, in salads and marinades, and with cauliflower and tomatoes

- mint with potatoes, in tabouleh, and with rice
- paprika with eggs, cheeses and in casseroles
- parsley in salads and with tomatoes
- rosemary with eggplant (aubergine), tomatoes and zucchini (courgettes)
- sage in bean, cheese or egg dishes, and in salads
- garlic with just about any savoury ingredient!

Stock up the pantry before you begin to roam through the varied world of vegetarian cookery. This will ensure you have the necessary ingredients for a successful dish always at hand and won't have to compromise on flavour.

Most supermarkets these days stock a huge variety of the ingredients you will need, but don't forget to explore delicatessens, and Asian and other ethnic food stores and markets, especially for condiments and unusual flavourings.

serving a vegetarian meal

Old habits die hard and the old tradition of meat and two vegetables can be very hard to break. But vegetarian eating can make things a whole lot easier.

When you don't have to make meat, chicken or fish the centrepiece of a meal, it becomes much easier to serve food buffet-style. Many ethnic cuisines demand this way of serving and eating, with platters of complementary dishes from which people help themselves, adding accompaniments of their choice.

Vegetarian food makes mealtime much more interesting because you can break all the 'rules'. Serve first courses as main courses, and change what you would normally serve as a main course into a starter. Make a soup the star of your meal. Except for the chapter 'Soups & starters', in which the recipes are grouped together because many people want a quick idea for a light meal, this book does not divide recipes into particular courses in the more traditional manner. The book is instead designed so that the cook can browse and plunder recipes at will.

ABOVE: Finish your vegetarian meal with a spectacular dessert such as the Free-form blueberry pie (page 227). It's easy to satisfy everybody's sweet tooth, and the juicy, tangy blueberries have plenty of vitamins, minerals and fibre as well as antioxidant properties.

When planning a meal, consider colour and texture as well as taste and nutritive value. Serve a Layered potato and apple bake (page 136) or Cauliflower and pasta bake (page 138) with a green salad or crisp-textured green vegetables, such as asparagus or snow peas (mangetout) to provide crunch and colour.

Make simple vegetable dishes and salads more interesting (and nutritious) by sprinkling them with chopped nuts or seeds — try a mixture of pumpkin and sesame seeds tossed in soy sauce and roasted in the oven. It's delicious with cucumber salad and even a simple green salad and will keep for months in the refrigerator in an airtight jar.

Incorporate lots of interesting breads when serving vegetarian foods, including flatbreads like lavash, chapattis, rotis, poppadums, tortillas and pitta.

The possibilities are almost endless.

soups & starters

Confess: who among us has ever felt like ordering two (or even three) first courses rather than just the usual one along with a main? First courses often seem more appealing and there is often a wider choice for vegetarians at the top of a menu. Here you're given free rein to realise that impulse: try a restorative soup with a gutsy antipasto. No matter how you pair these recipes, you'll love the meal.

red capsicum soup

✹ ✹

Preparation time: 20 minutes
Cooking time: 30 minutes
Serves 6

4 red capsicums (peppers)
4 tomatoes
60 ml (2 fl oz/¼ cup) olive oil
½ teaspoon dried marjoram
½ teaspoon dried mixed herbs
2 garlic cloves, crushed
1 teaspoon mild curry paste
1 red onion, sliced
1 leek, white part only, sliced
250 g (9 oz) green cabbage, chopped
1 teaspoon sweet chilli sauce

1   Cut the capsicums into quarters, then remove the seeds and membrane. Grill (broil) until the skin blackens and blisters. Place on a cutting board, cover with a tea towel (dish towel) and allow to cool before peeling and chopping. Set aside.

2   Score a cross in the base of the tomatoes. Place in a heatproof bowl and cover with boiling water. Leave for 30 seconds, then transfer to cold water and peel the skin away from the cross. Cut the tomatoes in half, scoop out the seeds and roughly chop the flesh. Set aside.

3   Heat the oil in a large saucepan. Add the herbs, garlic and curry paste. Stir over low heat for 1 minute, or until aromatic. Add the onion and leek and cook for 3 minutes, or until golden. Add the cabbage, capsicum, tomato and 1 litre (35 fl oz/4 cups) water. Bring to the boil, reduce the heat and simmer for 20 minutes. Remove from the heat.

4   Allow to cool slightly before transferring to a food processor and blending, in batches, until smooth. Return the soup to a clean saucepan, season to taste and stir the chilli sauce through. Reheat gently and serve hot.

red capsicum soup

fast mushroom soup

✹

Preparation time: 10 minutes
Cooking time: 25 minutes
Serves 4

60 g (2¼ oz) butter
2 onions, chopped
500 g (1 lb 2 oz) button mushrooms, chopped
30 g (1 oz/¼ cup) plain (all-purpose) flour
500 ml (17 fl oz/2 cups) milk
375 ml (13 fl oz/1½ cups) vegetable stock
sour cream, to serve
chopped flat-leaf (Italian) parsley, to serve

1   Heat the butter in a saucepan and fry the onion over medium heat for 5 minutes, or until lightly golden. Add the mushrooms and cook for a further 5 minutes, stirring often.

2   Add the flour and stir for 1 minute. Stir in the milk and stock. Reduce the heat and simmer, uncovered, for 10–15 minutes, or until the soup has thickened and the mushrooms are tender.

3   Serve topped with a dollop of sour cream sprinkled with the parsley.

puréeing soup

Be careful when puréeing hot soup in a blender or food processor as it can shoot out through the top and scald you. If possible, cool the soup before puréeing. If you must purée while the soup is hot, do so in small batches. Thin soups may also leak from a food processor — the best way to deal with this is to remove the vegetables from the soup with a slotted spoon and process them with a spoonful or two of the liquid. Mix the puréed vegetables back into the soup in the pan.

watercress soup

☀

Preparation time: 15 minutes
Cooking time: 25 minutes
Serves 4–6

100 g (3½ oz) butter
1 onion, chopped
4 spring onions (scallions), chopped
450 g (1 lb) watercress, trimmed and
    chopped
40 g (1⅓ oz/⅓ cup) plain (all-purpose)
    flour
750 ml (26 fl oz/3 cups) vegetable
    stock
sour cream or cream, to serve

1 Heat the butter in a large saucepan.
Add the onion, spring onion and
watercress and stir over low heat for
3 minutes, or until the vegetables have
softened. Add the flour and stir until
combined.
2 Gradually pour in the stock and 310 ml
(10¾ fl oz/1¼ cups) water. Stir until the
mixture is smooth and the soup boils and
thickens. Cover and simmer over low heat
for 10 minutes, or until the watercress
is tender.
3 Allow to cool slightly before
transferring to a food processor and
processing, in batches, until smooth.
Reheat gently and season to taste. Serve
with a swirl of sour cream or cream.

corn chowder

☀

Preparation time: 15 minutes
Cooking time: 30 minutes
Serves 8

90 g (3¼ oz) butter
2 large onions, finely chopped
1 garlic clove, crushed
2 teaspoons cumin seeds
1 litre (35 fl oz/4 cups) vegetable stock
2 potatoes, peeled and chopped
250 g (9 oz/1 cup) tinned
    creamed corn

corn chowder

400 g (14 oz/2 cups) corn kernels
3 tablespoons chopped flat-leaf (Italian)
    parsley
125 g (4½ oz/1 cup) grated cheddar
    cheese
2 tablespoons snipped chives

1 Heat the butter in large heavy-based
saucepan. Add the onion and cook over
medium–high heat for 5 minutes, or until
golden. Add the garlic and cumin seeds
and cook for 1 minute, stirring constantly.
Add the stock and bring to the boil. Add
the potato and reduce the heat. Simmer,
uncovered, for 10 minutes.
2 Add the creamed corn, corn kernels
and parsley. Bring to the boil, then reduce
the heat and simmer for 10 minutes. Stir
in the cheese and season to taste. Heat
gently until the cheese melts.
3 Serve sprinkled with the chives.

vegetable stock

Preheat the oven to 210°C (425°F/
Gas 6–7). Heat 2 tablespoons oil
in a large baking dish. Add 4 large
onions, 5 large carrots and 2 large
parsnips, all unpeeled and chopped;
toss to coat. Bake for 30 minutes,
then transfer to a large heavy-based
pot. Add 5 chopped celery stalks
(with leaves), 2 bay leaves, 1 fresh
bouquet garni, 1 teaspoon black
peppercorns and 3 litres (105 fl oz/
12 cups) water. Slowly bring to the
boil, reduce the heat and simmer,
uncovered, for 1 hour, or until the
liquid has reduced by half. Strain
through a fine sieve, discarding the
solids. Cool, then refrigerate. Makes
1.5 litres (52 fl oz/6 cups).

gazpacho

GARNISH
½ Lebanese (short) cucumber, seeded and finely diced
½ red capsicum (pepper), finely diced
½ green capsicum (pepper), finely diced
½ red onion, finely diced
½ ripe tomato, diced

1 Score a cross in the base of the tomatoes. Place in a heatproof bowl and cover with boiling water. Leave for 30 seconds, then transfer to cold water and peel the skin away from the cross. Cut the tomatoes in half, scoop out the seeds and roughly chop the flesh.
2 Soak the bread in cold water for 5 minutes, then squeeze out any excess liquid. Put the bread in a food processor with the tomato, capsicum, garlic, chilli, sugar and vinegar, then process until combined and smooth.
3 With the motor running, gradually add the oil to make a smooth, creamy mixture. Season to taste. Refrigerate for at least 2 hours. Add a little extra vinegar, if desired.
4 Mix all the garnish ingredients in a bowl. Put 2 ice cubes in each bowl of soup and serve the garnish in separate bowls.

fast spicy bean soup

☀

Preparation time: 15 minutes
Cooking time: 20 minutes
Serves 4

2 tablespoons olive oil
1 onion, chopped
2 garlic cloves, crushed
½ teaspoon chilli powder
2 x 420 g (15 oz) tins mixed beans, rinsed and drained
500 ml (17 fl oz/2 cups) vegetable stock
410 g (14½ oz) tin tomato purée
1 hard-boiled egg, finely chopped
finely chopped flat-leaf (Italian) parsley, to garnish

gazpacho

☀

Preparation time: 40 minutes
Cooking time: nil
Serves 4

1 kg (2 lb 4 oz) vine-ripened tomatoes
2 slices day-old white Italian bread, crust removed, broken into pieces
1 red capsicum (pepper), chopped
2 garlic cloves, chopped
1 small green chilli, chopped (optional)
1 teaspoon sugar
2 tablespoons red wine vinegar, plus extra to taste
2 tablespoons extra virgin olive oil
8 ice cubes

1 Heat the oil in a saucepan and fry the onion over medium heat for 5 minutes, or until soft. Add the garlic and chilli powder, stir-fry for 1 minute, then add the beans. Stir in the stock and passata and cook until heated through. Season to taste and serve, garnished with the egg and parsley.

NOTE: Combinations of beans such as red kidney, cannellini and borlotti are available in tins. If you prefer, you can use just one kind of bean.

spinach and lentil soup

✳

Preparation time: **10 minutes**
Cooking time: **1 hour 30 minutes**
Serves **4–6**

375 g (13 oz/2 cups) brown lentils
2 teaspoons olive oil
1 onion, finely chopped
2 garlic cloves, crushed
20 English spinach leaves, stalks removed, leaves finely shredded
1 teaspoon ground cumin
1 teaspoon finely grated lemon zest
500 ml (17 fl oz/2 cups) vegetable stock
2 tablespoons finely chopped coriander (cilantro)

1 Put the lentils in a large saucepan with 1.25 litres (44 fl oz/5 cups) water. Bring to the boil, then reduce the heat and simmer, uncovered, for 1 hour. Rinse and drain, then set aside.
2 In a separate saucepan, heat the oil. Add the onion and garlic and cook over medium heat for 5 minutes, or until golden. Add the spinach and cook for a further 2 minutes.
3 Add the lentils, cumin, lemon zest, stock and 500 ml (17 fl oz/2 cups) water to the pan. Mix together well, then simmer, uncovered, for 15 minutes.
4 Serve sprinkled with the coriander.

freezing soup

Some soups take a long time to cook, so it makes sense to prepare a big batch and freeze it for later use. Freeze in quantities that you're most likely to use — one serving, two servings, five servings — because once the soup has thawed it is unsafe to freeze it again. Cool the soup and pour it into airtight containers, cover tightly, then label and date. To thaw, place the container in the fridge up to 24 hours ahead, then reheat gently in a saucepan on top of the stove. If you're in a hurry, you can put the frozen soup in a saucepan and heat gently, or heat it in the microwave.

pumpkin soup with harissa

✳

Preparation time: 30 minutes
Cooking time: 25 minutes
Serves 6

2.5 kg (5 lb 8 oz) pumpkin (winter squash)
750 ml (26 fl oz/3 cups) vegetable stock
750 ml (26 fl oz/3 cups) milk
sugar, to taste

HARISSA
250 g (9 oz) fresh red chillies
1 tablespoon caraway seeds
1 tablespoon coriander seeds
2 teaspoons cumin seeds
4–6 garlic cloves
1 tablespoon dried mint
125 ml (4 fl oz/½ cup) extra virgin
   olive oil

1   Remove the skin and seeds from the pumpkin and cut into pieces. Place in a large saucepan with the stock and milk. Bring to the boil, then reduce the heat and simmer for 15–20 minutes, or until tender.
2   Allow to cool slightly before transferring to a food processor, and blending, in batches, until smooth. Season with a little sugar and black pepper. Return to a clean saucepan and gently reheat until ready to serve.
3   Meanwhile, make the harissa. Wearing rubber gloves, remove the stems of the chillies, split in half, remove the seeds and soften the flesh in hot water for 5 minutes. Drain and place in a food processor.
4   While the chillies are soaking, dry-fry the caraway, coriander and cumin seeds in a frying pan for 1–2 minutes, or until they become aromatic. Add the toasted seeds, garlic, mint and 1 teaspoon salt to the food processor. Gradually add the olive oil and process until a smooth, thick paste forms.
5   Serve the harissa in a bowl to stir through the soup.

NOTE: You can use dried red chillies in the harissa. Soak them in hot water for 30 minutes before using.

minestrone

✳

Preparation time: 30 minutes +
   overnight soaking time
Cooking time: 2 hours 45 minutes
Serves 6–8

250 g (9 oz/1¼ cups) haricot beans
2 tablespoons olive oil
2 onions, chopped
2 garlic cloves, crushed
4 tomatoes, peeled and chopped
3 tablespoons chopped parsley
2.25 litres (79 fl oz/9 cups) vegetable
   stock
60 ml (2 fl oz/¼ cup) red wine
1 carrot, chopped
1 turnip, chopped
2 potatoes, chopped
1 celery stalk, chopped
3 tablespoons tomato paste
   (concentrated purée)
1 zucchini (courgette), sliced
60 g (2¼ oz/½ cup) sliced green
   beans
80 g (2¾ oz/½ cup) elbow macaroni
shaved parmesan cheese, to serve

1   Soak the beans overnight in cold water. Drain the beans, add them to a saucepan of boiling water and simmer for 15 minutes. Drain and set aside.
2   Heat the oil in a saucepan over medium heat. Add the onion and garlic and cook, stirring, for 5 minutes, or until the onion is soft. Add the beans, tomato, parsley, stock and wine. Cover and simmer over low heat for 2 hours.
3   Stir in the carrot, turnip, potatoes, celery and tomato paste, then cover and simmer for 15–20 minutes.
4   Stir in the zucchini, green beans and macaroni. Cover and simmer for a final 10–15 minutes, or until the vegetables and pasta are tender. Season to taste and serve topped with shaved parmesan.

pumpkin soup with harissa

creamy corn and tomato soup

creamy corn and tomato soup

✳

Preparation time: 20 minutes
Cooking time: 15 minutes
Serves 4–6

3 tomatoes
1 teaspoon olive oil
1 teaspoon vegetable stock (bouillon) powder
1 onion, finely chopped
2 x 125 g (4½ oz) tin creamed corn
125 g (4½ oz) tin corn kernels, drained
410 g (14¼ oz) tin tomato purée
chilli powder, to taste
yoghurt or sour cream, to serve
warm tortillas, to serve

1 Score a cross in the base of the tomatoes. Place in a heatproof bowl and cover with boiling water. Leave for 30 seconds, then transfer to cold water and peel the skin away from the cross. Cut the tomatoes in half, scoop out the seeds and chop the flesh. Set aside.

2 Heat the oil in a large saucepan over medium heat. Add the stock powder and onion and cook for 5 minutes, or until the onion is soft.

3 Add the tomato, creamed corn, corn kernels and tomato passata. Season to taste with chilli powder and stir until heated through. Serve with a dollop of yoghurt or sour cream and warm tortillas.

green pea soup

✳

Preparation time: 20 minutes +
    2 hours soaking time
Cooking time: 1 hour 40 minutes
Serves 4–6

335 g (11¾ oz/1½ cups) dried
    green split peas
2 tablespoons olive oil
1 onion, finely chopped
1 celery stalk, thinly sliced
1 carrot, thinly sliced
1 tablespoon ground cumin
1 tablespoon ground coriander
2 teaspoons finely grated fresh ginger
1.25 litres (44 fl oz/5 cups) vegetable stock
310 g (11 oz/2 cups) frozen green peas
1 tablespoon chopped mint
yoghurt or sour cream, to serve

1 Soak the split peas in cold water for 2 hours. Drain the peas well.

2 Heat the oil in a large heavy-based saucepan over medium heat. Add the onion, celery and carrot. Cook for 3 minutes, stirring occasionally, until soft but not browned. Stir in the cumin, coriander and ginger and cook for 1 minute.

3 Add the split peas and stock and bring to the boil, then reduce the heat to low. Cover and simmer for 1½ hours, stirring occasionally. Add the frozen peas and stir to combine.

4 Allow to cool slightly before transferring to a food processor and blending, in batches, until smooth. Return to a clean pan and gently reheat. Season to taste, then stir in the mint. Serve with a swirl of yoghurt or sour cream.

antipasto

Appealing to the eye, emitting a mouthwatering scent and captivating the palate, these seductive appetisers entice the senses, whether eaten on their own or as a tempting introduction to a meal.

marinated roasted capsicums

Cut 1 large red, 1 large yellow, 1 large green and, if available, 1 large purple capsicum (pepper) into quarters, then remove the seeds and membrane. Grill (broil) until the skin blackens and blisters. Place on a cutting board, cover with a tea towel (dish towel) and allow to cool before peeling. Cut the flesh into thick strips and place in a bowl. Add 2 crushed garlic cloves, 2 tablespoons balsamic vinegar, 2 tablespoons shredded basil and 60 ml (2 fl oz/¼ cup) olive oil and gently mix. Cover and refrigerate for 3 hours. Return to room temperature before serving. Serve on toasted bruschetta or focaccia. Serves 4–6.

sweet and sour onion

Carefully peel 3 red onions (about 500 g/1 lb 2 oz), keeping the ends intact so that the layers stay together. Cut the onions into eighths and place in a non-stick baking dish. Combine 2 tablespoons wholegrain mustard, 2 tablespoons honey, 2 tablespoons red wine vinegar and 2 tablespoons olive oil. Brush the mixture over the onion, then cover and bake in a preheated 220°C (425°F/Gas 7) oven for 20 minutes. Uncover and bake for a further 15–20 minutes, or until the onion is soft and caramelised. Serves 4–6.

golden fried goat's cheese

Cut 250 g (9 oz) goat's cheese into slices 5 mm (¼ inch) thick. (It is best to use the small logs of goat's cheese for this recipe.) Dust lightly with seasoned flour. In a bowl, combine 80 g (2¾ oz/1 cup) fresh breadcrumbs, 45 g (1½ oz/½ cup) grated pecorino cheese and 1 teaspoon sweet paprika. Dip the cheese slices into 2 lightly beaten eggs, then gently toss to coat in the breadcrumb mixture. Refrigerate for 1 hour. Deep-fry the crumbed goat's cheese in batches in hot oil for 2 minutes, or until the crust is crisp and golden. Serve with your favourite relish or a sweet dipping sauce. Serves 4.

chargrilled spring onion and asparagus

Cut 12 asparagus spears and 12 spring onions (scallions) into 12 cm (4½ inch) lengths. Brush lightly with macadamia nut oil and cook on a preheated chargrill or barbecue for 3 minutes, or until the vegetables are tender. Drizzle with balsamic vinegar, sprinkle with black pepper and top with parmesan cheese shavings. Serves 4–6.

mushrooms in lime and chilli

Brush 250 g (9 oz) button mushrooms with vegetable oil; cook under a preheated grill (broiler), or on a barbecue grill, until tender. Combine 1 teaspoon chilli flakes, 1 tablespoon shredded lime zest, 1 crushed garlic clove, 1 tablespoon chopped coriander (cilantro), 1 teaspoon soft brown sugar, 2 tablespoons lime juice and 60 ml (2 fl oz/¼ cup) olive oil in a bowl. Toss the mushrooms in the mixture and refrigerate for 1 hour before serving. Serves 2–4.

carrot and orange soup

1 Melt the butter in a large heavy-based saucepan. Add the carrot and cook over medium heat for 10 minutes, stirring occasionally. Add the orange juice, stock and onion. Bring to the boil, add the thyme and season to taste. Reduce the heat, then cover and simmer for 20 minutes, or until the carrot is tender.

2 Allow to cool slightly before transferring to a food processor and blending, in batches, until smooth. Return the soup to a clean saucepan.

3 Reheat gently and serve with a dollop of sour cream, sprinkled with nutmeg.

french onion soup

☀

Preparation time: 20 minutes
Cooking time: 1 hour 45 minutes
Serves 4–6

60 g (2¼ oz) butter
1 kg (2 lb 4 oz) onions, sliced into fine rings
1 teaspoon sugar
3 tablespoons plain (all-purpose) flour
2.25 litres (79 fl oz/9 cups) vegetable stock
1 baguette, cut into 1 cm (½ inch) slices
65 g (2½ oz/½ cup) grated gruyère or
    cheddar cheese, plus extra, to serve

1 Melt the butter in a large saucepan. Add the onion and cook slowly over low heat for 20 minutes, or until tender. Add the sugar and flour and cook, stirring, for 1–2 minutes, or until the mixture is just starting to turn golden. Pour in the stock and bring to a simmer. Cover and cook over low heat for 1 hour, stirring occasionally. Season to taste.

2 Near serving time, preheat the oven to 180°C (350°F/Gas 4). Spread the baguette slices on a baking tray and bake for 20 minutes, turning once, until dry and golden. Top each slice with grated cheese and place under a hot grill (broiler) for 5 minutes, or until the cheese has melted.

3 Serve the soup topped with the toasted cheese croutons and sprinkled with some extra grated cheese.

melba toast

Toast thin slices of white or brown bread (with crusts) until golden on both sides. Using a serrated knife, cut off the crusts. Carefully slice the toast in half horizontally to make two pieces, each one with a toasted and an untoasted side. Scrape away the soft untoasted side and place the slices, untoasted side up, on a baking tray. Bake in a slow oven until they begin to curl and turn golden. Serve with soups and salads, or top and serve as finger food.

carrot and orange soup

☀

Preparation time: 20 minutes
Cooking time: 35 minutes
Serves 4

500 g (1 lb 2 oz) carrots, peeled
    and chopped
30 g (1 oz) butter
125 ml (4 fl oz/½ cup) orange juice
1–1.25 litres (35–44 fl oz/4–5 cups)
    vegetable stock
1 small onion, chopped
3–4 teaspoons chopped thyme
sour cream, to serve
freshly grated nutmeg, to serve

fast pasta soup

❋

Preparation time: **10 minutes**
Cooking time: **10 minutes**
Serves **4**

1 tablespoon olive oil
2 spring onions (scallions), chopped
150 g (5½ oz) snow peas (mangetout),
   trimmed and sliced
200 g (7 oz) mushrooms, sliced
2 garlic cloves, crushed
1 teaspoon finely grated fresh ginger
1 litre (35 fl oz/4 cups) vegetable stock
150 g (5½ oz) angel hair pasta

1 Heat the oil in a saucepan over
medium heat. Add the spring onion, snow
peas and mushrooms and and stir-fry for
a few minutes, or until just tender.
2 Add the garlic and ginger and stir for
a further minute. Pour in the stock and
bring to the boil.
3 Add the pasta to the boiling stock and
cook for 3 minutes, or until just tender.
Serve immediately.

grilled vegetables with garlic mayonnaise

❋ ❋

Preparation time: **30 minutes**
   + 30 minutes standing time
Cooking time: **15 minutes**
Serves **8**

2 eggplants (aubergines), cut into
   thin slices
4 small leeks, white part only
4 small zucchini (courgettes)
2 red capsicums (peppers)
8 large flat mushrooms

DRESSING
1 tablespoon balsamic vinegar
2 tablespoons dijon mustard
2 teaspoons dried oregano
250 ml (9 fl oz/1 cup) olive oil

GARLIC MAYONNAISE
2 egg yolks
1 tablespoon lemon juice
2 garlic cloves, crushed
250 ml (9 fl oz/1 cup) olive oil
1 tablespoon snipped chives
1 tablespoon chopped flat-leaf (Italian)
   parsley

1 Sprinkle the eggplant with salt and
leave to stand for 30 minutes. Rinse
under cold water, then pat dry with
paper towels.
2 Preheat the grill (broiler) to high.
Halve the leeks and zucchini lengthways.
Cut the capsicums in half, remove the
seeds and membrane, then cut each half
into four pieces.
3 To make the dressing, combine the
vinegar, mustard and oregano in a bowl,
then gradually whisk in the oil. Set aside.
4 Place the eggplant, leek, zucchini and
capsicum in a single layer on a flat grill
tray, then brush with some of the dressing.

Grill (broil) for 5 minutes, brushing
occasionally with dressing. Turn the
vegetables, add the mushrooms, cap side
up, to the grill tray and brush with the
dressing. Cook the vegetables for a further
10 minutes, or until tender, turning
the mushrooms once and brushing the
vegetables with the dressing.
5 Meanwhile, make the garlic
mayonnaise. Put the egg yolks, lemon
juice and garlic in a food processor or
blender and blend for 5 seconds, or until
combined. With the motor running,
slowly add the oil in a thin, steady
stream until the mayonnaise is thick
and creamy. Add the chives, parsley
and 1 tablespoon water and blend for
3 seconds, or until combined. Serve with
the grilled vegetables.

NOTE: Don't worry if the dressing
separates — simply brush it on as
required. The garlic mayonnaise can be
made several days ahead and refrigerated.

grilled vegetables with garlic mayonnaise

flavoured butters

Softened butter can be flavoured with chopped fresh herbs, garlic, blue cheese or mustard and used to liven up steamed or baked vegetables. Put the flavoured butter on a sheet of plastic wrap, roll into a log shape, wrap up tightly and refrigerate until firm. Slice and serve on top of hot vegetables.

mushrooms with herb nut butter

✳

Preparation time: 20 minutes
Cooking time: 20 minutes
Serves 4–6

12 large button mushrooms
1 tablespoon olive oil
1 small onion, finely chopped

HERB NUT BUTTER
40 g (1½ oz/¼ cup) blanched almonds
1 garlic clove, chopped
1 tablespoon lemon juice
3 tablespoons chopped parsley
3 teaspoons chopped thyme or
    1 teaspoon dried thyme
3 teaspoons chopped rosemary or
    1 teaspoon dried rosemary
1 tablespoon snipped chives
½ teaspoon sea salt
¼ teaspoon freshly ground
    black pepper
75 g (2¾ oz) butter, chopped

1 Preheat the oven to 180°C (350°F/ Gas 4). Brush a shallow baking dish with a little oil or melted butter. Remove and finely chop the mushroom stalks, then set aside.
2 Heat the oil in a small frying pan, then add the onion and cook over medium heat for 2–3 minutes, or until soft and golden. Add the chopped mushroom stalks and cook for 2 minutes, or until softened. Remove from the heat.
3 Put the herb nut butter ingredients in a food processor and blend for 20–30 seconds, or until smooth.

fast mushroom pastries

Cut a sheet of thawed frozen puff pastry into four. Brush with melted butter, sprinkle with sesame seeds and bake in a preheated 200°C (400°F/Gas 6) oven for 15 minutes, or until puffed and golden. Meanwhile, melt 40 g (1½ oz) butter in a frying pan; add 400 g (14 oz) sliced button mushrooms and cook for 10 minutes, or until tender. Stir in 170 ml (5½ fl oz/ ⅔ cup) cream and season to taste. Split the cooked pastry squares in half lengthways, then spoon the mushroom mixture over the bottom halves. Sprinkle with grated parmesan cheese, replace the tops and serve immediately. Serves 4.

4 Place the mushroom caps in the baking dish. Spoon equal amounts of the onion and mushroom mixture into each cap and smooth the surface. Top each mushroom with the herb nut butter.

5 Bake for 10–15 minutes, or until the mushrooms are cooked through and the butter has melted. Serve immediately.

NOTE: The mushrooms are best cooked just before serving, but you can assemble the caps up to 2 hours ahead. Refrigerate on a flat tray, covered with plastic wrap.

grating potatoes

Grated potato can be made into pancakes (see recipe below), or used for Swiss potato rösti. When making such dishes it is essential the potato is dry so that it fries rather than stews in the moisture. First, dry the whole peeled potato, then grate it, place in a colander and squeeze several times until you've squeezed out all the moisture. Dry the grated potato in a tea towel (dish towel) or on paper towels. This will take many paper towels or several tea towels, but is essential for a crisp finish. To make potato rösti, put the grated potato into a pan of hot butter and oil and press down well to make a flat cake. Brown on one side, then flip and brown the other side.

potato pancakes

✳

Preparation time: 20 minutes
Cooking time: 15 minutes
Serves 4–6

4 large potatoes, peeled
3 eggs, lightly beaten
4 spring onions (scallions),
    thinly sliced, plus extra to garnish
3 tablespoons cornflour (cornstarch)
2 tablespoons oat bran
vegetable oil, for pan-frying
grated fresh beetroot, to serve (optional)
sour cream, to serve (optional)

1 Coarsely grate the potatoes. Squeeze the excess moisture from the grated potato with your hands. Dry the grated potato well in tea towels (dish towels), then place in a large bowl. Add the eggs, spring onion, cornflour and oatbran and mix well to combine.

2 Working in batches, drop heaped tablespoons of the mixture into a well-oiled frying pan, flatten them slightly and cook over medium heat until golden brown on both sides and cooked through. Drain on paper towels.

3 Serve hot, garnished with extra spring onion, or beetroot and a dollop of sour cream if desired.

eggplant and zucchini pots with capsicum relish

✳ ✳

Preparation time: 30 minutes +
    20 minutes standing time
Cooking time: 40 minutes
Makes 6

1 large eggplant (aubergine),
    cut into 1 cm (½ inch) cubes
200 g (6½ oz) fresh ricotta
    cheese
310 g (11 oz/ 1¼ cups) sour
    cream
3 eggs
1 tablespoon cornflour (cornstarch)
125 g (4½ oz/1 cup) grated zucchini
    (courgette)
½ teaspoon freshly ground black
    pepper

CAPSICUM RELISH
185 ml (6 fl oz/¾ cup) malt
    vinegar
90 g (3¼ oz/⅓ cup) sugar
1 teaspoon yellow mustard seeds
1 green apple, peeled and chopped
1 pear, peeled and chopped
1 red capsicum (pepper), chopped
1 green capsicum (pepper),
    chopped

1 Preheat the oven to 210°C (415°F/Gas 6–7) and brush six 185 ml (6 fl oz/¾ cup) ramekins with oil. Sprinkle the eggplant with salt and leave to stand for 20 minutes. Rinse under cold water, then pat dry with paper towels.

2 Using electric beaters, beat the ricotta and sour cream in a small bowl until light and creamy. Add the eggs and cornflour and beat until smooth. Transfer to a large bowl and gently fold in the eggplant, zucchini and pepper.

3 Spoon the mixture evenly into the ramekins. Place in a deep baking dish. Pour enough hot water into the baking dish to come two-thirds up the side of the ramekins, then cover loosely with foil. Bake for 40 minutes, or until a skewer inserted into the centre of the ramekins comes out clean.

4 Meanwhile, make the capsicum relish. Put the vinegar, sugar and mustard seeds in a saucepan and cook, stirring, over low heat for 5 minutes, or until the sugar has dissolved and the mixture boils. Add the remaining ingredients, bring back to the boil, then reduce the heat and simmer, uncovered, for 30 minutes.

5 Serve the vegetable pots with the capsicum relish.

peeling asparagus

Not all asparagus needs to be peeled — thin asparagus hardly ever does, and there would not be much left to eat if you did. Thick asparagus is fine unpeeled if it's really fresh, but if you have any doubts, peel the stalks. Do this with a vegetable peeler, working from just under the tip towards the base. Laying the asparagus on a board will make this easier. Cut or snap off the base of the stalk as well, as the end tends to be woody.

asparagus with citrus hollandaise

asparagus with citrus hollandaise

☀

Preparation time: 15 minutes
Cooking time: 10 minutes
Serves 4

24 asparagus spears, woody ends trimmed
185 g (6½ oz) butter
4 egg yolks
1–2 tablespoons lemon, lime or orange juice
shavings of parmesan or pecorino cheese, to garnish (optional)

1 Put the asparagus in a saucepan of boiling water. Simmer for 2–4 minutes, or until just tender. Drain well and keep warm.
2 Meanwhile, melt the butter in a small saucepan. Skim any froth from the top and discard. Allow the butter to cool.

3 Put the egg yolks and 2 tablespoons water in a small saucepan and whisk for 30 seconds, or until pale and creamy. Place the pan over very low heat and continue whisking for 3 minutes, or until the mixture thickens. Remove from the heat. Add the cooled butter gradually, whisking constantly (leave the whey in the bottom of the pan). Stir in the citrus juice and season to taste.
4 Drizzle the sauce over the asparagus and serve garnished with cheese shavings, if desired.

grilled tomatoes with bruschetta

☀

Preparation time: 15 minutes
Cooking time: 35 minutes
Makes 12

6 large ripe tomatoes
½ teaspoon dried marjoram
80 ml (2½ fl oz/⅓ cup) olive oil
2 tablespoons red wine vinegar
1 teaspoon soft brown sugar
1 loaf of Italian bread, cut into 12 thick slices
olive oil, extra, to brush over bread
1 garlic clove, halved
110 g (3¾ oz/½ cup) chopped, marinated artichokes
1 tablespoon finely chopped flat-leaf (Italian) parsley
sea salt, for sprinkling

1 Preheat the grill (broiler) to medium–high. Cut tomatoes in half and gently squeeze out the seeds. Place the tomatoes, cut side down, in a shallow baking dish. Combine marjoram, oil, vinegar and sugar in a bowl. Mix well. Season to taste, then drizzle half the mixture over the tomatoes.
2 Grill (broil) the tomatoes for 30 minutes, turning them over halfway

during cooking. Drizzle the remaining oil mixture over the tomatoes, then remove from the heat and keep warm.

3 Liberally brush the bread slices on both sides with the extra oil. Toast under the hot grill on both sides until golden.

4 Rub the cut surface of the garlic over the bread. Place a tomato half on each slice and top with some artichoke. Sprinkle with the parsley and sea salt and serve immediately.

chilli puffs with curried vegetables

✸ ✸ ✸

Preparation time: **35 minutes**
Cooking time: **1 hour 25 minutes**
Makes **12**

4 yellow squash, thinly sliced
100 g (3½ oz) snow peas (mangetout), cut in half diagonally
1 carrot, cut into thin strips
50 g (1¾ oz) butter
2 onions, sliced
2 tablespoons mild curry paste
300 g (10½ oz) small oyster mushrooms
1 tablespoon lemon juice

CHOUX PASTRY
90 g (3¼ oz) butter
155 g (5½ oz/1¼ cups) plain (all-purpose) flour, sifted
¼ teaspoon chilli powder
4 eggs, lightly beaten

1 Preheat the oven to 210°C (425°F/ Gas 7). Sprinkle two 28 x 32 cm (11 x 12 inch) baking trays with a little water.

2 To make the choux pastry, combine the butter and 310 ml (10¾ fl oz/1¼ cups) water in a saucepan. Stir over low heat for 5 minutes, or until the butter has melted and the mixture comes to the boil. Remove from the heat, add the flour and chilli powder all at once and stir with a wooden spoon until just combined.

3 Return the pan to the heat and beat constantly with a wooden spoon over low heat for 3 minutes, or until the mixture thickens and comes away from the side and base of the pan. Transfer the mixture to a large bowl.

4 Using electric beaters, beat the mixture on high speed for 1 minute. Add the beaten egg gradually, beating until the mixture is stiff and glossy — this could take up to 5 minutes.

5 Place the mixture in mounds, measuring about 2 tablespoons each, onto the baking trays, spacing them about 10 cm (4 inches) apart. Sprinkle with a little water and bake for 20 minutes.

6 Turn the oven down to 180°C (350°F/ Gas 4) and bake for a further 25 minutes.

7 Cut a small slit into each pastry puff, to allow the excess steam to escape so the puffs can dry out. Bake for a final 25 minutes, or until the puffs are crisp and well browned. Transfer to a wire rack to cool.

8 Melt the butter in a frying pan and add the onion. Cook over low heat for 5 minutes, or until golden, then stir in the curry paste. Add all the vegetables and stir over high heat for 1 minute. Remove the vegetables from the heat and stir in the lemon juice.

9 Cut the cooled puffs in half lengthways and remove any uncooked mixture from the centres with a spoon. Fill the puffs with the curried vegetables and serve immediately.

goat's cheese

Although most cheeses are made from cow's milk, other animal milks are used to make some famous cheeses. Goat's cheese or chèvre has a very distinctive, tart flavour that may take some getting used to. Depending on its age, it ranges from fresh and soft to crumbly and dry. When very young, it is soft enough to spread and it matures to a chalky consistency.

avocado with lime and chilli

✳

Preparation time: 20 minutes
Cooking time: nil
Serves 6

2 ripe avocados
1 teaspoon finely grated lime zest
2 tablespoons lime juice
1 teaspoon soft brown sugar
1 tablespoon olive oil
1 tablespoon chopped flat-leaf (Italian)
   parsley
2–3 jalapeño chillies, seeded and diced

avocado with lime and chilli

1 Peel and slice the avocados and arrange on serving plates.
2 In a small bowl, mix together the remaining ingredients until well combined. Pour the dressing over the avocado and serve.

NOTE: The lime juice stops the avocados browning. Lemon juice can also be used.

goat's cheese salad

✳

Preparation time: 20 minutes
Cooking time: 15 minutes
Serves 4

4 x 100 g (3½ oz) goat's cheese logs
12 slices white bread
60 g (2¼ oz) mixed salad leaves
   (mesclun)
60 g (2¼ oz) rocket (arugula)
250 g (9 oz) cherry tomatoes, halved
1 tablespoon white wine vinegar
60 ml (2 fl oz/¼ cup) olive oil
½ teaspoon wholegrain mustard
snipped chives, to garnish

1 Preheat the oven to 180°C (350°F/ Gas 4). Cut each goat's cheese log into three slices; set aside. Using a biscuit (cookie) cutter, cut a round out of each slice of bread — the rounds must not be wider than the cheese slices or the edges will burn. Place the bread on a baking tray and bake for 10 minutes.
2 Place a slice of cheese on each piece of bread. Bake for a further 5 minutes, or until the cheese turns golden and bubbles.
3 Meanwhile, arrange a bed of salad leaves and rocket on serving plates; top with the tomato. Mix together the vinegar, oil and mustard until well combined, then drizzle over the salad leaves.
4 Place three cheese rounds on each salad. Garnish with chives and serve.

eggplant marinated in chermoula

✳

Preparation time: 10 minutes + 30 minutes
  standing + 1 hour refrigeration time
Cooking time: 10 minutes
Serves 4

2 eggplants (aubergines), sliced 1 cm
  (½ inch) thick
olive oil, for brushing

CHERMOULA
2 garlic cloves, crushed
1 tablespoon ground cumin
1 teaspoon ground cinnamon
¼ teaspoon cayenne pepper
1 teaspoon ground allspice
60 ml (2 fl oz/¼ cup) lemon juice
3 tablespoons chopped coriander (cilantro)
2 tablespoons chopped mint
125 ml (4 fl oz/½ cup) olive oil

1 Sprinkle the eggplant with salt and
leave to stand for 30 minutes. Rinse
under cold water, then pat dry with
paper towels.
2 Preheat the grill (broiler) to
medium–high. Brush the eggplant slices
liberally with olive oil and grill (broil) for
5 minutes on each side, or until golden
brown. Drain on paper towels.
3 Put the chermoula ingredients in a
large bowl and mix together well. Add
the eggplant and toss to coat. Cover and
marinate in the refrigerator for 1 hour.
4 Serve at room temperature.

eggplant fritters

eggplant fritters

✳

Preparation time: 20 minutes
  + 30 minutes standing time
Cooking time: 20 minutes
Makes 20

1 large, long eggplant (aubergine)
55 g (2 oz/½ cup) besan (chickpea flour),
  plus 2 tablespoons extra

¼ teaspoon freshly ground black
  pepper
30 g (1 oz/¼ cup) self-raising flour
2 eggs, lightly beaten
60 ml (2 fl oz/¼ cup) beer, chilled
2 teaspoons lemon juice
170 ml (5½ fl oz/⅔ cup) vegetable oil

YOGHURT DIP
200 g (7 oz) plain yoghurt
2 tablespoons finely grated onion
½ teaspoon sea salt
½ teaspoon dried mint
¼ teaspoon ground coriander
a pinch of ground cumin

1 Put the yoghurt dip ingredients in a
small bowl and beat until well combined.
Cover with plastic wrap and refrigerate
until required.
2 Cut the eggplant into 20 slices, each
about 5 mm (¼ inch) thick. Sprinkle the
eggplant with salt and leave to stand for
30 minutes. Rinse under cold water, then
pat dry with paper towels.
3 Combine 2 tablespoons besan and
pepper on a sheet of baking paper. Lightly
dust the eggplant slices in the mixture
and shake off any excess.
4 Sift the remaining flours into a medium
bowl and make a well in the centre. Add
the eggs, beer and lemon juice all at once.
Beat until all the liquid is incorporated
and the batter is free of lumps.
5 Heat the oil in a large heavy-based
frying pan over medium–high heat. Using
two forks, dip the floured eggplant slices
into the batter a few pieces at a time;
drain off the excess. Fry for 2 minutes, or
until golden and crisp underneath. Turn
the fritters over and cook the other side.
Transfer to a large plate and keep warm.
6 Repeat with the remaining batter and
eggplant. Serve with the yoghurt dip.

eating artichokes

Whole fresh artichokes are always eaten with the fingers, so be sure to provide finger bowls for diners, and a bowl for the discarded leaves. To eat artichokes, take off one leaf at a time. Dip the bottom of the leaf in mayonnaise and scrape off the fleshy base with your teeth. Towards the centre of the artichoke, the leaves are more tender and more of the leaf is edible.

artichokes with tarragon mayonnaise

✳ ✳

Preparation time: **30 minutes**
Cooking time: **35 minutes**
Serves **4**

4 globe artichokes
60 ml (2 fl oz/¼ cup) lemon juice

TARRAGON MAYONNAISE
1 egg yolk
1 tablespoon tarragon vinegar
½ teaspoon dijon mustard
170 ml (5½ fl oz/⅔ cup)
    olive oil

1 Trim the stalks from the base of the artichokes. Using scissors, trim the points from the outer leaves. Using a sharp knife, cut the tops from the artichokes. Brush all cut areas of the artichokes with the lemon juice to prevent discolouration.
2 Steam the artichokes for 30 minutes, or until tender, topping up the saucepan with boiling water if necessary. Remove from the heat and set aside to cool.
3 To make the tarragon mayonnaise, put the egg yolk, vinegar and mustard

fast salsa toasts

Cut a short baguette into six diagonal slices about 4 cm (1½ inches) thick. Toast one side under a preheated grill (broiler) until golden. Scrape some of the bread out from the untoasted side. Finely chop 2 small, ripe tomatoes, half a small red onion and a few pitted black olives; mix together, then spoon into the bread cavities. Top with 125 g (4½ oz) crumbled feta cheese and some fresh thyme. Drizzle lightly with olive oil, then grill (broil) until golden on top. Makes 6.

in a bowl. Using a wire whisk, beat for 1 minute. Add the oil a teaspoon at a time, whisking constantly; as the mayonnaise thickens, add the oil in a thin, steady stream. Continue whisking until all the oil is added, then season to taste. Transfer to a small bowl.

4 Arrange the cooled artichokes on a serving platter. Serve with the tarragon mayonnaise.

crudités with garlic sauce

❊

Preparation time: 30 minutes
Cooking time: 20 minutes
Serves 4–6

a selection of fresh vegetables, cut into batons, to serve
crusty bread or toasted flatbread, to serve (optional)

GARLIC SAUCE
2 large old potatoes, peeled and cubed
4–5 garlic cloves, crushed
1 tablespoon white wine vinegar
lemon juice, to taste
freshly ground white pepper, to taste
80 ml (2½ fl oz/⅓ cup) olive oil

1 Cover and refrigerate the vegetables until required.
2 To make the garlic sauce, cook the potato in a saucepan of boiling water for 15 minutes, or until tender. Drain well, place in a bowl, then mash until smooth. Add the garlic and vinegar and mix well. Stir in a little lemon juice and season to taste with salt and white pepper.
3 Add the oil a few drops at a time, beating well after each addition. Continue adding the oil and beating until the mixture is quite smooth and thick — this may take up to 5 minutes.
4 Serve the garlic sauce warm with the vegetables, and crusty bread or toasted flatbread if desired.

NOTE: The garlic sauce is often made using almonds and soaked white bread instead of potato. Substitute 35 g (1¼ oz/⅓ cup) ground almonds and 90 g (3 oz) of stale white bread that has been soaked in water and squeezed dry. Blend in a food processor, adding the oil in drops while the motor is running. The consistency should be that of a thick mayonnaise. If the mixture is too thick, add a little more oil or lemon juice.

marinated baby mushrooms

❊

Preparation time: 30 minutes +
    at least 1 hour marinating time
Cooking time: nil
Serves 6–8

500 g (1 lb 2 oz) button mushrooms, halved
125 ml (4 fl oz/½ cup) olive oil
125 ml (4 fl oz/½ cup) white wine vinegar
3 garlic cloves, chopped
2 tablespoons chopped parsley
2 teaspoons chopped red chilli
1 teaspoon caster (superfine) sugar

1 Wipe the mushrooms with paper towels and trim the stalks to the level of the caps. Place the caps in a large bowl.
2 In a large bowl, mix together the remaining ingredients and season to taste. Pour the marinade over the mushrooms and toss to combine. Cover with plastic wrap and refrigerate for at least 1 hour.
3 Serve at room temperature, as part of an antipasto platter if desired.

NOTE: The mushrooms can be marinated for up to 2 days, depending on how intensely flavoured you like them. Turn them occasionally as they marinate.

crudités with garlic sauce

vegetable strudel

fast peach relish
Peel and roughly chop 6 large peaches and place in a heavy-based saucepan. Add 1 tablespoon finely chopped preserved ginger, 2 tablespoons soft brown sugar, 2 finely chopped spring onion (scallions), ¼ teaspoon mixed spice, 2 whole cloves, 4 whole black peppercorns, 2 tablespoons malt vinegar and 2 teaspoons soy sauce. Stir over medium heat until the sugar dissolves. Cover and simmer gently for 15 minutes, or until soft and pulpy. Discard the cloves and peppercorns and allow to cool, then serve with pakoras or samosas. Refrigerate any remaining relish in an airtight container. Makes about 750 g (1 lb 10 oz/3 cups).

vegetable strudel

✹ ✹

Preparation time: 30 minutes
Cooking time: 35 minutes
Serves 4–6

12 English spinach leaves
2 tablespoons olive oil
1 onion, thinly sliced
1 red capsicum (pepper), cut into strips
1 green capsicum (pepper), cut into strips
2 zucchini (courgettes), sliced
2 slender eggplants (aubergines), sliced
6 sheets filo pastry
40 g (1½ oz) butter, melted
4 tablespoons finely shredded basil leaves
60 g (2¼ oz/½ cup) grated cheddar cheese
2 tablespoons sesame seeds

1 Preheat the oven to 210°C (415°F/ Gas 6–7). Grease a baking tray with melted butter or oil.
2 Wash the spinach leaves thoroughly, then steam or microwave them until they are just softened. Squeeze out any excess moisture and spread the leaves out to dry.
3 Heat the oil in a frying pan over medium heat. Add the onion and cook for 3 minutes. Add the capsicum, zucchini and eggplant and cook, stirring, for 5 minutes, or until the vegetables have softened. Season to taste and set aside to cool.
4 Brush a sheet of filo pastry with the melted butter, then top with a second sheet. Repeat with the remaining pastry, brushing with butter between each layer.

5 Place the spinach, cooled vegetable mixture, basil and cheese along one long side of the pastry, about 5 cm (2 inches) in from the edge. Fold the sides over the filling, then fold the short end over and roll up tightly.
6 Place the strudel, seam side down, on the baking tray. Brush with the remaining melted butter and sprinkle with the sesame seeds. Bake for 25 minutes, or until golden brown and crisp. Serve immediately.

samosas

✹

Preparation time: 30 minutes
Cooking time: 50 minutes
Makes about 24

2 potatoes, peeled
80 g (2¾ oz/½ cup) frozen peas
3 tablespoons currants
2 tablespoons chopped coriander (cilantro)
2 tablespoons lemon juice
1 tablespoon soy sauce
1 teaspoon ground cumin
1 teaspoon chilli powder

½ teaspoon chopped red chilli
¼ teaspoon ground cinnamon
4 sheets ready-rolled frozen puff
    pastry, thawed
vegetable oil, for pan-frying

MINT SAUCE
125 g (4½ oz/½ cup) plain yoghurt
125 ml (4 fl oz/½ cup) buttermilk
3 tablespoons chopped mint
½ teaspoon ground cumin

1 Cook the potato in a saucepan of boiling water for 20 minutes, or until tender. Drain well, then chop finely and place in a bowl.
2 Add the peas, currants, coriander, lemon juice, soy sauce, cumin, chilli powder, chilli and cinnamon and mix together well.
3 Cut the pastry into rounds using a 10 cm (4 inch) cutter. Place heaped teaspoons of the potato mixture on one side of each round. Fold the pastry over the filling to make a semi-circle. Press the edges together firmly with a fork to seal.
4 Heat 2 cm (¾ inch) oil in a saucepan; add the samosas in batches and cook for 2–3 minutes on each side, or until golden brown and puffed. Drain on paper towels.
5 Combine the mint sauce ingredients in a small bowl and stir until smooth. Serve with the hot samosas.

vegetable pakoras

☀

Preparation time: **30 minutes**
Cooking time: **20 minutes**
Serves 4

35 g (1¼ oz/⅓ cup) besan (chickpea
    flour)
40 g (1½ oz/⅓ cup) self-raising flour
45 g (1¾ oz/⅓ cup) soy flour
½ teaspoon ground turmeric
1 teaspoon cayenne pepper
½ teaspoon ground coriander
1 small green chilli, seeded and
    finely chopped
1 teaspoon salt

200 g (7 oz) cauliflower
150 g (5½ oz) orange sweet potato
175 g (6 oz) eggplant (aubergine)
175 g (6 oz/1 bunch) asparagus,
    woody ends trimmed
vegetable oil, for deep-frying

RAITA
2 Lebanese (short) cucumbers, peeled,
    seeded and finely chopped
250 g (9 oz/1 cup) plain yoghurt
1 teaspoon ground cumin
1 teaspoon mustard seeds
½ teaspoon finely grated fresh ginger
paprika, to garnish (optional)

1 To make the raita, mix the cucumber and yoghurt in a bowl. Dry-fry the cumin and mustard seeds in a small frying pan over medium heat for 1 minute, or until fragrant and lightly browned, then add to the yoghurt mixture. Stir in the ginger, season to taste and mix together well.

Garnish with paprika, if desired. Cover and refrigerate until ready to serve.
2 Sift the besan, self-raising and soy flours into a bowl, then add the ground spices, chilli and salt. Gradually whisk in 250 ml (9 fl oz/1 cup) cold water until a batter forms. Set aside for 15 minutes.
3 Meanwhile, preheat the oven to 120°C (235°F/Gas 1–2). Cut the cauliflower into small florets. Cut the sweet potato and eggplant into 5 mm (¼ inch) slices, and cut the asparagus into 6 cm (2½ inch) lengths.
4 Fill a wok one-third full of oil and heat to 170°C (325°F), or until a cube of bread dropped into the oil browns in 20 seconds. Working in small batches, dip the vegetables in the batter, then fry for 1–2 minutes, or until pale golden. Remove with a slotted spoon and drain on paper towels. Keep warm in the oven until all the vegetables are cooked.
5 Serve hot, with raita or plain yoghurt.

snacks & party food

Beautifully presented party food always creates a sensation, and the vegetarian variety is no exception. Leave the tired old party pies and ribbon sandwiches on the shelf and impress your guests with this tempting array of inspired suggestions. When the party is over, pack up any leftovers, and enjoy them the next day as you relive the whole event.

swiss cheese

Both gruyère and emmental cheeses are often called 'Swiss cheese'. They are, however, quite different. Gruyère has only a few holes the size of peas, while emmental has eyes the size of cherries. From the chef's point of view, the important difference is in the texture of the cheeses when cooked: gruyère is often preferred as emmental becomes stringy when melted.

fast french sandwich

Cut two diagonal slices of crusty French bread; spread each with butter. Top one slice with Swiss cheese and a little wholegrain mustard; place the other slice on top and press firmly. Beat together an egg and a dash of milk; season with salt and pepper and add some finely chopped fresh herbs. Dip the sandwich in the egg mixture, turning to soak both sides. Melt a little butter in a frying pan. When sizzling, cook the sandwich for 2–3 minutes on each side, or until golden. Serve at once, on its own or with a salad. Serves 1.

cheese and mushroom pies

✹ ✹

Preparation time: 30 minutes
Cooking time: 35 minutes
Makes 6

40 g (1½ oz) butter
2 garlic cloves, crushed
500 g (1 lb 2 oz) button mushrooms, sliced
1 small red capsicum (pepper), finely chopped
165 g (5¾ oz/⅔ cup) sour cream
3 teaspoons wholegrain mustard
125 g (4½ oz/1 cup) finely grated gruyère or cheddar cheese

6 sheets ready-rolled puff pastry
1 egg, lightly beaten, to glaze

1 Preheat the oven to 190°C (375°F/ Gas 5). Lightly grease two baking trays.
2 Melt the butter in a large frying pan. Add the garlic and mushrooms and cook over medium heat, stirring occasionally, for 15 minutes, or until the mushrooms are tender and the liquid has evaporated. Remove from the heat and leave to cool. Stir in the capsicum.
3 Combine the sour cream, mustard and half the cheese. Cut twelve circles with a 14 cm (5½ inch) diameter from the pastry. Spread the sour cream mixture over six of the circles, leaving a 1 cm (½ inch) border. Top each with the mushroom mixture, then sprinkle with

the remaining cheese, reserving some for sprinkling over the pies. Brush the outer edges with beaten egg, then place the remaining pastry rounds over the filling, sealing the edges with a fork.

4 Brush the tops with egg and sprinkle with the remaining cheese. Place on baking trays and bake for 20 minutes, or until lightly browned and puffed.

polenta chillies

※ ※

Preparation time: 30 minutes
  + 2 hours chilling time
Cooking time: 15 minutes
Makes 12

330 g (11¾ oz) jar of mild, whole
  chillies
60 g (2¼ oz/½ cup) grated cheddar
  cheese
100 g (3½ oz) soft cream cheese
40 g (1½ oz/⅓ cup) plain (all-purpose)
  flour
2 eggs, lightly beaten
110 g (3¾ oz/¾ cup) polenta
75 g (2¾ oz/¾ cup) dry
  breadcrumbs
vegetable oil, for deep-frying
sour cream, to serve (optional)

1 Select twelve large, similar-sized chillies from the jar. Drain well and dry with paper towels. With a sharp knife, cut a slit down the length of one side of each chilli. Remove all the seeds and membrane. Combine the cheddar and cream cheese, then fill each chilli with the mixture.

2 Put the flour on a large plate and beat the eggs in a small bowl. Combine the polenta and breadcrumbs in a small plastic bag, then transfer to a large plate. Roll each chilli in the flour, shake off the excess, dip in the egg, then roll in the breadcrumb mixture to thoroughly coat. Place on a plate and refrigerate for 1 hour.

3 Re-dip each chilli in the egg, then re-roll in the breadcrumbs. Refrigerate for a further 1 hour.

4 Fill a heavy-based saucepan one-third full of oil and heat to 180°C (350°F), or until a cube of bread dropped into the oil browns in 15 seconds. Fry the chillies in small batches until golden and drain on paper towels. Serve with sour cream, if desired.

spring rolls

※ ※

Preparation time: 45 minutes
  + 20 minutes soaking time
Cooking time: 20 minutes
Makes 20

4 dried Chinese mushrooms
vegetable oil, for stir-frying and
  deep-frying
2 garlic cloves, crushed
1 tablespoon finely grated fresh ginger
150 g (5½ oz) fried tofu, cut into
  fine strips
1 large carrot, cut into very fine
  batons
70 g (2½ oz/½ cup) tinned water
  chestnuts, chopped
6 spring onions (scallions), chopped
150 g (5½ oz/3 cups) shredded
  Chinese cabbage (wong bok)
1 tablespoon soy sauce
freshly ground white pepper, to taste
pinch of sugar
1 tablespoon cornflour (cornstarch)
10 large spring roll wrappers

1 Soak the dried mushrooms in boiling water for 20 minutes. Drain and squeeze to remove any excess liquid. Slice the mushroom caps and discard the hard stems.

2 Heat 1 tablespoon oil in a large wok, over high heat, swirling gently to coat the base and side. Stir-fry the garlic, ginger, tofu, carrot and water chestnuts for 30 seconds. Add the spring onion and cabbage and cook for 1 minute, or until the cabbage has just softened. Add the soy sauce and some salt, white pepper and sugar to taste. Add the mushroom and set aside to cool.

3 Mix the cornflour with 2 tablespoons water to form a paste. Keep the spring roll wrappers covered with a clean damp tea towel (dish towel) while you work. Place two wrappers on a board, one on top of the other. (The rolls are made with two layers of wrappers.) Cut into four squares, then brush the edges of each square with a little cornflour paste. Place about 1 tablespoon of the filling in the centre of one square. With a corner facing you, roll up the wrapper firmly, folding in the sides as you roll. Repeat with the remaining wrappers and filling.

4 Fill a deep heavy-based saucepan one-third full of oil and heat to 180°C (350°F), or until a cube of bread dropped into the oil browns in 15 seconds. Deep-fry the spring rolls, about four at a time, for 3 minutes, or until golden. Drain on paper towels and serve.

rice vermicelli

Rice vermicelli are dried noodles made from rice flour. Their thickness and widths vary slightly. Commonly used in stir-fries and soups, they need to be soaked briefly in hot water or boiled until soft, and drained before use. (Follow the instructions on the packet.) Some recipes require fried rice vermicelli — it separates and puffs up when deep-fried; a little goes a long way, so always deep-fry in small quantities.

spinach and olive turnovers

✳ ✳ ✳

Preparation time: 1 hour 20 minutes
  + 1 hour chilling time
Cooking time: 15 minutes
Makes 30

250 g (8 oz/2 cups) plain (all-purpose)
  flour
200 g (7 oz) butter, cut into small cubes
1 egg, lightly beaten

FILLING
60 g (2 oz) English spinach leaves
100 g (3½ oz) feta cheese
2 tablespoons chopped pitted black
  olives
2 teaspoons chopped fresh rosemary
1 garlic clove, crushed

2 tablespoons lightly toasted
  pistachio nuts, finely chopped
1 egg, lightly beaten

1 Sift the flour into a large bowl and stir in the butter until just combined. Make a well in the centre, add about 150 ml (5 fl oz) water and mix to a slightly sticky dough using a flat-bladed knife, adding more water if necessary.
2 Gather the dough together, then turn out onto a well-floured surface and lightly press together until almost smooth, taking care not to overwork the dough.
3 Roll the dough out to a 20 x 40 cm (8 x 16 inch) rectangle, trying to keep the corners fairly square. Fold the top third of the pastry down, then fold the bottom third of the pastry up over it. Make a quarter turn to the right so that the edge of the top fold is on the right. Re-roll the pastry to a 20 x 40 cm (8 x 16 inch)

rectangle, and repeat the folding step. Wrap in plastic wrap and refrigerate for 30 minutes.
4 Repeat the previous step, giving a roll, fold and turn twice more. Refrigerate for a further 30 minutes.
5 To make the filling, wash the spinach leaves and dry thoroughly. Shred finely and place in a bowl. Crumble the feta over the spinach; add the remaining filling ingredients and stir until well combined. Set aside.
6 Preheat the oven to 180°C (350°F/ Gas 4). Brush a large baking tray with melted butter or oil. Roll out the pastry on a well-floured surface to a 3 mm (⅛ inch) thickness, then cut out 30 rounds using an 8 cm (3 inch) cutter.
7 Place two teaspoons of the filling in the centre of each pastry round; fold in half and pinch the edges to seal. Place on the baking tray, brush lightly with beaten egg and bake for 15 minutes, or until golden and crisp. Serve hot.

NOTE: The multiple folding and rolling process is essential to give the pastry its flaky character. To toast pistachio nuts, spread them on a baking tray and toast under a moderately hot grill (broiler) for 1–2 minutes.

fast bruschetta with herbs and capers

Toast one or two slices of thick crusty Italian bread or a mini pizza base until lightly golden on both sides. Rub each slice or base with a little crushed garlic, then top with chunks of vine-ripened or egg (roma) tomato. Sprinkle with sea salt and freshly ground black pepper and some fresh herbs such as basil or lemon thyme. Quickly deep-fry some capers until they turn crisp and have opened up like flowers. Drain the capers and sprinkle on top of the tomato. Serve immediately with parmesan cheese shavings or sour cream. Serves 1.

eggplant and capsicum focaccia

✹

Preparation time: 20 minutes
Cooking time: 10 minutes
Serves 4

2 tablespoons olive oil
1 small eggplant (aubergine), cut into
    1 cm (½ inch) slices
1 large focaccia (about 30 x 30 cm/
    12 x 12 inches)
90 g (3¼ oz/⅓ cup) tomato paste
    (concentrated purée)
1 small onion, thinly sliced
1 small red capsicum (pepper), cut into
    thin strips
3 tablespoons chopped coriander (cilantro)
    leaves
60 g (2¼ oz/½ cup) grated cheddar cheese
25 g (1 oz/¼ cup) shredded parmesan cheese

1 Heat the oil in a large frying pan.
Add the eggplant slices and cook over
medium–high heat for 2 minutes on each
side, or until soft and just golden. Drain
on paper towels.
2 Preheat the grill (broiler) to medium–
high. Cut the focaccia into four squares,
then in half horizontally. Toast each side
until golden.
3 Spread each square with the tomato
paste. Layer the eggplant, onion,
capsicum, coriander and the combined
cheeses on each square. Grill (broil) for
2–3 minutes, or until the cheese has
melted. Serve immediately.

dolmades

✹ ✹ ✹

Preparation time: 1 hour
Cooking time: 1 hour 15 minutes
Makes about 50

125 ml (4 fl oz/½ cup) olive oil, plus
    2 tablespoons, extra
6 spring onions (scallions), chopped
150 g (5½ oz/¾ cup) long-grain white rice

dolmades

3 tablespoons chopped mint
2 tablespoons chopped dill
170 ml (5½ fl oz/⅔ cup) lemon juice
35 g (1¼ oz/¼ cup) currants
40 g (1½ oz/¼ cup) pine nuts
235 g (8½ oz) packaged vine leaves
    (about 50)

1 Heat the oil in a saucepan over
medium heat. Add the spring onion and
cook for 1 minute. Stir in the rice, mint,
dill and half the lemon juice. Season to
taste. Add 250 ml (9 fl oz/1 cup) water
and bring to the boil, then reduce the
heat, cover and simmer for 20 minutes.
Remove the lid and mix the currants and
pine nuts through. Cover with a paper
towel, then the lid, then set aside to cool.
2 Meanwhile, rinse the vine leaves and
gently separate. Drain, then dry on paper
towels. Trim any thick stems with scissors.
Line the base of a 20 cm (8 inch) saucepan
with any torn or misshapen leaves. Choose
the larger leaves for filling, and use the
smaller leaves to patch up any gaps.

3 Place a leaf on a surface, shiny side
down. Spoon a tablespoon of the rice
mixture into the centre. Bring in the sides
and roll up tightly from the stem end.
Place seam side down, with the stem end
closest to you, in the saucepan, arranging
them close together in a single layer.
4 Pour in the remaining lemon juice, the
2 tablespoons extra oil and about 185 ml
(6 fl oz/¾ cup) water to just cover the
dolmades. Cover with an inverted plate,
then place a tin of food on the plate to
firmly compress the dolmades and keep
them in place while cooking. Cover with
the lid.
5 Bring to the boil, then reduce the heat
and simmer for 45 minutes. Remove from
the heat and leave to cool in the pan.
Serve at room temperature.

NOTE: Covered with the cooking liquid,
the dolmades will keep in the refrigerator
for up to 2 weeks.

herb pepper crisps with blue cheese dip

90 g (3¼ oz/⅓ cup) crème fraîche
   or sour cream
chives, to garnish

1 Preheat the oven to 180°C (350°F/ Gas 4). Brush each sheet of lavash bread with the butter. Sprinkle with the herb pepper seasoning and chives.
2 Cut each lavash sheet into 20 squares. Cut each piece in half to make triangles. Place on baking trays and bake in batches for 5 minutes, or until crisp. Remove from the oven and allow to cool.
3 To make the blue cheese dip, beat the cheese and butter in a small bowl using electric beaters until smooth and creamy. Add the wine, mint, rosemary and oregano and mix well. Fold the crème fraîche through and season to taste. Spoon the mixture into serving dishes and garnish with chives. Serve with the crisps.

NOTE: The crisps may be stored in an airtight container for up to 2 weeks.
   As a variation, combine 2 crushed garlic cloves with the melted butter before brushing over the bread. Sprinkle with grated parmesan cheese and chives. Cut into squares, then triangles, and bake.

To peel garlic easily, place the clove of garlic on a board. Lay a wide-bladed knife on top and give a sharp blow with the heel of the hand.

herb pepper crisps with blue cheese dip

☀

Preparation time: 30 minutes
Cooking time: 10 minutes
Serves 10

4 sheets lavash or other unleavened bread
90 g (3¼ oz) butter, melted
herb pepper seasoning, to sprinkle
1 tablespoon finely snipped chives

BLUE CHEESE DIP
250 g (9 oz) blue vein cheese, chopped
60 g (2¼ oz) butter, softened
1 tablespoon sweet white wine
2 teaspoons chopped mint
1 teaspoon chopped rosemary
2 teaspoons chopped oregano

mediterranean squares

☀

Preparation time: 15 minutes
Cooking time: 15 minutes
Makes about 20

1 red onion, sliced
3 tablespoons pitted black olives, sliced
1 red capsicum (pepper), cut into thin strips
1 green capsicum (pepper), cut into thin strips
2 tablespoons basil, finely shredded
3 teaspoons balsamic vinegar
5 garlic cloves, crushed
60 ml (2 fl oz/¼ cup) oil
3 garlic cloves, crushed, extra
1 large focaccia (about 30 x 40 cm/
   12 x 16 inches)
90 g (3¼ oz/¾ cup) grated cheddar cheese

1 Preheat the oven to 180°C (350°F/ Gas 4). Line a baking tray with foil.

2 Combine the onion, olives, capsicums, basil, vinegar and 2 crushed garlic cloves in a bowl. Mix together well, then cover and set aside.

3 Combine the oil and remaining garlic in a small bowl. Using a serrated knife, split the focaccia through the centre. Brush the focaccia halves with the garlic oil, then arrange the capsicum mixture evenly over the bottom half of the focaccia. Sprinkle with the cheese and top with the remaining piece of focaccia.

4 Place on the baking tray and bake for 15 minutes, or until the cheese has melted. Cut into squares to serve.

cheese, basil and pine nut triangles

✳ ✳

Preparation time: 40 minutes
Cooking time: 15 minutes
Makes 28

125 g (4½ oz) feta cheese, crumbled
125 g (4½ oz/½ cup) ricotta cheese
2 tablespoons chopped basil
3 tablespoons pine nuts, toasted
1 egg, lightly beaten
14 sheets filo pastry
125 g (4½ oz) butter, melted

1 Preheat the oven to 190°C (375°F/ Gas 5). Lightly grease two large baking trays.

2 Combine the feta, ricotta, basil, pine nuts and egg in a bowl. Season to taste and set aside.

3 Place a sheet of pastry on a work surface and brush all over with melted butter. Top with another sheet of pastry and brush with more butter. Cut the double layer of pastry lengthways into four strips.

4 Place 3 teaspoons of the cheese mixture on the end of each pastry strip. Fold the pastry over and up to enclose the filling and form a triangle. Brush the triangles with butter and place on the baking trays. Repeat with the remaining pastry and filling.

5 Bake for 15 minutes, or until golden brown. Serve hot.

VARIATION: Heat 1 tablespoon vegetable oil in a saucepan over medium heat. Add 1 finely chopped onion, 2 crushed garlic cloves and 2 small finely chopped red chillies. Cook, stirring, for 2–3 minutes, or until the onion is tender. Stir in 425 g (15 oz) drained and mashed tinned pinto or red kidney beans, 250 g (9 oz/1 cup) ready-made tomato salsa and 2 tablespoons chopped coriander; mix well. Place a teaspoon of the bean mixture onto each pastry sheet. Sprinkle with a little grated cheddar cheese, fold into triangles and bake. Serve with sour cream and guacamole.

fast savoury bites

Brush four ready-rolled puff pastry sheets with melted butter or oil. Place on four greased baking trays. Thinly spread two sheets with tomato paste (concentrated purée) and the others with dijon mustard. Top the tomato sheets with drained and quartered marinated artichoke hearts, some sliced black olives, finely shredded basil, grated mozzarella cheese and a sprinkle of crushed garlic. Top the mustard sheets with thin wedges of egg (roma) tomatoes, chopped fresh herbs and thin slices of camembert cheese. Bake in a preheated 210°C (415°F/Gas 6–7) oven 10–15 minutes. Cut into triangles for serving. Serves 2–6.

tangy tomato dip with pitta crisps

✳

Preparation time: 20 minutes
Cooking time: 15 minutes
Makes 2 cups

2 tablespoons olive oil
1 onion, chopped
2 garlic cloves, crushed
2 small red chillies, chopped
400 g (14 oz) tin chopped tomatoes
2 pimiento peppers, chopped
2 tablespoons lemon juice
4 tablespoons chopped parsley
3 pitta bread pockets
3 tablespoons sour cream

1 Preheat the oven to 180°C (350°F/ Gas 4). Split the pitta pockets in half and cut each half into eight wedges; brush with a little oil. Place in a single layer on a baking tray and bake for 10 minutes, or until golden and crisp.
2 Meanwhile, heat the oil in a saucepan over medium heat. Add the onion, garlic and chillies and cook, stirring, for 5 minutes, or until the onion has softened. Add the tomatoes, pimientos and lemon juice and bring to the boil. Reduce the heat to low, then simmer for 5 minutes, or until the sauce has thickened. Remove from the heat and stir in the parsley.
3 Spoon the tomato dip into a bowl and top with the sour cream. Serve warm or cold, with the pitta crisps.

baba ghanoush

✳

Preparation time: 20 minutes
Cooking time: 50 minutes
Makes about 2 cups

2 large eggplants (aubergines)
3 garlic cloves, crushed
½ teaspoon ground cumin
80 ml (2½ fl oz/⅓ cup) lemon juice
2 tablespoons tahini

a pinch of cayenne pepper
1½ tablespoons olive oil
1 tablespoon chopped flat-leaf (Italian) parsley
black olives, to garnish
toasted crusty bread or pitta crisps, to serve

1 Preheat the oven to 200°C (400°F/ Gas 6). Prick the eggplants several times with a fork, then cook over an open flame for 5 minutes, or until the skin is black and blistered. Transfer to a baking tray and bake for 40–45 minutes, or until the eggplants are very soft and wrinkled. Place in a colander and leave to stand over a bowl for 30 minutes to drain off any bitter juices.
2 Carefully peel the skin from the eggplants and chop the flesh. Place in a food processor with the garlic, cumin, lemon juice, tahini, cayenne pepper and oil. Process until smooth and creamy. Season with salt and stir in the parsley.
3 Spoon into a flat bowl or onto a plate and garnish with olives. Serve with toasted crusty bread or pitta bread.

avocado salsa

✳

Preparation time: 15 minutes
Cooking time: 1 minute
Makes 6

1 teaspoon ground coriander
1 teaspoon ground cumin
2 large avocados

baba ghanoush

1 tablespoon lime juice
1 tomato
1 red onion, finely chopped
1 small red capsicum (pepper)
3 tablespoons chopped coriander
   (cilantro)
2 tablespoons olive oil
4–5 drops Tabasco sauce
corn chips, to serve

1 Put the ground spices in a small frying pan and stir over medium heat for 1 minute, or until aromatic. Set aside.
2 Cut the avocados in half, remove the stones and carefully peel. Finely chop the flesh, place in a bowl and toss lightly with the lime juice. Cut the tomato in half horizontally, remove the seeds, then finely chop the flesh. Add to the avocado with the remaining ingredients and gently mix. Cover and refrigerate until required.
3 Serve the salsa at room temperature, with corn chips.

potato and cashew samosas

✸ ✸

Preparation time: **20 minutes**
Cooking time: **40 minutes**
Makes **16**

1 tablespoon olive oil
3 all-purpose potatoes, peeled and
   finely diced
2 teaspoons finely chopped ginger
100 g (3½ oz/⅔ cup) roasted unsalted
   cashew nuts, chopped
15 g (½ oz/¼ cup) shredded coconut
60 ml (2 fl oz/¼ cup) coconut cream
3 tablespoons chopped coriander (cilantro)
   leaves
4 sheets shortcrust (pie) pastry
vegetable oil, for deep-frying

1 Heat the oil in a large heavy-based frying pan over medium heat. Cook the potato and ginger for 8 minutes, stirring constantly. Add the cashews, coconut, coconut cream and coriander. Stir well

to combine and season to taste. Set aside and leave to cool.
2 Cut each pastry sheet into four. Place quarter-cupfuls of the filling in the centre of each square, then brush the pastry edges with water. Press the edges together and twist to seal. Refrigerate for 15 minutes.
3 Fill a large heavy-based saucepan one-third full of oil and heat to 180°C (350°F), or until a cube of bread dropped into the oil browns in 15 seconds. Deep-fry the samosas in batches for 6 minutes, or until golden and crisp. Drain on paper towels and serve immediately.

NOTE: Serve with a dip made from plain yoghurt, finely chopped cucumber, chopped chilli and mint, if desired.

avocados

An avocado that is ready to eat should be firm, but just yield to pressure when gently squeezed. The skin should be blemish-free. There are three common varieties of avocado. Hass has a rough knobbly skin that changes from green to purple-black. Fuerte is more pear-shaped, with a thinner, smoother green skin. There is also a small cocktail avocado that is only about 5 cm (2 inches) long.

fast crispy kefalotyri cheese sticks

Cut 500 g (1 lb 2 oz) kefalotyri cheese into sticks 1 cm (½ inch) thick. Dip in water and toss to coat in a mixture of 125 g (4 oz/1 cup) plain (all-purpose) flour, 100 g (3⅓ oz/1 cup) dry breadcrumbs, 2 tablespoons sweet paprika, 1 teaspoon ground cumin and 1 tablespoon chopped parsley. Repeat the dipping process, then cover with plastic wrap and refrigerate until needed. Pan-fry in hot oil until crisp — don't overcook or the cheese will start to melt through the crust. Gruyère or romano cheese may be used instead of kefalotyri. Serves 6–8.

herb ice cubes

Place a few mint or basil leaves (or any other large-leaf herbs you like) into ice cube trays, either singly or in sprigs. Cover with water and freeze. Herb ice cubes look wonderful added to summer drinks — borage flowers are especially suitable.

nachos with guacamole

❋

Preparation time: **20 minutes**
Cooking time: **5 minutes**
Serves **4**

400 g (14 oz) tin red kidney beans, rinsed and drained
450 g (1 lb/2 cups) ready-made tomato salsa
250 g (9 oz) corn chips
250 g (9 oz/2 cups) grated cheddar cheese
90 g (3¼ oz/⅓ cup) sour cream

GUACAMOLE
1 large avocado
1 spring onion (scallion), finely chopped
1 small tomato, finely chopped
1 tablespoon lemon juice

1 Preheat the oven to 180°C (350°F/ Gas 4). Mix the beans together with about 4 tablespoons of the salsa, then divide the bean mixture among four ovenproof serving plates. Cover with corn chips and grated cheese. Bake for 3–5 minutes, or until the cheese has melted.
2 Meanwhile, make the guacamole. Cut the avocado in half, discard the skin and stone and place the flesh in a bowl. Mash lightly with a fork, then stir in the remaining guacamole ingredients and some freshly ground black pepper.
3 To assemble the nachos, spoon the guacamole and sour cream over the corn chips. Top with the remaining salsa and serve.

mushrooms en croûte

✳

Preparation time: 40 minutes
Cooking time: 20–25 minutes
Makes 48

8 slices white bread, crusts
   removed
90 g (3¼ oz) butter, melted
1 tablespoon olive oil
1 garlic clove, crushed
½ small onion, finely chopped
375 g (13 oz) small button mushrooms,
   thinly sliced
1 tablespoon dry sherry
2 teaspoons cornflour
90 g (3¼ oz/⅓ cup) sour cream
1 tablespoon finely chopped
   parsley
1 teaspoon finely chopped thyme
3 tablespoons shredded parmesan
   cheese

1 Preheat the oven to 180°C (350°F/
Gas 4). Line a baking tray with foil.
Brush both sides of each bread slice
with melted butter. Cut each slice in
half down the middle, then cut each half
into thirds. Place on the baking tray and
bake for 5–10 minutes, or until golden
and crisp.
2 Heat the oil in a large frying pan
over low heat. Add the garlic and
onion and cook, stirring, until the onion
is soft. Add the mushrooms and cook
over medium heat for 5 minutes, or
until tender. Season to taste and add
the sherry.
3 Blend the cornflour and sour
cream; add to the mushroom mixture
and stir until the mixture boils and
thickens. Remove from the heat, then
stir in the parsley and thyme. Set aside
to cool.
4 Spread some mushroom mixture onto
each croûte. Sprinkle with parmesan.
Place on a baking tray and bake for
5 minutes, or until heated through.

individual herb tarts

✳

Preparation time: 20 minutes
Cooking time: 35 minutes
Makes 18

18 slices white bread, crusts removed
40 g (1½ oz) butter, softened

HERB FILLING
2 eggs
2 tablespoons milk
125 ml (4 fl oz/½ cup) cream
2 teaspoons chopped chives
1 teaspoon chopped dill
1 teaspoon chopped thyme
1 tablespoon chopped parsley
2 tablespoons grated parmesan
   cheese

1 Preheat the oven to 210°C (415°C/
Gas 6–7). Grease two 12-hole muffin or
patty pan trays. Cut the bread into rounds
using a 7 cm (2¾ inch) plain biscuit
(cookie) cutter. Flatten out each round
with a rolling pin.
2 Spread both sides of each bread round
with the butter, then gently press into
the muffin holes. Bake for 10 minutes,
or until lightly browned and crisp — do
not overcook.
3 Turn the oven down to 180°C (350°F/
Gas 4). To make the herb filling, combine
the eggs, milk, cream and herbs in a bowl
and mix well. Pour the mixture into the
bread cases and sprinkle with the parmesan.
4 Bake for 25 minutes, or until the filling
is lightly browned and has set. Serve hot.

mushrooms

If mushrooms need to be
cleaned, they should be wiped
with a damp cloth — washing
will make them soggy. Always
store fresh mushrooms in a
paper bag in the refrigerator.
Storing them in a plastic bag or
container will make them sweat
and deteriorate quickly.

fast parmesan lace biscuits

Finely shred 100 g (3½ oz) good-quality parmesan cheese. Combine in a small
bowl with 1 tablespoon finely chopped parsley, 1 tablespoon chopped chives
and ¼ teaspoon paprika. Heat a non-stick frying pan over medium–high heat.
Sprinkle a heaped tablespoon of the cheese mixture in the pan, in a round about
5 cm/2 inches in diameter. Cook until melted and bubbling, then remove the pan
from the heat. When the bubbling subsides and the cheese firms slightly, lift the
crisp out of the pan with a spatula and place onto paper towels. Repeat with the
remaining mixture. Makes 8 crisps.

parmesan and pesto toasts

✳

Preparation time: 15 minutes
+ 15 minutes freezing time
Cooking time: 5 minutes
Serves 8–10

1 baguette
16 large sun-dried tomatoes,
    thinly sliced
150 g (5½ oz) parmesan cheese,
    thinly shaved

PESTO
1 large handful basil
2 tablespoons snipped chives
50 g (1¾ oz/⅓ cup) pine nuts
2–3 garlic cloves
60 ml (2 fl oz/¼ cup) olive oil

1　Freeze the whole baguette for
15 minutes, or until firm.
2　Preheat the grill (broiler) to high.
Cut the baguette into very thin slices,
using a sharp serrated knife. Briefly grill
(broil) the slices until they are golden
brown on both sides.
3　Put all the pesto ingredients in a food
processor and blend for 20–30 seconds,
or until smooth.
4　Spread the pesto over the baguette
toasts. Top with the sun-dried tomato
and parmesan and serve.

eggplant sandwiches

✳

Preparation time: 30 minutes +
    30 minutes standing time
Cooking time: 20 minutes
Serves 4

3 eggplants (aubergines)
olive oil, for pan-frying
pinch of ground cumin (optional)
2 red capsicums (peppers),
    cut into large, flat pieces
10–12 sun-dried tomatoes, cut into strips

200 g (7 oz) ricotta or goat's cheese
4 tablespoons small basil leaves, plus extra,
    to garnish

1　Cut the eggplants lengthways into
slices about 1 cm (½ inch) thick. Choose
the eight largest slices and place on a
tray or board. Refrigerate the remaining
eggplant slices (see Note). Sprinkle the
eight reserved eggplant slices with salt
and allow to stand for 30 minutes. Rinse
well and pat dry with paper towels.
2　Heat a large frying pan over medium
heat. Pour in enough oil to cover the
base. When the oil is hot, add the
eggplant slices, a few at a time. Cook for
2–3 minutes on each side, or until brown.
Drain on paper towels and season each
slice with sea salt and freshly ground
black pepper. Sprinkle with cumin,
if desired.
3　Meanwhile, grill (broil) the capsicum
until the skin blackens and blisters. Place
on a cutting board, cover with a tea towel
(dish towel) and allow to cool before
peeling and chopping. Set aside.
4　On each of four serving plates, place
a slice of eggplant. Spread the slices
with the cheese, then top with sun-dried
tomato and capsicum, reserving some for
garnishing. Sprinkle with basil leaves,
then cover each with a second slice of
eggplant. Garnish with the remaining
capsicum, sun-dried tomato and extra
basil leaves.

NOTE: The unused eggplant slices will
last a day or two in the refrigerator. Finely
chop and then sauté in olive oil with
crushed garlic; season well and spread on
toast or on pitta bread as a snack, or add
to a soup or casserole.

sweet and spicy nuts

✳

Preparation time: 20 minutes
Cooking time: 15 minutes
Serves 6–8

250 g (9 oz/1⅔ cups) blanched almonds
250 g (9 oz/2½ cups) pecans
3 tablespoons sugar
1 teaspoon salt
½ teaspoon freshly ground
    black pepper
1 teaspoon ground cinnamon
a pinch of ground cloves
½ teaspoon curry powder
¼ teaspoon ground cumin

1　Preheat the oven to 180°C (350°F/
Gas 4). Place the nuts on a large baking
tray and bake for 5–10 minutes, or until
golden and crisp. Remove from the oven
and allow to cool.
2　Combine the remaining ingredients in
a small bowl. Mix well.
3　Heat a large frying pan over medium
heat. Add the nuts and sprinkle with the
spice mixture. Cook, shaking the frying
pan often, for 5 minutes, or until the nuts
turn golden — the sugar will melt and
coat the nuts. If the nuts stick together,
separate them with a wooden spoon.
4　Remove the nuts from the heat and
spread on a lightly oiled baking tray
to cool. Store in an airtight container
until required.

the vegetarian party

Bright, fresh vegetarian food is perfect for
parties. Make pizzas from lavash bread, spread
with a tapenade of sun-dried tomatoes and
olives; serve them warm, cut into wedges, as
you hand out drinks chilled with herb ice cubes
(see page 64). Also popular are large colourful
platters of roasted and marinated vegetables
such as capsicum (pepper), zucchini (courgette)
and eggplant (aubergine) — these vegetables
taste just as good at room temperature as they
do warm. Cut them into pieces and serve with a
variety of breads.

parmesan and pesto toasts

pies, flans & pizza

A deliciously familiar and much-loved way to combine fresh vegetables with crisp pastry, and often a creamy sauce, home-baked pies also have a healthy dollop of nostalgia buried deep within their crusts. These pastry- and dough-based recipes, whether a rich, classic onion tart or piquant tomato pizzettas, will travel from picnic to party, light lunch to family meal, with scarcely a single golden crumb out of place.

spinach pie

✹

Preparation time: **35 minutes**
Cooking time: **45 minutes**
Serves **6–8**

500 g (1 lb 2 oz) English spinach
olive oil, for pan-frying and brushing
6 spring onions (scallions), finely chopped
6 eggs
125 g (4½ oz) feta cheese, crumbled
90 g (3¼ oz/¾ cup) grated cheddar cheese
16 sheets filo pastry
1 tablespoon poppy seeds or sesame seeds

1 Preheat the oven to 210°C (425°F/Gas 6–7). Grease a 25 x 30 cm (10 x 12 inch) baking dish.
2 Wash the spinach thoroughly and shred finely. Place in a large saucepan with just the water that is still clinging to the leaves. Cover and cook over low heat for 2 minutes, or until just wilted. Allow to cool, then squeeze out any excess water. Spread the leaves out to dry.
3 Heat 1 tablespoon oil in a small frying pan and gently cook the spring onion for 3 minutes, or until soft. Transfer to a large bowl. Add 5 eggs and lightly beat. Season well, then add the spinach, feta and cheddar and stir until the cheeses are distributed evenly.
4 Place one sheet of pastry in the baking dish, letting the edges overhang. Cover the remaining pastry with a clean, damp tea towel (dish towel) to stop it drying out. Brush the pastry in the dish with oil, then repeat with another seven layers of pastry, brushing each lightly with oil.
5 Spread the spinach mixture over the pastry, then fold the edges in. Brush each remaining sheet of pastry lightly with oil and place on top of the pie. Tuck the edges down the sides. Lightly beat the remaining egg and brush it over the pie.
6 Sprinkle with poppy seeds and bake for 35–40 minutes, or until the pastry is golden. Serve immediately.

vegetable pasties

✹

Preparation time: **40 minutes**
Cooking time: **40 minutes**
Makes **12**

1 potato
1 carrot
1 parsnip
100 g (3½ oz) pumpkin (winter squash)
2 teaspoons vegetable oil

picnic pies

Most vegetable pies taste just as good at room temperature as they do hot and so are perfect as picnic food. If they've been refrigerated, you may like to warm them up in the oven before you leave the house. Wrap them in foil for transporting.

spinach pie

1 onion, finely chopped
125 ml (4 fl oz/½ cup) vegetable stock
50 g (1¾ oz/⅓ cup) fresh or frozen peas
1 tablespoon finely chopped flat-leaf
   (Italian) parsley
3 sheets frozen puff pastry, thawed
1 egg, lightly beaten
tomato sauce (ketchup), to serve

1 Preheat the oven to 210°C (425°F/
Gas 6–7). Lightly grease a baking
tray. Peel the potato, carrot, parsnip
and pumpkin and cut into 1 cm
(½ inch) cubes.
2 Heat the oil in a frying pan over
medium heat and cook the onion for
2 minutes, or until soft. Add the potato,
carrot, parsnip, pumpkin and stock
and bring to the boil. Reduce the heat
and simmer, stirring occasionally, for
10 minutes, or until the vegetables are
soft and the liquid has evaporated. Stir in
the peas and parsley and allow to cool.
3 Using a plate as a guide, cut four
12 cm (5 inch) circles from each sheet
of pastry. Place 1 level tablespoon of the
vegetable mixture onto each round, brush
the edges with water and fold the pastry
over so the edges meet. Crimp the edges
together to seal.
4 Brush the pasties with beaten egg
and place on the baking tray. Bake for
25 minutes, or until puffed and golden.
Serve with tomato sauce.

individual pot pies

✳

Preparation time: 40 minutes
Cooking time: 45 minutes
Serves 6

1 potato
150 g (5½ oz) pumpkin (winter squash)
1 large carrot
1 red capsicum (pepper)
150 g (5½ oz/2½ cups) small broccoli
   florets
1 tablespoon olive oil
1 onion, finely chopped
50 g (1¾ oz) butter

individual pot pies

2 tablespoons plain (all-purpose) flour
375 ml (13 fl oz/1½ cups) milk
125 g (4½ oz/1 cup) grated cheddar cheese
2 egg yolks, plus 1 lightly beaten egg
cayenne pepper, to taste
2 sheets ready-rolled puff pastry
1 teaspoon poppy seeds

1 Preheat the oven to 210°C (425°F/
Gas 6–7). Grease six 250 ml (9 fl oz/1 cup)
ramekins or dariole moulds.
2 Peel the potato, pumpkin and carrot
and cut into 1 cm (½ inch) cubes. Cut
the capsicum into 1 cm (½ inch) squares.
Steam or microwave the potato, pumpkin,
carrot and broccoli until just tender.
Drain well and place in a large bowl.
3 Heat the oil in a frying pan over
medium heat. Add the onion and capsicum
and cook for 2 minutes, or until softened.
Add to the vegetable mixture.

4 Melt the butter in a saucepan.
Add the flour and stir over low heat for
2 minutes, or until lightly golden. Add
the milk gradually, stirring until smooth.
Stir over medium heat for 3 minutes, or
until the mixture boils and thickens. Boil
for another minute, then remove from the
heat and cool slightly. Stir in the cheese
and egg yolks until smooth, then season
to taste with cayenne pepper and salt.
Add the sauce to the vegetables and
stir to combine.
5 Divide the mixture among the
ramekins. Cut six circles from the pastry
to fit the top of the ramekins, then press
the edges to seal. Brush with the beaten
egg and sprinkle with poppy seeds. Bake
for 30 minutes, or until golden brown.

NOTE: These pies are best eaten on the
day they are made.

silverbeet pie

4 Sprinkle the pistachios around the pastry-lined pie dish. Combine the silverbeet, raisins and cheeses and spread over the pistachios. Whisk the eggs with the cream and nutmeg, then pour over the silverbeet mixture.
5 Roll out the remaining pastry to cover the top of the pie, then trim the edges with a sharp knife. Press the edges together to seal. Brush the pie top with the beaten egg and decorate with pastry trimmings. Bake for 45 minutes, or until golden. Serve warm.

NOTE: This pie is best eaten on the day it is made.

harvest pie

❀ ❀

Preparation time: 40 minutes +
   30 minutes chilling time
Cooking time: 1 hour
Serves 6

250 g (9 oz/2 cups) plain
   (all-purpose) flour
125 g (4½ oz) butter, chopped
60 ml (2 fl oz/¼ cup) iced water
1 egg, lightly beaten

FILLING
1 tablespoon olive oil
1 onion, finely chopped
1 small red capsicum (pepper), chopped
1 small green capsicum (pepper), chopped
150 g (5½ oz) pumpkin (winter squash),
   chopped
1 small potato, chopped
100 g (3½ oz/1⅔ cups) broccoli florets
1 carrot, chopped
50 g (1¾ oz) butter
30 g (1 oz/¼ cup) plain (all-purpose) flour
250 ml (9 fl oz/1 cup) milk
2 egg yolks
60 g (2¼ oz/½ cup) grated cheddar cheese

1 Sift the flours into a large bowl. Using your fingertips, rub in the butter until the mixture resembles fine breadcrumbs. Add almost all the water and mix with a flat-

silverbeet pie

❀ ❀

Preparation time: 20 minutes
   + 30 minutes chilling time
Cooking time: 50 minutes
Serves 6–8

250 g (9 oz/2 cups) plain
   (all-purpose) flour
80 g (2¾ oz/½ cup) wholemeal
   (whole-wheat) flour
125 g (4½ oz) butter, chopped
80 ml (2½ fl oz/⅓ cup) iced water
1 egg, lightly beaten

FILLING
800 g (1 lb 12 oz) silverbeet
   (Swiss chard), stalks discarded
70 g (2½ oz/½ cup) chopped pistachio nuts
40 g (1½ oz/⅓ cup) chopped raisins
35 g (1¼ oz/⅓ cup) grated parmesan
   cheese
60 g (2¼ oz/½ cup) grated cheddar
   cheese

3 eggs
170 ml (5½ fl oz/⅔ cup) cream
¼ teaspoon freshly grated nutmeg

1 Sift the flours into a large bowl. Using your fingertips, rub in the butter until the mixture resembles fine breadcrumbs. Add almost all the water and mix with a flat-bladed knife, using a cutting action, until the mixture forms a firm dough, adding a little more water if necessary. Turn out onto a lightly floured work surface and press together until smooth.
2 Roll out two-thirds of the pastry and use it to line a greased 23 cm (9 inch) pie dish. Wrap the remaining pastry in plastic wrap, then refrigerate both the wrapped pastry and the pie dish for 30 minutes.
3 Preheat the oven to 180°C (350°F/Gas 4). To make the filling, wash the silverbeet leaves thoroughly, then shred finely. Steam or microwave for 3 minutes, or until tender. Allow to cool, then squeeze out any excess moisture. Spread the leaves out to dry.

bladed knife, using a cutting action, until the mixture forms a firm dough, adding a little more water if necessary. Turn out onto a lightly floured work surface and press together until smooth.

2 Divide the dough in half. Roll out one portion and use it to line a deep 21 cm (8¼ inch) fluted flan (tart) tin. Refrigerate for 30 minutes. Meanwhile, roll the remaining pastry out to a 25 cm (10 inch) circle. Cut the pastry into strips and lay half of them on a sheet of baking paper, leaving a 1 cm (½ inch) gap between each strip. Interweave the remaining strips to form a lattice pattern. Cover with plastic wrap and refrigerate, keeping it flat, until firm.

3 Preheat the oven to 180°C (350°F/ Gas 4). Cut a sheet of baking paper to cover the pastry-lined flan tin. Place over the pastry, then spread a layer of baking beads or uncooked rice over the paper. Bake for 10 minutes, then remove the paper and beads. Bake for another 10 minutes, or until lightly golden. Remove from the oven and leave to cool.

4 Meanwhile, make the filling. Heat the oil in a frying pan over medium heat. Add the onion and cook for 2 minutes, or until softened. Add the capsicums and cook, stirring, for 3 minutes. Set aside.

5 Steam or boil the remaining vegetables until just tender. Drain well, cool, then mix in a bowl with the onion and capsicum.

6 Melt the butter in a small saucepan. Add the flour and cook, stirring, for 2 minutes. Add the milk gradually, stirring until smooth. Stir over medium heat for 3 minutes, or until the mixture boils and thickens. Boil for another minute, then remove from the heat and cool slightly. Stir in the egg yolks and cheese until smooth. Pour the sauce over the vegetables and stir to combine.

7 Spoon the mixture into the pastry case and brush the edges with beaten egg. Using the baking paper to lift it, invert the pastry lattice over the vegetables. Remove the paper, trim the pastry edges and brush with beaten egg, sealing it to the cooked pastry. Brush the top with egg and bake for 30 minutes, or until golden brown.

pastry secrets

The secret of a light and crisp pastry is to make sure the dough is not overworked. Whether the mixing is done by hand or with a food processor, as long as you do it quickly, the dough will be easy to handle and roll. The amount of liquid required varies depending on the flour, so it must be added gradually, in small amounts until the mixture just comes together. The pastry should then be gathered up into a ball, wrapped and refrigerated. Pastry should always be cooked in a preheated oven, never one that has not yet reached the required temperature.

harvest pie

potatoes

Nature's ultimate comfort food has a long history of keeping famine at bay and families together — and with so many varieties and unlimited ways to cook it, the potato's staying power seems assured.

crispy potato wedges

Scrub and pat dry 8 sebago potatoes, then cut into thick wedges. Brush the wedges lightly with olive oil and sprinkle with sea salt and sweet paprika (or chilli powder for a spicier flavour). Bake in a preheated 220°C (425°F/Gas 7) oven for 35–40 minutes, or until crisp and golden. Serves 4.

classic potato gnocchi

Boil 1.25 kg (2 lb 12 oz) unpeeled desiree or pontiac potatoes in salted water until tender. Rinse and allow to cool slightly, then peel and mash (don't use a food processor). Place the mashed potato on a lightly floured surface. Make a well in the centre and add 2 egg yolks and 125 g (4 oz/1 cup) plain flour. Knead to form a soft dough. If the dough is too sticky, add more flour — the amount needed will differ with the type of potato used. Coat your hands with flour, then divide the mixture into eight pieces and roll into logs 3 cm (1¼ inches) thick and 22 cm (8½ inches) long. Cut the logs into 1 cm (½ inch) lengths and roll the pieces over the prongs of a lightly floured fork. Cook the gnocchi in a large pan of salted boiling water until they float to the surface. Serve with your favourite pasta sauce. Serves 4.

rosemary oven-roasted potatoes

Peel and chop 500 g (1 lb 2 oz) kipfler (fingerling) or other new potatoes into 1 cm (½ inch) cubes. Place in a non-stick baking dish and drizzle with 60 ml (2 fl oz/¼ cup) olive oil. Sprinkle with sea salt and freshly ground black pepper and toss 2 tablespoons rosemary sprigs through. Bake in a preheated 220°C (425°F/Gas 7) oven for 45 minutes, turning frequently, until crisp and golden. Serves 4.

warm and spicy potato salad

Peel and thickly slice 1 kg (2 lb 4 oz) pontiac potatoes. Heat 125 ml (4 fl oz/½ cup) olive oil in a large non-stick frying pan; add the sliced potatoes, 2 tablespoons tomato paste (concentrated purée), ½ teaspoon ground turmeric and 1 teaspoon each chilli flakes, saffron threads, black mustard seeds and cumin seeds. Cook over medium heat for 5 minutes, then stir in 375 ml (13 fl oz/1½ cups) vegetable stock and 2 bay leaves. Bring to the boil, reduce the heat, then cover and simmer for 30 minutes, or until the potato is tender. Stir in 3 tablespoons chopped mint and serve with plain yoghurt. Serves 4–6.

potatoes with crème fraîche and avocado salsa

Place 500 g (1 lb 2 oz) new potatoes in a large non-stick baking tray. Drizzle with 3 tablespoons olive oil and sprinkle with sea salt. Bake in a preheated 200°C (400°F/Gas 6) oven for 40 minutes, or until crisp and golden. Finely chop 1 small red onion, 1 small red chilli, 1 tomato and 1 peach. Place in a bowl with 1 crushed garlic clove, 1 chopped avocado, 1 tablespoon lime juice and 2 tablespoons chopped coriander (cilantro); gently mix together. Serve with the potatoes topped with a dollop of crème fraîche or sour cream. Serves 4.

tomato and bocconcini flan

bocconcini

Bocconcini are small rounds of fresh mozzarella cheese. They are usually served in salads to retain their delicate texture. If you cook them, be careful to do so only briefly or they will become dry and leathery.

tomato and bocconcini flan

✷ ✷

Preparation time: 20 minutes
  + 30 minutes chilling time
Cooking time: 50 minutes
Serves 6

185 g (6½ oz/1½ cups) plain
  (all-purpose) flour
100 g (3½ oz) butter, chopped
1 egg, lightly beaten with 2 tablespoons
  cold water

FILLING
5–6 roma (plum) tomatoes
1 tablespoon olive oil
8 bocconcini (fresh baby mozzarella cheese),
  about 220 g (7¾ oz), sliced
6 spring onions (scallions), chopped
2 tablespoons chopped rosemary

1 Process the flour and butter in a food processor for 10 seconds, or until fine and crumbly. With the motor running, gradually add the egg and process until the mixture just comes together. Turn out onto a lightly floured surface and gather into a smooth dough. Cover with plastic wrap and refrigerate for 30 minutes.
2 Preheat the oven to 210°C (425°F/ Gas 6–7). On a floured board, roll out the pastry to fit a 23 cm (9 inch) round, loose-based flan (tart) tin. Ease the pastry into the tin and trim the edges. Cut a sheet of baking paper to cover the pastry-lined flan tin. Place over the pastry, then spread a layer of baking beads or uncooked rice over the paper. Bake for 15 minutes, then remove the paper and beads. Bake for another 10 minutes, or until the pastry is lightly golden. Remove from the oven and leave to cool.
3 Turn the oven down to 180°C (350°F/ Gas 4). To make the filling, cut the tomatoes in half, sprinkle with sea salt and drizzle with the oil. Place in a baking dish, cut side up, and bake for 15 minutes.
4 Arrange the tomatoes, cut side up, in the pastry shell. Arrange the bocconcini and spring onion between the tomatoes. Scatter with the rosemary and season to taste. Bake for 10 minutes, then remove from the oven and allow to cool for 10 minutes before serving.

individual pumpkin and curry quiches

✷ ✷

Preparation time: 30 minutes
  + 30 minutes chilling time
Cooking time: 40 minutes
Serves 8

185 g (6½ oz/1½ cups) plain
  (all-purpose) flour
125 g (4½ oz/½ cup) cream cheese, chopped
125 g (4½ oz) butter, chopped

FILLING
1 tablespoon olive oil
2 onions, finely chopped
3 garlic cloves, crushed

1 teaspoon curry powder
3 eggs
125 ml (4 fl oz/½ cup) thick (double/heavy) cream
350 g (12 oz) pumpkin (winter squash), cooked and mashed
2 teaspoons cumin seeds

1 Sift the flour into a large bowl. Using your fingertips, rub in the cream cheese and butter until the mixture is smooth and comes together in a ball. Turn out onto a lightly floured surface and knead for 10 seconds, or until smooth. Cover with plastic wrap and refrigerate for 30 minutes.
2 Preheat the oven to 210°C (425°F/Gas 6–7). Grease eight deep 10 cm (4 inch) flan (tart) tins and line with baking paper. Divide the pastry into eight equal portions, then roll out until large enough to line the tins. Trim the edges and bake for 15 minutes, or until lightly browned. Remove from the oven.
3 Turn the oven down to 180°C (350°F/Gas 4). To make the filling, heat the oil in a small frying pan over low heat. Add the onion and garlic and cook, stirring, for 5 minutes, or until softened. Add the curry powder and stir for 1 minute. Spoon the mixture into the pastry cases, spreading it evenly.
4 In a large bowl, beat the eggs, cream and pumpkin until combined. Pour into the pastry cases, then sprinkle with the cumin seeds. Bake for 20 minutes, or until the filling has set.

rocket, basil and leek quiche

✲✲

Preparation time: 30 minutes
Cooking time: 1 hour 10 minutes
Serves 4–6

185 g (6½ oz/1½ cups) plain (all-purpose) flour
125 g (4½ oz) butter, chopped
1–2 tablespoons iced water

FILLING
1 tablespoon olive oil
1 large leek, white part only, thinly sliced
2 garlic cloves, crushed
150 g (5½ oz) rocket (arugula), stalks removed, leaves finely shredded
2 eggs
125 ml (4 fl oz/½ cup) milk
125 ml (4 fl oz/½ cup) cream
basil leaves, to garnish
parmesan cheese shavings, to garnish (optional)

1 Sift the flour into a bowl. Using your fingertips, rub in the butter until the mixture resembles fine breadcrumbs. Add the water and mix with a flat-bladed knife, using a cutting action, until the mixture forms a soft dough. Turn out onto a lightly floured work surface and knead for 10 seconds, or until smooth. Cover with plastic wrap and refrigerate for 30 minutes.
2 Preheat the oven to 210°C (425°F/Gas 6–7). Roll out the pastry until it is large enough to cover the base and side of a shallow 23 cm (9 inch) flan (tart) tin. Cut a sheet of baking paper to cover the pastry-lined flan tin. Place over the pastry, then spread a layer of baking beads or uncooked rice over the paper. Bake for 10 minutes, then remove the paper and beads. Bake for another 5 minutes, or until lightly golden. Remove from the oven and leave to cool.
3 Turn the oven down to 180°C (350°F/Gas 4). To make the filling, heat the oil in a frying pan over low heat. Add the leek and garlic and cook for 5 minutes, or until the leek is soft. Add the rocket and cook for 1 minute. Remove from the heat and allow to cool.
4 Spoon the leek mixture into the pastry shell, spreading it evenly. Combine the eggs, milk and cream in a large bowl and whisk until smooth. Pour the mixture into the pastry shell.
5 Bake for 50 minutes, or until the filling has set and is golden. Serve topped with basil and shaved parmesan, if desired.

rocket, basil and leek quiche

tomato and olive flan

✷ ✷

Preparation time: 20 minutes
   + 30 minutes chilling time
Cooking time: 40 minutes
Serves 4–6

250g (9 oz/2 cups) plain (all-purpose) flour
90 g (3¼ oz) butter, chopped
1 egg yolk, lightly beaten with
   1 tablespoon water

FILLING
6 small tomatoes
15 g (½ oz) butter
3 large onions, thinly sliced
2 tablespoons olive oil
1–2 tablespoons dijon mustard
1 teaspoon sugar
2 tablespoons shredded basil
125 g (4½ oz/1 cup) pitted black
   olives, sliced
135 g (4¾ oz/1 cup) grated gruyère cheese

1   Put the flour and butter in a food processor and process for 30 seconds, or until fine and crumbly. With the motor running, gradually add the egg yolk and process until the mixture just comes together. Turn out onto a lightly floured work surface and gather into a smooth dough. Cover with plastic wrap and refrigerate for 30 minutes.

2   Preheat the oven to 210°C (425°F/ Gas 6–7). Brush a deep 20 cm (8 inch) flan (tart) tin with melted butter or oil. Coat the base and sides of the tin evenly with flour and shake off any excess.

3   Roll out the pastry until large enough to fit the baking tin. Trim the edges with a sharp knife. Cut a sheet of baking paper to cover the tin. Place over the pastry, then spread a layer of baking beads or uncooked rice over the paper. Bake for 15 minutes, then remove the paper and beads and leave the pastry to cool.

4   Meanwhile, score a cross in the base of the tomatoes. Place in a heatproof bowl and cover with boiling water. Leave for 30 seconds, then transfer to cold water and peel the skin away from the cross. Cut the tomatoes in half, scoop out the seeds and chop the flesh.

olives

The golden rule when buying olives is to get the best you can afford. Two of the most delicious varieties are the purple-black kalamata from Greece, and the tiny dark-brown niçoise olives from France. If a recipe specifies using a certain type it is best to try to find it.

5 Melt the butter in a frying pan over medium heat. Cook the tomato and onion for 5 minutes, or until soft. Remove from the heat and drain off the excess liquid.
6 Mix together the oil and mustard to make a smooth paste. Spread over the base, then spoon the tomato over the top. Mix together the sugar, basil and olives and sprinkle over the flan. Sprinkle with gruyère and bake for 20 minutes, or until the pastry is crisp and the cheese is brown.

swiss onion tart

✳

Preparation time: 30 minutes
Cooking time: 1 hour 10 minutes
Serves 4

2 sheets frozen shortcrust pastry
2 tablespoons oil
3 medium onions, sliced
125 g (4 oz/½ cup) sour cream
2 eggs
65 g (2¼ oz/½ cup) grated Gruyére cheese
cayenne pepper

1 Preheat the oven to 210°C (415°F/ Gas 6–7). Thaw the pastry and fit the sheets, overlapping where necessary, into a 20 cm (8 inch) fluted flan tin; trim edges. Place on a baking tray. Cut a sheet of baking paper large enough to cover the pastry-lined tin. Spread a layer of dried beans or rice evenly over the paper. Bake the pastry shell for 10 minutes. Discard the paper and beans or rice. Bake for another 5 minutes or until the pastry is lightly golden. Reduce the oven temperature to 180°C (350°F/Gas 4).
2 Heat the oil in a saucepan over medium–low heat. Cook the onion, stirring often, for 15 minutes or until golden and very tender. Spread over pastry base.
3 Whisk together the sour cream and eggs until smooth. Add the cheese and stir until combined. Pour the egg mixture over the onion and sprinkle lightly with cayenne pepper. Bake for 40 minutes or until filling is set. Serve warm or cold.

baking blind

Baking a pastry case blind ensures the pastry base is crisp and cooked thoroughly. Once the pastry is in the tin, lay a sheet of baking paper over it, to cover the base and sides. Spread a layer of uncooked rice, dried beans or baking beads over the base to stop the pastry rising.

Bake in a preheated oven for the time stated, then remove the rice, beans or beads and paper. Return the pastry to the oven until lightly golden, then prepare the filling as directed. The rice or beans (dried chickpeas are also good) can be kept in a separate jar and reused whenever needed.

potato pizza with onion
and goat's cheese

low heat. Add the onion, cover and cook, stirring occasionally, for 20–30 minutes, or until golden and glossy. Remove from the heat and set aside.

4 Preheat the oven to 210°C (425°F/ Gas 6–7). Generously oil a pizza tray or two small baking trays. Turn the dough out onto a lightly floured surface. Gently punch down and knead for another 2 minutes. Put the dough on the tray and press out to fit. Top with the onion, capsicum and olives, then crumble the goat's cheese over the top and sprinkle with freshly ground black pepper. Bake for 20–25 minutes, or until the base is crisp. Serve immediately.

NOTE: The caramelised onions can be prepared a day in advance. Be sure to cook them over low heat so they become sweet and delicious. If they burn they will be bitter.

mini pizzas

✹

Preparation time: **20 minutes**
Cooking time: **25 minutes**
Serves **4**

1 tablespoon oil
1 small green capsicum (pepper),
   cut into short, thin strips
150 g (5½ oz) mushrooms, thinly
   sliced
1 zucchini (courgette), thinly
   sliced
4 mini pizza bases
160 g (5½ oz/⅔ cup) ready-made
   napoletana pasta sauce
400 g (14 oz) tin artichokes, drained
   and quartered
125 g (4 oz) tin corn kernels,
   drained
150 g (5½ oz/1 cup) grated mozzarella
   cheese

1 Preheat the oven to 210°C (425°F/ Gas 6–7). Lightly grease two baking trays.
2 Heat the oil in a frying pan over medium heat. Add the capsicum,

potato pizza with onion and goat's cheese

✹ ✹

Preparation time: **30 minutes**
   + 1 hour 30 minutes proving time
Cooking time: **55 minutes**
Serves **4**

125 ml (4 fl oz/½ cup) warm milk
4 teaspoons dried yeast
½ teaspoon sugar
165 g (5¾ oz/¾ cup) mashed potato
125 g (4 oz/1 cup) plain
   (all-purpose) flour
2 tablespoons chopped parsley

TOPPING
2 tablespoons olive oil
1 kg (2 lb 4 oz) red onions, thinly sliced

200 g (7 oz) roasted red capsicum
   (pepper), cut into strips
90 g (3¼ oz/½ cup) black olives
50 g (1¾ oz) goat's cheese

1 Combine the milk, yeast and sugar in a small bowl. Cover with plastic wrap and leave in a warm place for 10 minutes, or until foamy.
2 Put the mashed potato, flour and parsley in a large bowl. Add the yeast mixture, season well and mix until a soft dough forms. Turn out onto a lightly floured surface and knead for 10 minutes, or until the dough is smooth and springs back when pressed. Place in a large, lightly oiled bowl, cover with plastic wrap and leave in a warm place for 1–1½ hours, or until the dough has doubled in size.
3 Meanwhile, make the topping. Heat the oil in a heavy-based saucepan over

mushroom and zucchini and cook, stirring, for 3 minutes, or until softened, then set aside to cool.

3 Spread the pizza bases with pasta sauce. Top with the sautéed vegetables, the artichoke and corn. Sprinkle with mozzarella and place on the baking trays.

4 Bake for 15–20 minutes, or until the cheese has melted and the pizza bases are crisp. Serve immediately.

spanish pizza

✹ ✹

Preparation time: 30 minutes
  + 15 minutes proving time
Cooking time: 45 minutes
Serves 4–6

2 teaspoons dried yeast
1 teaspoon caster (superfine) sugar
280 g (10 oz/2¼ cups) plain
  (all-purpose) flour

TOPPING
10 English spinach leaves,
  shredded
1 tablespoon olive oil
2 onions, chopped
2 garlic cloves, crushed
400 g (14 oz) tin chopped tomatoes,
  drained
12 pitted black olives, chopped

1 Preheat the oven to 210°C (425°F/ Gas 6–7). Grease a 25 x 30 cm (10 x 12 inch) Swiss roll tin (jelly roll tin).

2 Combine the yeast, sugar and flour in a large bowl. Gradually add 250 ml (9 fl oz/1 cup) lukewarm water and mix to a smooth dough. Turn out onto a lightly floured surface and knead for 10 minutes, or until the dough is smooth and springs back when pressed. Place in a large, lightly oiled bowl, cover with plastic wrap and leave in a warm place for 15 minutes, or until the dough has doubled in size.

3 Meanwhile, make the topping. Put the spinach in a large saucepan, cover and cook on low heat for 3 minutes. Drain and

leave to cool, then squeeze out the excess moisture with your hands. Set aside.

4 Heat the oil in a frying pan over low heat. Add the onion and garlic and cook, stirring, for 5–6 minutes. Add the tomato, season with freshly ground black pepper and simmer gently for 5 minutes.

5 Turn the dough out onto a lightly floured surface. Gently punch down and knead for 2 minutes. Put the dough in the roll tin and press out to fit. Top with the spinach, then the tomato mixture. Sprinkle the olives on top.

6 Bake for 25–30 minutes, or until the base is crisp. Cut into small squares or fingers and serve hot or cold.

pizza bases

Traditionally, pizza bases are made from the local baker's leftover bread dough. They can also be made from scone dough or shortcrust pastry. Pitta, Lebanese, lavash and Turkish (pide) breads also make good pizza bases.

pancakes, fritters & omelettes

Good all-rounders, these scrumptious savoury dishes provide a perfect kickstart to a busy Saturday or a delightful late supper for friends after the movies. No matter what time you serve your first stack of aromatic herbed potato pancakes or a tangy chilli frittata, rest assured you'll get calls for an encore.

polenta

Polenta, also known as cornmeal, is made from ground dried corn and is bright yellow in colour. Polenta also refers to the dish made from cornmeal. This is a thick, porridge-like mixture that is usually left to set, and then brushed with oil and fried or grilled.

mexican polenta pancakes with avocado

✳

Preparation time: 30 minutes
 + 20 minutes chilling time
Cooking time: 20 minutes
Serves 4–6

50 g (1¾ oz/¼ cup) polenta
60 g (2 oz/½ cup) plain
 (all-purpose) flour
¼ teaspoon baking powder
¼ teaspoon salt
1 teaspoon sugar
250 ml (9 fl oz/1 cup) buttermilk
2 eggs
30 g (1 oz) butter, melted
vegetable oil, for pan-frying
160 g (5½ oz/⅔ cup) sour cream

AVOCADO FILLING
1 large ripe avocado
8 spring onions (scallions),
 finely chopped
2 ripe tomatoes, seeded and
 finely chopped
1 teaspoon chilli sauce,
 or to taste
2 teaspoons lemon juice

1 Sift the polenta, flour, baking powder, salt and sugar into a bowl. Make a well in the centre. Beat the buttermilk, eggs and butter until smooth, then add to the dry ingredients. Beat until the liquid is incorporated and the batter is free of lumps. Cover with plastic wrap and set aside for 20 minutes.

2 Meanwhile, make the avocado filling. Mash the avocado flesh in a bowl. Add half the spring onion, the tomato, chilli sauce and lemon juice. Mix well, season to taste, then cover and refrigerate for 20 minutes.

3 Brush a small frying pan with oil and heat over medium heat. Pour in enough batter to thinly cover the base of the pan. Cook until golden underneath, then turn the pancake over and cook the other side. Transfer to a plate, cover with a tea towel (dish towel) and keep warm. Repeat with the remaining batter, oiling the pan as necessary.

4 Spoon some avocado filling on one half of each pancake, then fold the other half over. Serve with sour cream, sprinkled with the remaining spring onion.

potato and pumpkin pancakes

✳

Preparation time: **25 minutes**
Cooking time: **25 minutes**
Makes **10**

250 g (9 oz) potato, cooked and mashed
250 g (9 oz) pumpkin (winter squash), cooked and mashed
30 g (1 oz) butter
3 spring onions (scallions), finely chopped
2 eggs, lightly beaten
30 g (1 oz/¼ cup) plain (all-purpose) flour
2 tablespoons self-raising flour
¼ teaspoon ground nutmeg
a pinch of cayenne pepper
¼ teaspoon salt
2 tablespoons vegetable oil

1 Put the potato and pumpkin in a food processor with the butter. Process until smooth, then transfer to a bowl. Stir in the spring onion and eggs.

2 Sift the flours, spices and salt into a bowl. Add to the pumpkin mixture and stir well to combine.

3 Heat half the oil in a non-stick frying pan over medium heat. Cook heaped tablespoons of the mixture for 2 minutes, then turn and cook for 2–3 minutes, or until golden. Drain on paper towels and keep warm. Repeat with the remaining mixture, adding more oil to the pan as necessary. Serve warm.

fast thai corn pancakes

Place the kernels of 2 corn cobs in a bowl. Add 2 finely chopped spring onions (scallions), 2 tablespoons finely chopped coriander (cilantro) stems, 2 crushed garlic cloves, 2 teaspoons drained and crushed tinned green peppercorns, 2 tablespoons cornflour (cornstarch), 2 beaten eggs, 1 tablespoon fish sauce (optional) and 2 teaspoons soft brown sugar. Beat with a wooden spoon until well combined. Heat a little vegetable oil in a heavy-based frying pan over medium–high heat. Spoon tablespoons of the batter into the pan and cook in batches until golden on both sides. Drain on paper towels and serve immediately. Serves 4–6.

potato and herb fritters

✳

Preparation time: 25 minutes
Cooking time: 10 minutes
Serves 4–6

625 g (1 lb 6 oz/4 cups) finely
    grated potato
185 g (6½ oz/1½ cups) finely grated
    orange sweet potato
3 tablespoons finely snipped chives
1 tablespoon finely chopped oregano
2 tablespoons finely chopped flat-leaf
    (Italian) parsley
2 eggs, lightly beaten
30 g (1 oz/¼ cup) plain (all-purpose) flour
1 tablespoon olive oil
250 g (9 oz/1 cup) light sour cream
dill sprigs, to garnish

1 In a bowl, combine the potato, sweet potato, herbs and egg. Sift the flour over the top and stir with a wooden spoon until just combined.
2 Heat the oil in a large heavy-based frying pan over medium–high heat. Spoon heaped tablespoons of the mixture into the pan and cook for 4 minutes on each side, or until golden. Serve warm, topped with sour cream and dill sprigs.

fried green tomatoes

✳

Preparation time: 15 minutes
Cooking time: 10 minutes
Serves 4–6

90 g (3¼ oz/¾ cup) plain (all-purpose)
    flour
½ teaspoon ground white pepper
1 teaspoon salt
35 g (1¼ oz/¼ cup) polenta
1 egg
185 ml (6 fl oz/¾ cup) milk
vegetable oil, for pan-frying
4 green tomatoes (about 500 g/1 lb 2 oz),
    cut into thick slices

1 Sift the flour, pepper and salt into a bowl. Add the polenta and stir to combine, then make a well in the centre.
2 Lightly whisk together the egg and milk, then gradually add to the flour mixture. Whisk the batter until just combined — do not overbeat.
3 Heat about 1 cm (½ inch) of oil in a frying pan over medium heat.
4 Working in batches, dip the tomato into the batter and drain off the excess. Fry for 1 minute on each side, turning only once with tongs. Drain on paper towels and serve immediately.

NOTE: Red tomatoes can also be used.

mixed grated vegetable frittata

✳

Preparation time: 25 minutes
Cooking time: 15 minutes
Serves 2–4

60 ml (2 fl oz/¼ cup) olive oil
1 onion, finely chopped
1 small carrot, grated
1 small zucchini (courgette),
    grated
125 g (4½ oz/1 cup) grated pumpkin
    (winter squash)
4 tablespoons finely diced jarlsberg
    or cheddar cheese
½ teaspoon salt
½ teaspoon freshly ground
    black pepper
5 eggs, lightly beaten

1 Heat 2 tablespoons of the oil in a frying pan over medium heat. Add the onion and cook, stirring, for 5 minutes,

potato and herb fritters

or until the onion is soft. Add the carrot, zucchini and pumpkin, then cover and cook over low heat for 3 minutes.

2 Transfer the mixture to a bowl and allow to cool. Stir in the cheese, salt, pepper and eggs and mix together well.

3 Heat the remaining oil in a small frying pan over medium heat. Add the egg mixture and shake the pan to spread the mixture evenly over the base. Reduce the heat to low and cook for 5 minutes, or until the mixture is set almost all the way through; tilt the pan and lift the edges of the frittata occasionally during cooking to allow the uncooked egg to flow underneath.

4 Remove the frittata to a plate, cut into wedges and serve.

chilli and coriander frittata

✳

Preparation time: **25 minutes**
Cooking time: **30 minutes**
Serves **6**

3 all-purpose potatoes, peeled and
    cut into small cubes
2 tablespoons olive oil
2 banana chillies, seeded and sliced
1 onion, finely chopped
1 small red chilli, thinly sliced
1 tablespoon chopped coriander (cilantro)
    leaves
5 eggs

1 Cook the potatoes in a large saucepan of boiling water for 10 minutes, or until just tender. Drain well and set aside.

2 Meanwhile, heat half the oil in a non-stick frying pan over medium heat. Cook the banana chilli for 2 minutes, or until softened. Remove from the pan and set aside.

3 Heat the remaining oil in the pan and cook the onion and red chilli over medium heat for 3 minutes, or until soft. Add the potato and toss to combine, then remove from the pan and set aside.

4 Return half the banana chilli to the pan and sprinkle with the coriander. Spread half the potato mixture over the top. Sprinkle with the remaining banana chilli and the remaining potato mixture.

5 Preheat the grill (broiler) to medium–high. Beat the eggs in a bowl, then pour into the frying pan. Reduce the heat and cook over medium–low heat for 8 minutes, or until the egg is almost cooked through, then place under the grill for 4 minutes to cook the top.

6 Invert the frittata onto a plate. Allow to cool, then cut into wedges and serve.

green tomatoes

Green tomatoes are not a separate variety but are simply unripe red tomatoes. They became popular during the Depression years in the southern states of America as a tasty, light summer meal. It is easy to confuse green tomatoes with tomatillos — these are small green fruit that closely resemble the tomato. As well as being fried, green tomatoes are also excellent pickled or made into a spicy sauce.

vegetable chips

Paper-thin or rough and chunky, chips are loved by everyone — and they don't even have to be made from potatoes, as these clever ideas prove.

beetroot chips

Peel 500 g (1 lb 2 oz) beetroots (beets). Using a sharp vegetable peeler or a knife, cut them into paper-thin slices. Heat 750 ml (26 fl oz/3 cups) vegetable oil in a saucepan over medium–high heat. Working in batches, cook the beetroot chips until crisp and browned. Drain on paper towels and keep warm in a preheated 180°C (350°F/Gas 4) oven while cooking the remainder. Serve with whole-egg mayonnaise blended with chopped fresh herbs of your choice.

crispy sweet potato discs

Peel 500 g (1 lb 2 oz) orange sweet potato. Using a sharp vegetable peeler or a knife, cut into thin slices. Heat 750 ml (26 fl oz/3 cups) vegetable oil in a saucepan over medium–high heat. Working in batches, cook the sweet potato discs until crisp and golden. Drain on paper towels and keep warm in a preheated 180°C (350°F/Gas 4) oven while cooking the remainder. Serve with whole-egg mayonnaise blended with lime juice and curry powder.

zucchini ribbons

Using a sharp vegetable peeler, cut 500 g (1 lb 2 oz) large zucchini (courgettes) into ribbons by running the peeler lengthwise along each zucchini. Lightly beat 4 eggs in a bowl; in another bowl combine 100 g (3½ oz/1 cup) dry breadcrumbs and 1 tablespoon chopped fresh herbs. Heat 750 ml (26 fl oz/3 cups) vegetable oil in a saucepan over medium–high heat. Working in batches, dip the zucchini ribbons into the egg, then the breadcrumbs, and cook until golden. Drain on paper towels and keep warm in a preheated 180°C (350°F/Gas 4) oven while cooking the remainder. Serve with a dipping sauce made from chopped sun-dried tomatoes and plain yoghurt.

golden potato chips

Cut 500 g (1 lb 2 oz) scrubbed old potatoes into thick country-style chips or wedges. Heat 750 ml (26 fl oz/3 cups) vegetable oil in a saucepan over medium–high heat. Working in batches, cook the chips until lightly golden; drain on paper towels. Repeat with the remaining potato. Just before serving, re-fry the potatoes in batches until crisp and golden. Sprinkle with sea salt and malt vinegar, if desired.

pumpkin crisps

Peel 500 g (1 lb 2 oz) butternut pumpkin (squash) and cut into crinkle-cut slices. Heat 750 ml (26 fl oz/3 cups) vegetable oil in a saucepan over medium–high heat. Working in batches, cook the pumpkin slices until crisp and golden. Drain on paper towels and keep warm in a preheated 180°C (350°F/Gas 4) oven while cooking the remainder. Serve hot.

carrot and herb ribbons

Peel 500 g (1 lb 2 oz) carrots, then cut into ribbons by running a sharp peeler lengthwise along each carrot. Rinse and dry a large handful of basil leaves. Heat 750 ml (26 fl oz/3 cups) vegetable oil in a saucepan over medium–high heat. Working in batches, cook the carrot and basil until crisp. Drain on paper towels and keep warm in a preheated 180°C (350°F/Gas 4) oven while cooking the remainder. Serve with a dipping sauce of sweet chilli sauce, lime juice and chopped coriander (cilantro).

cheese soufflé omelette

cheese soufflé omelette

☼

Preparation time: **10 minutes**
Cooking time: **5 minutes**
Serves **2–4**

5 eggs, separated
2 teaspoons lemon juice
20 g (¾ oz) butter
85 g (3 oz/⅔ cup) grated cheddar cheese
chopped herbs, to serve (optional)

1 Preheat the grill (broiler) to high. Put the egg yolks, lemon juice and 2 teaspoons water in a small bowl. Season with sea salt and freshly ground black pepper. Using electric beaters, beat on high for 2 minutes, or until pale and creamy.
2 Place the egg whites in a small, dry, bowl. Using electric beaters or a wire whisk, beat until firm peaks form. Using a metal spoon, gently fold the egg whites into the yolk mixture.
3 Melt the butter in a deep, non-stick frying pan over high heat. When the butter is foaming, add the egg mixture and swirl the pan to spread the mixture evenly over the base. Cook for 1 minute without stirring, then remove from the heat and sprinkle with the cheese.
4 Grill (broil) for 2–3 minutes, or until the omelette is puffed and golden. Cut into serving portions and serve immediately, as the omelette may deflate quickly. Sprinkle with chopped fresh herbs, if desired.

NOTE: The omelette is delicious accompanied by pan-fried mushrooms, or tomatoes that have been halved, sprinkled with cheese and then grilled.

eggs

Many vegetarians eat eggs and dairy foods, and can obtain a significant amount of calcium and protein by doing so. Free-range eggs are produced in an environment where the hens are allowed to move about and feed naturally, rather than be confined in batteries. These eggs are therefore preferable for people with health and humanitarian concerns.

omelette rolls

✻

Preparation time: 10 minutes
Cooking time: 10 minutes
Makes 5

4 eggs
2 teaspoons soy sauce
2 teaspoons peanut oil

1 Place the eggs, soy sauce and 2 tablespoons water in a bowl. Beat with a wire whisk for 2 minutes.
2 Heat a small non-stick frying pan over high heat and brush with the oil. Pour in one-fifth of the egg mixture, then swirl the pan to spread the mixture evenly over the base. Cook for 20 seconds, or until the egg has almost set. Remove the pan from the heat.
3 Using a spatula, roll the omelette from one end, forming a roll. Transfer to a warm plate and cover with a tea towel (dish towel).
4 Repeat with the remaining egg mixture, to make five omelette rolls. Serve warm.

NOTE: For extra flavour, spread the top with some pesto or olive tapenade, or top with a filling of your choice. Roll them up tightly and cut into rounds for serving.

creamy omelette

✻

Preparation time: 5 minutes
Cooking time: 5 minutes
Serves 2

3 eggs
60 ml (2 fl oz/¼ cup) cream
20 g (¾ oz) butter
chopped herbs, to serve

1 Place the eggs and cream in a bowl and season with sea salt and freshly ground black pepper. Beat with a wire whisk for 2 minutes.
2 Heat the butter in a small non-stick frying pan over medium heat. When the butter is foaming, pour in the egg mixture all at once. Stir with a wooden spoon for 15 seconds.
3 Cook until the egg mixture is almost set, tilting the pan and lifting the edges of the omelette occasionally to allow the uncooked egg to flow underneath.
4 When the egg mixture has almost set, fold the omelette in half using a spatula — the centre of the omelette should still be moist and creamy.
5 Sprinkle with herbs and serve.

NOTE: Instead of folding the omelette, you can complete the cooking process by covering the pan with a lid for about 2 minutes.

omelettes

Omelettes come in many shapes and forms, and each country has its own traditional variety. The French make their folded omelettes to incorporate many diffent fillings, both sweet and savoury. The Italians have frittata, a more substantial dish that is cooked on both sides and cut into wedges to serve. Spanish omelette, which is called tortilla in Spain, is similar to frittata, but is always made from cooked potatoes that are set with eggs.

omelette rolls with olive tapenade filling

pasta & noodles

The Italians have been enjoying spaghetti and macaroni since the days of ancient Rome, but it's only in the past few decades that all manner of pasta has found its way into our kitchens, each variety able to assume a dozen or more tantalising guises when sauced and presented. From spicy Oriental noodles to the splendidly simple spaghetti tossed with rocket, here is an introduction to the countless possibilities of pasta.

pumpkin and herb ravioli

ravioli

For a light texture, the dough for ravioli should be rolled as thinly as possible, but it also needs to be thick enough to remain intact during handling and cooking. The knack of obtaining the most manageable thickness will come naturally once you've made it once or twice.

pumpkin and
herb ravioli

✸ ✸

Preparation time: 30 minutes
  + 30 minutes resting time
Cooking time: 1 hour 15 minutes
Serves 6

500 g (1 lb 2 oz) pumpkin (winter squash), peeled and cut into chunks
¼ teaspoon freshly grated nutmeg
220 g (7¾ oz/1¾ cups) plain (all-purpose) flour
3 eggs, lightly beaten
15 sage leaves
15 flat-leaf (Italian) parsley leaves
125 g (4½ oz) butter, melted
finely grated parmesan cheese, to serve

1 Preheat the oven to 180°C (350°F/ Gas 4). Bake the pumpkin on an oiled baking tray for 1 hour, or until tender. Allow to cool, then peel and place in a bowl with the nutmeg. Mash with a fork.

2 Meanwhile, place the flour and eggs in a food processor. Blend for 30 seconds, or until the mixture forms a dough. Transfer to a lightly floured surface and knead for 3 minutes, or until smooth and elastic. Cover with a clean tea towel (dish towel) and leave to rest for 30 minutes.
3 Roll out half the dough to form a rectangle about 2 mm (¹⁄₁₆ inch) thick. Roll out the remaining half to form a rectangle slightly larger than the first.
4 On the first rectangle, place heaped teaspoons of the pumpkin mixture in straight rows, at intervals about 5 cm (2 inches) apart. Flatten each pumpkin mound slightly, then place one whole sage or parsley leaf on top of each mound.
5 Lightly brush between the pumpkin mounds with water. Place the second sheet of dough on top, then press down gently between the pumpkin mounds to seal. Cut into squares with a knife or a fluted cutter.
6 Bring a large saucepan of water to the boil. Drop in the ravioli a few at a time and cook for 4 minutes, or until just tender. Remove using a slotted spoon and place in a heated serving dish. Sprinkle with salt and pepper, toss with the melted butter and parmesan and serve.

NOTE: Ravioli can be made several hours in advance — refrigerate in layers between sheets of baking paper to stop them sticking together. Cook just before serving.

fettuccine with
zucchini and
crisp-fried basil

✸

Preparation time: 15 minutes
Cooking time: 15 minutes
Serves 6

500 g (1 lb 2 oz) fettuccine or tagliatelle
250 ml (9 fl oz/1 cup) olive oil
1 handful of basil leaves
60 g (2¼ oz) butter
2 garlic cloves, crushed

500 g (1 lb 2 oz) zucchini (courgettes), grated
75 g (2¾ oz/¾ cup) grated parmesan cheese

1 Cook the pasta in a large saucepan of rapidly boiling salted water until al dente. Drain and return to the pan.
2 While the pasta is cooking, heat the oil in a small frying pan over medium heat. Add a few basil leaves at a time and cook for 1 minute, or until crisp. Remove with a slotted spoon and drain on paper towels. Repeat with the remaining basil leaves and set aside.
3 Heat the butter in a deep heavy-based saucepan over low heat until foaming. Add the garlic and cook for 1 minute. Add the zucchini and cook, stirring, for 1–2 minutes, or until softened.
4 Add the zucchini mixture to the hot pasta. Add the parmesan and toss well. Serve garnished with the fried basil leaves.

NOTE: The basil leaves can be fried up to 2 hours in advance. Allow to cool, then store in an airtight container.

tagliatelle with green olives and eggplant

❈

Preparation time: 20 minutes
Cooking time: 20 minutes
Serves 4

500 g (1 lb 2 oz) tagliatelle
2 tablespoons olive oil
2 garlic cloves, crushed
1 large eggplant (aubergine), cut into small cubes
175 g (6 oz/1 cup) green olives, pitted and chopped
125 ml (4 fl oz/½ cup) lemon juice

2 tablespoons chopped flat-leaf (Italian) parsley
50 g (1¾ oz/½ cup) grated parmesan cheese

1 Cook the pasta in a large saucepan of rapidly boiling salted water until al dente. Drain and return to the pan.
2 While the pasta is cooking, heat the oil in a heavy-based frying pan over medium heat. Add the garlic and stir for 30 seconds, then add the eggplant and cook, stirring frequently, for 6 minutes, or until tender. Stir in the olives and lemon juice and season to taste.
3 Add the sauce to the hot pasta and toss. Serve sprinkled with the parsley and parmesan.

NOTE: If you prefer, the eggplant can be salted to draw out any bitter juices. Sprinkle the cut eggplant liberally with salt and leave to stand for 30 minutes. Rinse well before using.

tagliatelle with green olives and eggplant

ribbon noodles

Ribbon or flat noodles come in various widths. Tagliatelle and fettuccine are fairly similar and can be interchanged in recipes. Tagliatelle is traditionally the wider of the two. Pappardelle is wider still, while tagliolini is the narrowest.

cooking pasta ahead

If you are cooking for a large crowd, cook the pasta in batches and place in a baking dish. Stir a little oil through, cover with a damp tea towel (dish towel) and keep the pasta warm in a low oven. Alternatively, you can reheat the cooked pasta in a microwave oven.

tagliatelle with asparagus and herbs

❈

Preparation time: 15 minutes
Cooking time: 15 minutes
Serves 4–6

500 g (1 lb 2 oz) tagliatelle
150 g (5½ oz) asparagus
40 g (1½ oz) butter
1 tablespoon chopped flat-leaf (Italian) parsley
1 tablespoon chopped basil
310 ml (10¾ fl oz/1¼ cups) cream
50 g (1¾ oz/½ cup) grated parmesan cheese, plus extra shavings, to serve

1 Cook the pasta in a large saucepan of rapidly boiling salted water until al dente. Drain and return to the pan.
2 While the pasta is cooking, trim the woody ends off the asparagus and cut the spears into short pieces. Melt the butter in a saucepan over medium heat, add the asparagus and stir for 2 minutes, or until just tender.
3 Add the parsley, basil and cream and cook for 2 minutes, then season to taste. Add the parmesan and stir until thoroughly combined.
4 Add the sauce to the hot pasta and toss. Serve scattered with shaved parmesan.

blue cheese tagliatelle

❈

Preparation time: 15 minutes
Cooking time: 20 minutes
Serves 6

500 g (1 lb 2 oz) tagliatelle
30 g (1 oz) butter
1 garlic clove, crushed
2 zucchini (courgettes), sliced
100 ml (3½ fl oz) white wine
100 g (3½ oz) blue cheese, crumbled
300 ml (10½ fl oz) cream
grated parmesan cheese, to serve
chopped flat-leaf (Italian) parsley, to garnish

1 Cook the pasta in a large saucepan of rapidly boiling salted water until al dente. Drain and return to the pan.

fast pasta with mushrooms and mascarpone

Melt 30 g (1 oz) butter in a non-stick frying pan. Add 10 thinly sliced flat or field mushrooms and cook over medium heat until soft and golden. Stir in 1–2 crushed garlic cloves and 125 g (4½ oz) mascarpone cheese. Stir over low heat until the cheese has melted and is smooth; stir in a little cream if the mixture is too thick. Add some chopped parsley and season to taste. Toss through hot pasta and serve. Serves 2.

tagliatelle with asparagus and herbs

2 While the pasta is cooking, melt the butter in a frying pan over medium–low heat. Add the garlic and zucchini and cook for 3 minutes, or until the zucchini is tender. Stir in the wine, cheese, cream and a pinch of freshly ground black pepper. Simmer for 10 minutes.

3 Add the sauce to the hot pasta and toss. Serve sprinkled with parmesan and parsley.

thyme

A tiny-leafed but tough herb, thyme has an affinity with Mediterranean vegetables such as eggplant (aubergine), zucchini (courgette) and capsicum (pepper). Lemon thyme is superb in stuffing mixes. Thyme is easy to grow in a sunny corner in even the smallest garden and it's well worth the effort — home-dried or frozen thyme is far superior in flavour to commercially powdered or dried products. To dry thyme, hang bunches in a warm place, then rub the leaves off and store them in an airtight jar.

spaghetti with fresh tomato sauce

✺

Preparation time: 15 minutes +
   2 hours chilling time
Cooking time: 15 minutes
Serves 4

4 spring onions (scallions), finely chopped
4 firm, ripe tomatoes, thinly sliced
8 stuffed green olives, chopped
2 tablespoons capers, drained and chopped
2 cloves garlic, crushed
½ teaspoon dried oregano
4 tablespoons chopped parsley
80 ml (2½ fl oz/⅓ cup) olive oil
500 g (1 lb 2 oz) thin spaghetti
basil leaves, to garnish (optional)

1 Put the spring onion, tomato, olives and capers in a bowl. Add the garlic, oregano, parsley and oil and mix well. Cover and refrigerate for at least 2 hours.

2 Cook the pasta in a large saucepan of rapidly boiling salted water until al dente. Drain and return to the pan.

3 Add the cold sauce to the hot pasta and toss. Serve garnished with basil, if desired.

cheese tortellini with nutty herb sauce

cheese tortellini with nutty herb sauce

✺

Preparation time: 15 minutes
Cooking time: 15 minutes
Serves 4–6

500 g (1 lb 2 oz) ricotta-filled fresh or
   dried tortellini or ravioli
60 g (2¼ oz) butter
100 g (3½ oz/1 cup) walnuts, finely chopped
100 g (3½ oz/⅔ cup) pine nuts
2 tablespoons chopped flat-leaf (Italian) parsley
2 teaspoons thyme
60 g (2¼ oz/¼ cup) ricotta cheese
60 ml (2 fl oz/¼ cup) cream

1 Cook the pasta in a large saucepan of rapidly boiling salted water until al dente.

Drain the pasta and return it to the pan to keep warm.

2 While the pasta is cooking, melt the butter in a heavy-based frying pan over medium heat until foaming. Add the walnuts and pine nuts and cook, stirring, for 5 minutes, or until golden brown. Add the parsley and thyme and season to taste.

3 Beat the ricotta with the cream. Add the nut mixture to the hot pasta and toss. Serve topped with the ricotta cream.

fettuccine with creamy mushroom and bean sauce

✹

Preparation time: **20 minutes**
Cooking time: **20 minutes**
Serves **4**

280 g (10 oz) fettuccine
2 tablespoons olive oil
1 onion, chopped
2 garlic cloves, crushed
250 g (9 oz) mushrooms, thinly sliced
125 ml (4 fl oz/½ cup) white wine
310 ml (10¾ fl oz/1¼ cups) cream
125 ml (4 fl oz/½ cup) vegetable stock
1 egg
250 g (9 oz) green beans, trimmed and
    thinly sliced diagonally
3 tablespoons chopped basil
35 g (1¼ oz/¼ cup) sun-dried tomatoes,
    cut into strips
100 g (3½ oz/⅔ cup) pine nuts, toasted
    (see Note)
shaved parmesan cheese, to serve
herb sprigs, to serve (optional)

1 Cook the pasta in a large saucepan of rapidly boiling salted water until al dente. Drain and return to the pan.
2 While the pasta is cooking, heat the oil in a large heavy-based frying pan over medium heat. Add the onion and garlic and cook for 3 minutes, or until the onion has softened. Add the mushrooms and cook, stirring, for 1 minute. Pour in the wine, cream and stock. Bring to the boil, then reduce the heat and simmer for 10 minutes.
3 Lightly beat the egg in a small bowl. Stirring constantly, add a little of the cooking liquid. Pour the mixture slowly into the pan, stirring constantly for 30 seconds. Keep the heat low — if the mixture boils, it will curdle.
4 Add the beans, basil, pine nuts and sun-dried tomato and stir until heated through. Season to taste.
5 Serve the sauce over the pasta, garnished with parmesan shavings and herb sprigs, if desired.

green beans

Today there are literally dozens of varieties of green beans to choose from. Whatever type you buy, they should be crisp and bright: the beans should literally snap when bent. Avoid any limp or overly matured beans with tough-looking pods. Most beans need topping and tailing, and some types still need to have the strings removed.

NOTE: Toast the pine nuts in a dry frying pan over medium heat, stirring constantly, until they are golden brown and fragrant. Watch carefully as they will burn easily.

semolina gnocchi

❋

Preparation time: 20 minutes +
   1 hour chilling time
Cooking time: 40 minutes
Serves 4

750 ml (26 fl oz/3 cups) milk
½ teaspoon ground nutmeg
85 g (2¾ oz/⅔ cup) semolina
1 egg, beaten
150 g (5½ oz/1½ cups) grated
   parmesan cheese
60 g (2¼ oz) butter, melted
125 ml (4 fl oz/½ cup) thick
   (double/heavy) cream
75 g (2½ oz/½ cup) grated
   mozzarella cheese
mixed salad, to serve

1 Line a deep 28 x 18 x 3 cm (11 x 7 x 1¼ inch) Swiss roll tin (jelly roll tin) with baking paper.
2 Place the milk and half the nutmeg in a saucepan and season well with sea salt and freshly ground black pepper. Bring to the boil, then reduce the heat to medium and gradually stir in the semolina. Cook, stirring occasionally, for 5–10 minutes, or until the semolina is very stiff. Remove from the heat and stir in the egg and 100 g (3½ oz/1 cup) of the parmesan. Spread the mixture in the roll tin and refrigerate for 1 hour, or until firm.
3 Preheat the oven to 180°C (350°F/ Gas 4). Cut the semolina into rounds using a floured 4 cm (1½ inch) cutter. Arrange in a greased shallow baking dish.
4 Pour the melted butter over the top, then the cream. Combine the remaining nutmeg, parmesan and mozzarella and sprinkle over the semolina.
5 Bake for 20–25 minutes, or until golden. Serve with a mixed salad.

semolina

Semolina is durum wheat that is more coarsely ground than normal wheat flour. The finest semolina is used for making Italian gnocchi and good-quality pasta, while medium-ground semolina is used in a variety of desserts, from milk or fruit puddings to sweet cakes.

fast pasta with breadcrumb sauce

Cook 500 g (1 lb 2 oz) spiral pasta or farfalle in a large saucepan of rapidly boiling salted water until al dente. Drain and return to the pan. While the pasta is cooking, put 5 slices of brown bread in a food processor and pulse for 30 seconds to make fine crumbs. Heat 60 ml (2 fl oz/¼ cup) olive oil in a large, heavy-based frying pan over low heat. Add the breadcrumbs and 3 crushed garlic cloves and cook, stirring, for 3 minutes, or until crisp and golden. Toss through the hot pasta with 2 tablespoons finely chopped parsley and 45 g (1½ oz/½ cup) grated pecorino cheese and some freshly ground black pepper. Serve garnished with fresh herbs, if desired. Serves 4–6.

mushrooms

A valuable source of vitamins and fibre, with a flavour all their own, these cultivated fungi are adaptable vegetables, fitting in perfectly with both light modern dishes and heavier rustic fare.

pesto-filled mushrooms

Place 2 large handfuls of basil leaves in a food processor with 3 crushed garlic cloves, 80 g (2¾ oz/½ cup) toasted pine nuts and 50 g (1¾ oz/½ cup) grated parmesan cheese. Process until finely chopped, then gradually add 80 ml (2½ fl oz/⅓ cup) olive oil and blend until well combined. Remove the stems from 14 mushrooms that are small enough for finger food, then brush the mushrooms lightly with macadamia nut oil. Cook, gill side down, on a preheated chargrill or barbecue until the mushrooms are lightly browned. Turn the mushrooms over and spoon a level tablespoon of pesto into each cap. Serve immediately. Makes 14.

golden mushroom tart

Heat 2 tablespoons olive oil in a frying pan over medium heat. Add 2 thinly sliced onions and 1 tablespoon red wine vinegar and cook, stirring, for 20 minutes, or until the onion has caramelised. Remove from the pan and cool slightly on paper towels. Melt 60 g (2¼ oz) butter in the frying pan, then add 350 g (12 oz) assorted mushrooms and cook for 5 minutes, or until tender. Drain off any excess liquid, season to taste and cool on paper towels. Preheat the oven to 200°C (400°F/Gas 6). Place a sheet of puff pastry on a non-stick baking tray and bake for 10 minutes. Very gently and quickly spread the caramelised onion over the puff pastry, leaving a 2 cm (¾ inch) border. Top with the mushrooms, then sprinkle with some marjoram and 25 g (1 oz/¼ cup) grated parmesan cheese. Bake for another 10 minutes, or until the pastry is golden. Serves 4.

mushroom yoghurt dip

Heat 1 tablespoon oil in a frying pan over medium heat. Add 2 crushed garlic cloves and 4 finely chopped spring onions (scallions) and cook for 3 minutes. Add 225 g (8 oz) chopped button mushrooms and cook for 5 minutes, or until golden brown. Remove from the heat and drain off any excess liquid, then transfer to a bowl. Stir in 200 g (7 oz) Greek-style yoghurt, 1 teaspoon ground cumin and 2 tablespoons chopped lemon thyme. Use as a dip with crudités, grissini sticks, corn chips or sliced baguette.

marinated mushrooms

Pour 250 ml (9 fl oz/1 cup) apple cider vinegar and 125 ml (4 fl oz/½ cup) orange juice into a saucepan. Add 1 tablespoon coriander seeds, 2 rosemary sprigs and 1 bay leaf and bring to the boil. Add 500 g (1 lb 2 oz) button mushrooms and simmer for 3 minutes. Remove with a slotted spoon, reserving the cooking liquid, and spoon into a sterilised jar. Boil the cooking liquid until reduced by half. Replace the rosemary sprigs and bay leaf with fresh ones, then stir in 80 ml (2½ fl oz/⅓ cup) olive oil. Pour the liquid over the mushrooms and seal with a layer of olive oil. Refrigerate for up to 1 month.

wild mushroom stuffing

Melt 60 g (2¼ oz) butter in a frying pan over medium heat. Add 1 finely chopped onion and cook for 3 minutes, or until golden. Add 225 g (8 oz) mixed mushrooms (oyster, Swiss brown, enoki, button) and cook for 5 minutes. Transfer the mixture to a bowl, then add 60 g (2¼ oz/2 cups) croutons, 3 tablespoons chopped fresh herbs, 95 g (3¼ oz/½ cup) cooked brown rice, 60 ml (2 fl oz/¼ cup) milk and 1 lightly beaten egg and mix well. Use the mixture to stuff cooked potatoes, eggplants (aubergines) and capsicums (peppers), or to fill omelettes and crepes.

tagliatelle with tomato and walnut sauce

✳

Preparation time: 20 minutes
Cooking time: 30 minutes
Serves 4–6

4 ripe tomatoes
1 tablespoon olive oil
1 onion, finely chopped
1 celery stalk, finely chopped
1 carrot, grated
2 tablespoons chopped parsley
1 teaspoon red wine vinegar
60 ml (2 fl oz/¼ cup) white wine

75 g (2½ oz/½ cup) toasted walnuts
    (see Note), chopped
500 g (1 lb 2 oz) tagliatelle
grated parmesan cheese, to serve

1 Score a cross in the base of the tomatoes. Place in a heatproof bowl and cover with boiling water. Leave for 30 seconds, then transfer to cold water and peel the skin away from the cross. Cut the tomatoes in half, scoop out the seeds and chop the flesh. Set aside.
2 Heat half the oil in a heavy-based saucepan over low heat. Add the onion and celery and cook for 5 minutes, stirring regularly. Add the tomato, carrot, parsley, vinegar and wine. Bring to the

boil, then reduce the heat and simmer for 25 minutes. Season to taste.
3 While the sauce is simmering, cook the pasta in a large saucepan of rapidly boiling salted water until al dente. Drain and return to the pan.
4 Add the sauce to the hot pasta and toss. Serve topped with the walnuts and sprinkled with parmesan.

NOTE: Italians often use roma (plum) tomatoes for sauces — use them if they are available. You will need 6–8 for this recipe as they are quite small.

To toast walnuts, heat 1 tablespoon oil in a medium frying pan, add the walnuts and stir over low heat for 5 minutes.

To peel tomatoes easily, score a cross with a sharp knife in the base of each tomato. Cover with boiling water and leave for 2 minutes.

Drain the tomatoes and plunge into cold water. Peel the skin in a downwards motion, away from the cross, and discard the skin.

herb and pepper fettuccine

☀

Preparation time: 5 minutes
Cooking time: 20 minutes
Serves 4

500 g (1 lb 2 oz) fettuccine
60 g (2¼ oz) butter
2 garlic cloves, crushed
2 tablespoons finely chopped sage
2 tablespoons finely chopped basil
2 tablespoons finely chopped oregano
2 teaspoons freshly ground black pepper
grated parmesan cheese, to serve

1 Cook the pasta in a large saucepan of rapidly boiling salted water until al dente. Drain and return to the pan.
2 While the pasta is cooking, melt the butter over medium heat until foaming. Add the garlic, herbs and black pepper.
3 Add the herb mixture to the hot pasta and toss. Serve sprinkled with parmesan.

pasta with pesto

pasta with sun-dried tomato pesto

☀

Preparation time: 15 minutes
Cooking time: 15 minutes
Serves 6

500 g (1 lb 2 oz) spiral pasta
150 g (5½ oz) sun-dried tomatoes
   in olive oil, drained
50 g (1¾ oz/½ cup) finely grated
   parmesan cheese
50 g (1¾ oz/⅓ cup) pine nuts
25 g (¾ oz/½ cup) basil leaves
80 ml (2½ fl oz/⅓ cup) olive oil
150 g (5½ oz) asparagus spears,
   chopped
250 g (9 oz) cherry tomatoes, halved

1 Cook the pasta in a large saucepan of rapidly boiling salted water until al dente. Drain and return to the pan.

2 While the pasta is cooking, place the sun-dried tomato in a food processor with the parmesan, pine nuts and basil. Process until finely chopped. With the motor running, slowly pour in the oil until combined.
3 Place the asparagus in a heatproof bowl. Cover with boiling water and leave for 2 minutes; drain.
4 Add the pesto to the hot pasta and toss to combine. Toss the asparagus through the pasta with the cherry tomatoes and serve.

pasta with pesto

☀

Preparation time: 10 minutes
Cooking time: 15 minutes
Serves 4

400 g (14 oz) spinach tagliatelle
2 large handfuls of basil leaves, plus extra,
   to garnish (optional)

4 garlic cloves, chopped
50 g (1¾ oz/⅓ cup) pine nuts
100 g (3½ oz/1 cup) grated
   parmesan cheese
185 ml (6 fl oz/¾ cup) olive oil

1 Cook the pasta in a large saucepan of rapidly boiling salted water until al dente. Drain and return to the pan.
2 While the pasta is cooking, put the basil, garlic and pine nuts in a food processor and process until finely chopped. Add the parmesan and blend until well combined. With the motor running, slowly pour in the oil.
3 Toss through pesto through the hot pasta to coat well. Season to taste and serve garnished with basil leaves, if desired.

NOTE: As a variation, you can toast 40 g (1½ oz/¼ cup) pine nuts, extra, in a dry frying pan and add them to the pasta just before serving.

worcestershire sauce

Worcestershire sauce is a sharply flavoured sauce used sparingly to give zest to a range of dishes. Made from an old Indian recipe, it contains tamarind, vinegar, soy sauce, molasses, garlic, anchovies and various other tropical fruits and spices.

ricotta-filled ravioli with tomato sauce

❋ ❋

Preparation time: 35 minutes
  + 30 minutes resting time
Cooking time: 50 minutes
Serves 4–6

125 g (4½ oz/1 cup) plain
  (all-purpose) flour
1 egg
1 tablespoon olive oil

TOMATO SAUCE
1 kg (2 lb 4 oz) ripe tomatoes
1 tablespoon olive oil
1 onion, chopped
1 carrot, chopped
2 garlic cloves, crushed
50 g (1¾ oz) tomato paste
  (concentrated purée)
1 teaspoon soft brown sugar
125 ml (4 fl oz/½ cup)
  vegetable stock
1 tablespoon worcestershire sauce
30 g (1 oz) chopped basil, plus extra,
  to garnish

FILLING
250 g (9 oz/1 cup) ricotta cheese
½ tablespoon chopped flat-leaf parsley
1 egg yolk

1 Sift the flour into a bowl and make a well in the centre. Add the egg, oil and 1 teaspoon water to the well, then gradually incorporate into the flour. Turn out onto a lightly floured surface and knead until smooth and elastic. Cover and leave to rest for 30 minutes.

2 While the pastry is resting, make the tomato sauce. Score a cross in the base of the tomatoes. Place in a heatproof bowl and cover with boiling water. Leave for 30 seconds, then transfer to cold water and peel the skin away from the cross. Cut the tomatoes in half, scoop out the seeds and chop the flesh. Set aside.

3 Heat the oil in a large heavy-based saucepan over medium–low heat. Add the onion, carrot and garlic and cook, stirring, for 5–7 minutes. Add the tomato, tomato paste, sugar, stock, worcestershire sauce and basil. Bring to the boil, reduce to a simmer, then cover and cook for 30 minutes. Leave to cool slightly, then briefly process the mixture in a food processor. Keep warm.

4 In a small bowl, combine all the filling ingredients and mix well.

5 Roll out half the dough to form a rectangle about 2 mm (1⁄16 inch) thick. Roll out the remaining half to form a rectangle slightly larger than the first.

6 On the first rectangle, place heaped teaspoons of the filling mixture in straight rows, at intervals about 5 cm (2 inches) apart. Flatten each mound slightly.

7 Lightly brush between the mounds with water. Place the second sheet of dough on top, then press down gently between the mounds to seal. Cut into squares with a knife or a fluted cutter.

8 Bring a saucepan of water to the boil. Drop in the ravioli a few at a time and cook for 8–10 minutes, or until just tender. Remove using a slotted spoon and place in a heated serving dish. Spoon the sauce over, garnish with extra basil and serve.

pasta and vegetable salad

✻

Preparation time: **15 minutes**
Cooking time: **15 minutes**
Serves **4–6 as an accompaniment**

250 g (9 oz) bow pasta
250 g (9 oz) broccoli, broken
 into florets

250 g (9 oz) green beans, trimmed
 and cut diagonally
125 g (4½ oz) snow peas (mangetout),
 topped and tailed
250 g (9 oz) cherry tomatoes, cut in half
80 ml (2½ fl oz/⅓ cup) olive oil
60 ml (2 fl oz/¼ cup) white wine
 vinegar
2 teaspoons mustard powder
snow pea (mangetout) sprouts or herbs,
 to garnish

1 Cook the pasta in a large saucepan of rapidly boiling salted water until al dente. Drain well and rinse with cold water; set aside.

2 Plunge the broccoli, beans and snow peas into a saucepan of boiling water. Rinse immediately in cold water, then drain well. Place in a bowl with the cherry tomatoes.

3 In a small bowl, mix together the oil, vinegar, mustard and some freshly ground black pepper until well combined.

4 Add the pasta to the vegetables and drizzle with the dressing. Toss well and serve garnished with sprouts or your favourite herbs.

ravioli with herbs

✻

Preparation time: **15 minutes**
Cooking time: **10 minutes**
Serves **6**

2 tablespoons olive oil
1 garlic clove, halved
800 g (1 lb 12 oz) ricotta-filled ravioli
60 g (2¼ oz) butter, chopped
2 tablespoons chopped flat-leaf parsley
4 tablespoons chopped basil
2 tablespoons snipped chives
grated parmesan cheese, to serve (optional)

1 Combine the oil and garlic in a small bowl; set aside.

2 Cook the pasta in a large saucepan of rapidly boiling salted water until al dente. Drain and return to the pan.

3 Add the oil to the hot pasta, discarding the garlic. Add the butter and herbs, toss well and season to taste. Serve sprinkled with parmesan, if desired.

NOTE: As a variation, you could use coriander (cilantro) instead of parsley.

ravioli with herbs

sweet and sour noodles and vegetables

☀

Preparation time: 15 minutes
Cooking time: 15 minutes
Serves 4–6

200 g (7 oz) thin fresh egg noodles
60 ml (2 fl oz/¼ cup) vegetable oil
1 green capsicum (pepper), sliced
1 red capsicum (pepper), sliced
2 celery stalks, sliced diagonally
1 carrot, sliced diagonally
250 g (9 oz) button mushrooms, sliced
4 fresh baby corn, sliced lengthways
3 teaspoons cornflour (cornstarch)

2 tablespoons malt vinegar
1 teaspoon chopped chilli
2 teaspoons tomato paste
   (concentrated purée)
2 vegetable stock (bouillon) cubes, crumbled
1 teaspoon sesame oil
440 g (15½ oz) tin pineapple pieces in
   natural juice
3 spring onions (scallions), sliced
   diagonally

1 Add the noodles to a large saucepan of boiling water and cook for 3 minutes. Drain, rinse well under cold running water and drain again. Set aside.
2 Heat the vegetable oil in a wok or large frying pan. Add the green and red capsicums, celery, carrot and mushrooms and stir-fry for 5 minutes over high heat. Add the corn and noodles. Reduce the heat to low and stir-fry for 2 minutes.
3 Blend the cornflour and vinegar in a small bowl until smooth. Stir in the chilli, tomato paste, stock cubes, sesame oil and undrained pineapple pieces.
4 Pour the pineapple mixture into the wok and stir-fry over medium heat for 5 minutes, or until the mixture boils and the sauce thickens.
5 Serve topped with the spring onion.

sweet and sour noodles and vegetables

chilli satay noodles

☀

Preparation time: 10 minutes
Cooking time: 10 minutes
Serves 4–6

500 g (1 lb 2 oz) thin fresh egg noodles
1 tablespoon vegetable oil
1 teaspoon sesame oil
50 g (1¾ oz/⅓ cup) peanuts
2 small red chillies, chopped
4 slender eggplants (aubergines), sliced
200 g (7 oz) sugar snap peas
100 g (3½ oz) bean sprouts, tails trimmed
60 g (2¼ oz/¼ cup) crunchy peanut butter
1 tablespoon hoisin sauce
80 ml (2½ fl oz/⅓ cup) coconut milk
2 tablespoons lime juice
1 tablespoon sweet chilli sauce

fast cheese and noodle omelette

Place 85 g (3 oz) instant noodles and the contents of the flavouring sachet in a heatproof bowl. Cover with boiling water and soak for 2–3 minutes, or until the noodles are soft; drain well. Heat 30 g (1 oz) butter in a non-stick frying pan. Add some chopped red capsicum (pepper) and sliced onion and cook for 1–2 minutes. Add the noodles and cook briefly then pour in 3 lightly beaten eggs. Cook over medium heat for 3–5 minutes, shaking the pan occasionally to prevent sticking. When the egg is almost cooked, sprinkle with grated cheddar cheese and some chopped fresh herbs. Cook briefly under a hot grill (broiler) until the omelette is golden and cooked through. Sprinkle with freshly ground black pepper and serve. Serves 2–4.

1 Add the noodles to a large saucepan of boiling water and cook for 3 minutes. Drain, rinse well under cold running water and drain again. Set aside.

2 Heat the oils in a wok or large frying pan over high heat. Add the peanuts and toss for 1 minute, or until golden. Add the chillies, eggplant and sugar snap peas and stir-fry for 2 minutes.

3 Reduce the heat to medium and add the noodles and sprouts. Toss for 1 minute, or until combined.

4 Blend the peanut butter, hoisin sauce, coconut milk, lime juice and chilli sauce until almost smooth. Add to the noodles and toss over medium heat until the noodles are coated and the sauce is heated. Serve hot.

vegetarian rice noodles

✳

Preparation time: **10** minutes
Cooking time: **10** minutes
Serves **4–6**

8 dried Chinese mushrooms
250 g (9 oz) dried rice vermicelli noodles
2 tablespoons vegetable oil
3 garlic cloves, chopped
4 cm (1½ inch) knob of fresh ginger, finely grated
100 g (3½ oz) tofu puffs, cut into 2.5 cm (1 inch) cubes
1 carrot, cut into thin shreds
100 g (3½ oz) green beans, trimmed and cut into 2.5 cm (1 inch) lengths
½ red capsicum (pepper), cut into fine strips
2 tablespoons soy sauce
1 tablespoon fish sauce (optional)
2 teaspoons soft brown sugar
100 g (3½ oz) bean sprouts, tails trimmed, plus extra, to garnish
75 g (2½ oz/1 cup) finely shredded cabbage
sweet chilli sauce and lime cheeks, to serve

1 Soak the mushrooms in a small bowl of hot water for 20 minutes; drain and slice. Meanwhile, soak the noodles in a large

vegetarian rice noodles

bowl of hot water for 1–4 minutes, or until soft; drain well.

2 Heat the oil in a wok or large heavy-based frying pan over high heat. Add the garlic, ginger and tofu and stir-fry for 1 minute. Add the carrot, beans, capsicum and mushroom and stir-fry for 2 minutes.

3 Add the soy sauce, fish sauce and sugar and toss well. Cover and steam for 1 minute, then add the noodles, sprouts and cabbage. Toss well, cover and steam for 30 seconds.

4 Garnish with extra bean sprouts. Serve with sweet chilli sauce and lime cheeks.

noodles

To cook fresh Chinese noodles, bring a large pot of water to the boil — no need to add salt or oil. Add the noodles and cook until just past al dente stage. To stop the cooking process, run the noodles under cold water and toss a little oil through so they don't stick together.

chilli cashew noodles

chilli cashew noodles

※

Preparation time: **15 minutes**
Cooking time: **10 minutes**
Serves **4**

200 g (7 oz) thin fresh egg noodles
2 teaspoons chilli oil
60 ml (2 fl oz/¼ cup) vegetable oil
3 red chillies, seeded and cut into thin strips
80 g (2¾ oz/½ cup) roasted cashew nuts
1 red capsicum (pepper), thinly sliced
2 celery stalks, sliced diagonally
2 tablespoons chopped spring onions
   (scallions)
225 g (8 oz) tinned whole baby corn, drained
100 g (3½ oz) bean sprouts, tails trimmed
1 tablespoon soy sauce
2 tablespoons sweet chilli sauce

1 Add the noodles to a large saucepan
of boiling water and cook for 3 minutes.
Drain, rinse well under cold running
water and drain again. Set aside.

2 Heat the oils in a wok or large frying
pan over medium heat. Add the chilli and
stir-fry for 1 minute. Add the cashews and
toss for 1 minute, or until golden. Add
the capsicum, celery, spring onion, corn
and sprouts to the pan and stir-fry for a
further 3 minutes, or until tender.
3 Stir in the noodles and the soy and
sweet chilli sauce. Toss until the noodles
are heated through and the ingredients
are well combined. Serve hot.

curry flavoured noodles

※

Preparation time: **25 minutes**
Cooking time: **15 minutes**
Serves **4**

250 g (9 oz) thick fresh noodles
60 ml (2 fl oz/¼ cup) vegetable oil
2 garlic cloves, sliced

1 onion, thinly sliced
1 red capsicum (pepper), cut into long,
   thin strips
1 small cucumber, unpeeled, cut into long,
   thin strips
2 teaspoons mild curry powder
125 ml (4 fl oz/½ cup) vegetable stock
2 teaspoons dry sherry
1 tablespoon soy sauce
½ teaspoon sugar
3 spring onions (scallions), sliced
   diagonally

1 Add the noodles to a large saucepan
of boiling water and cook for 3 minutes.
Drain, rinse well under cold running
water and drain again. Set aside.
2 Heat the oil in a wok or large frying
pan over medium heat. Add the garlic,
onion and capsicum and stir-fry for
3 minutes. Add the cucumber and curry
powder and stir-fry for another 3 minutes.
3 Add the combined stock, sherry, soy
sauce and sugar and stir until the mixture
comes to the boil.

4 Add the noodles and spring onion and stir-fry until the noodles are heated through and the ingredients are well combined. Serve hot.

noodles with vegetables and herbs

✳

Preparation time: **20 minutes**
Cooking time: **25 minutes**
Serves **4–6**

2 tomatoes
30 g (1 oz) butter
2 teaspoons vegetable oil
1 onion, sliced
1 celery stalk, sliced
1 carrot, sliced on the diagonal
1 small red chilli, seeded and cut
    into thin strips
1 tablespoon taco seasoning mix
2 tablespoons tomato paste
    (concentrated purée)
125 ml (4 fl oz/½ cup) red wine
1 bay leaf
125 ml (4 fl oz/½ cup) vegetable stock
2 teaspoons chopped basil
2 teaspoons chopped flat-leaf
    (Italian) parsley
375 g (13 oz) thin fresh rice noodles

1 Score a cross in the base of each tomato. Put in a heatproof bowl and cover with boiling water. Leave for 30 seconds, then transfer to cold water, drain and peel away the skin from the cross. Cut the tomatoes into wedges and remove the seeds.
2 Heat the butter and oil in a large saucepan over medium heat. Add the onion, celery, carrot and chilli and cook for 5 minutes. Add the seasoning mix, tomato, tomato paste, wine, bay leaf and stock and bring to the boil. Reduce the heat to low and simmer, covered, for 15 minutes, stirring occasionally. Stir in the herbs.
3 Meanwhile, add the noodles to a large saucepan of boiling water and cook for

3 minutes. Drain, rinse well under cold running water and drain again. Toss with the sauce and serve.

noodles in black bean sauce

✳

Preparation time: **10 minutes**
Cooking time: **15 minutes**
Serves **4**

375 g (13 oz) thin fresh egg noodles
1 teaspoon vegetable oil
1 teaspoon sesame oil
1 tablespoon finely grated fresh ginger
4 garlic cloves, crushed
1 tablespoon dried, salted black beans,
    rinsed well and chopped
2 tablespoons hoisin sauce
1 tablespoon black bean sauce
1 tablespoon sugar
125 ml (4 fl oz/½ cup) vegetable stock
225 g (8 oz) tin sliced bamboo shoots,
    drained
3 spring onions (scallions), cut diagonally
    into long thin shreds

1 Add the noodles to a large saucepan of boiling water and cook for 3 minutes. Drain, rinse well under cold running water and drain again. Set aside.
2 Heat the oils in a wok or large frying pan over low heat. Add the ginger and garlic and stir-fry for 2 minutes. Add the black beans and stir for 2 minutes.
3 Add the hoisin and black bean sauces, sugar and stock and toss to combine. Simmer for 5 minutes, or until the liquid is slightly reduced and thickened.
4 Add the bamboo shoots, spring onion and noodles and stir-fry until the noodles are heated through and the ingredients are well combined. Serve hot.

noodles in black bean sauce

grains & pulses

Spilling out in a cornucopia of fabulous forms — from couscous to red lentils, chickpeas to millet — these wholesome staples are nutritious as well as delicious. When teamed with one another, or with nuts, they provide a diet complete in protein. They also provide the cook with an infinite number of recipe possibilities, inspired by national favourites from all around the world.

chickpea curry

☀

Preparation time: 15 minutes
Cooking time: 40 minutes
Serves 4

1 tablespoon ghee or oil
2 onions, thinly sliced
4 garlic cloves, crushed
1 teaspoon chilli powder
1 teaspoon ground turmeric
1 teaspoon paprika
1 tablespoon ground cumin
1 tablespoon ground coriander
1 teaspoon sea salt
2 x 400 g (14 oz) tins chickpeas,
    rinsed and drained
400 g (14 oz) tin chopped tomatoes
1 teaspoon garam masala
warm chappatis or naan bread,
    to serve

1 Heat the ghee in a frying pan over medium heat. Add the onion and garlic and cook, stirring, for 5 minutes, or until the onion is soft. Stir in the chilli powder, turmeric, paprika, cumin, coriander and salt. Cook, stirring, for 1 minute.
2 Add the chickpeas and tomato and stir until combined. Cover and simmer over low heat for 20 minutes, stirring occasionally.
3 Stir in the garam masala, then cover and simmer for a final 10 minutes.
4 Serve with chapattis or naan bread.

vegetable couscous

☀

Preparation time: 40 minutes
Cooking time: 30 minutes
Serves 4–6

60 ml (2 fl oz/¼ cup) olive oil
2 small onions, thinly sliced
1 teaspoon ground turmeric
½ teaspoon chilli powder
2 teaspoons finely grated fresh ginger
1 cinnamon stick
2 carrots, thickly sliced
2 parsnips, thickly sliced
375 ml (13 fl oz/1½ cups)
    vegetable stock
300 g (10½ oz) pumpkin (winter squash),
    cut into small cubes
250 g (9 oz) cauliflower, cut into
    small florets
2 zucchini (courgettes), cut into thick slices
400 g (14 oz) tin chickpeas, rinsed and
    drained
a pinch of saffron threads
2 tablespoons chopped coriander
    (cilantro)
2 tablespoons chopped flat-leaf (Italian)
    parsley
230 g (8 oz/1¼ cups) instant
    couscous
30 g (1 oz) butter

1 Heat 2 tablespoons of the oil in a large saucepan over medium heat. Add the onion and cook, stirring occasionally, for 3 minutes, or until the onion is soft. Add

chickpea curry

couscous

Couscous is made from semolina flour, rolled into tiny pellets. It is a staple of North African cooking, and is traditionally steamed over a pot of stew. The most common couscous is an 'instant' variety, which needs only to be combined with hot water and left to stand for a couple of minutes. Butter and oil are then forked through the grains. Couscous also refers to the whole dish of a stew served over couscous grains.

mushroom risotto

fast red lentil soup

Heat 1 tablespoon vegetable oil in a saucepan over medium heat. Add 1 finely chopped onion and cook, stirring, for 3 minutes, or until soft. Add 250 g (9 oz/1 cup) red lentils, 400 g (14 oz) tin chopped tomatoes and 1 litre (35 fl oz/4 cups) vegetable stock. Bring to the boil, then reduce the heat and simmer for 20 minutes. Stir in 2 tablespoons chopped basil and serve topped with a small dollop of sour cream. Serves 4.

1 Soak the porcini mushrooms in 500 ml (17 fl oz/2 cups) warm water for 30 minutes. Remove the mushrooms from the liquid, then chop and set aside.

2 Pour the mushroom liquid into a saucepan, through a fine sieve lined with a paper towel. Add the stock and bring to the boil. Reduce the heat, then cover and keep at a low simmer.

3 Meanwhile, heat half the oil and 40 g (1½ oz) of the butter in a frying pan over high heat. Add all the mushrooms and the garlic and cook, stirring, for 10 minutes, or until the mushrooms are soft. Reduce the heat to low and cook for a further 5 minutes. Increase the heat, add the vermouth and cook for 2–3 minutes, or until evaporated. Set aside.

4 Heat the remaining oil and 20 g (¾ oz) butter in a saucepan over medium heat. Add the onion and cook for 10 minutes, or until soft. Add the rice and stir for 1–2 minutes, or until coated. Pour in 125 ml (4 fl oz/½ cup) stock and stir constantly until the liquid is absorbed. Continue adding more stock, 125 ml (4 fl oz/½ cup) at a time, stirring for 20–25 minutes, or until the rice is creamy and tender.

5 Remove from the heat and stir in the mushrooms, parmesan and remaining butter. Season to taste and serve.

the turmeric, chilli powder and ginger and cook, stirring, for another minute.

2 Add the cinnamon stick, carrot, parsnip and stock and stir to combine. Cover and bring to the boil, then reduce the heat and simmer for 5 minutes, or until the vegetables are almost tender.

3 Add the pumpkin, cauliflower and zucchini and simmer for 10 minutes. Stir in the chickpeas, saffron, coriander and parsley and simmer, uncovered, for 5 minutes. Remove the cinnamon stick.

4 Place the couscous in a heatproof bowl and add 250 ml (9 fl oz/1 cup) hot water. Allow to stand for 5 minutes. Stir in the remaining oil and the butter and fluff up the grains with a fork.

5 Serve the vegetables on a bed of couscous.

NOTE: The vegetables may be cooked up to a day in advance and refrigerated. The couscous, however, is best prepared just before serving.

mushroom risotto

✹ ✹

Preparation time: 15 minutes
  + 30 minutes soaking time
Cooking time: 1 hour
Serves 4–6

20 g (¾ oz) dried porcini mushrooms
1 litre (35 fl oz/4 cups) vegetable stock
2 tablespoons olive oil
100 g (3½ oz) butter, chopped
750 g (1 lb 10 oz) small cup or Swiss brown mushrooms, stems trimmed, caps sliced
3 garlic cloves, crushed
80 ml (2½ fl oz/⅓ cup) dry white vermouth
1 onion, finely chopped
440 g (15½ oz/2 cups) arborio rice
150 g (5½ oz/1½ cups) grated parmesan cheese

falafel with tomato salsa

✹ ✹

Preparation time: 30 minutes
+ 30 minutes standing time
+ 4 hours soaking time
Cooking time: 25 minutes
Serves 6

FALAFEL
440 g (15½ oz/2 cups) dried chickpeas
1 small onion, finely chopped
2 cloves garlic, crushed
2 tablespoons chopped parsley
1 tablespoon chopped coriander (cilantro)
2 teaspoons ground cumin
½ teaspoon baking powder
vegetable oil, for deep-frying

TOMATO SALSA
2 tomatoes, peeled and finely chopped
¼ Lebanese (short) cucumber, finely chopped
½ green capsicum (pepper), finely chopped
2 tablespoons chopped parsley
1 teaspoon sugar
2 teaspoons chilli sauce
½ teaspoon freshly ground black pepper
1 lemon, finely grated zest and juice

1 To make the falafel, first soak the chickpeas in cold water overnight.
2 Rinse and drain the chickpeas, then place in a food processor and blend for 30 seconds, or until finely ground. Add the remaining falafel ingredients and 1 tablespoon water and process for 10 seconds, or until the mixture forms a rough paste. Cover and leave to stand for 30 minutes.
3 Place all the tomato salsa ingredients in a bowl and mix to combine. Set aside.
4 Shape heaped tablespoons of the falafel mixture into balls, squeezing out any excess liquid.
5 In a deep, heavy-based saucepan, heat about 5 cm (2 inches) oil over medium–high heat. Working in batches, lower the felafel balls into the oil using a large spoon and cook for 3–4 minutes, or until browned. Remove the balls using a slotted spoon and drain on paper towels.
6 Serve the falafel hot or cold on a bed of tomato salsa, or in pitta bread with the salsa and hummus.

NOTE: If the falafel mixture is too wet to form into balls, stir in a small amount of plain (all-purpose) flour to help bind it.

sweet and spicy lentils

✹

Preparation time: 10 minutes
+ overnight soaking time
Cooking time: 35 minutes
Serves 6

140 g (5 oz/¾ cup) green lentils
1 small onion, finely chopped
½ teaspoon ground cumin
½ teaspoon ground cinnamon
4 cloves
250 ml (9 fl oz/1 cup) orange juice

1 Soak the lentils in cold water overnight.
2 Drain the lentils and place in a saucepan with the remaining ingredients. Pour in 185 ml (6 fl oz/¾ cup) water and bring to the boil.
3 Reduce the heat and simmer, stirring occasionally, for 30 minutes, or until the liquid has been absorbed and the lentils are very soft. Remove the cloves.
4 Serve the lentils hot or cold, with your favourite Mexican dish.

mushroom risotto fritters

✹ ✹

Preparation time: 20 minutes
+ at least 1 hour 15 minutes chilling time
Cooking time: 40 minutes
Serves 4

1 tablespoon olive oil
20 g (¾ oz) butter
1 onion, finely chopped
220 g (7¾ oz/1 cup) arborio or short-grain rice
150 g (5½ oz/1¾ cups) thinly sliced button mushrooms
810 ml (28 fl oz/3¼ cups) vegetable stock
35 g (1¼ oz/⅓ cup) grated parmesan cheese
vegetable oil, for pan-frying

1 Heat the oil and butter in a heavy-based saucepan over medium heat. Add the onion and cook, stirring, for 3 minutes, or until softened. Add the rice and stir to coat. Cook for 2 minutes, then add the mushrooms and cook for 3 minutes, or until the mushrooms are soft.
2 Meanwhile, bring the stock to the boil in a small saucepan. Reduce the heat, then cover and keep at a simmer.
3 Add 125 ml (4 fl oz/½ cup) stock to the rice mixture and stir constantly until the liquid is absorbed. Continue adding more stock, 125 ml (4 fl oz/½ cup) at a

falafel

Falafel has become so popular in Israel that it has almost acquired the status of a national dish. Served in a pocket of pitta bread, with salad and any spicy relish, or with salad and a yoghurt and herb dressing, these crisp little savoury balls made from ground chickpeas make a healthy, wonderful lunch or snack.

time, stirring for 20–25 minutes, or until
the rice is creamy and tender. Stir in the
parmesan and remove from the heat.
Transfer the mixture to a bowl, allow to
cool, then refrigerate for at least 1 hour.
4 With wet hands, shape 2 tablespoons
of the rice mixture into flat rounds.
Refrigerate for 15 minutes.
5 Heat 2.5 cm (1 inch) oil in a non-stick
frying pan over medium heat. Working in
batches, cook the fritters for 3–4 minutes
on each side, or until golden and crisp.
Drain on paper towels.
6 Serve hot.

onion and
parmesan pilaff

☀

Preparation time: **15 minutes**
Cooking time: **30 minutes**
Serves **6**

60 g (2¼ oz) butter
3 onions, chopped
2 garlic cloves, crushed
400 g (14 oz/2 cups) basmati rice
1.25 litres (44 fl oz/5 cups) vegetable
    stock
235 g (8½ oz/1½ cups) fresh or
    frozen peas
50 g (1¾ oz/½ cup) finely grated
    parmesan cheese
1 large handful flat-leaf (Italian) parsley,
    chopped

1 Melt the butter in a large saucepan
over low heat. Add the onion and garlic
and cook for 5 minutes, or until the onion
is soft and golden.
2 Add the rice and stock; bring to
the boil and stir once. Reduce the heat
to low and simmer, uncovered, for
5 minutes, or until almost all the liquid
has been absorbed.
3 Stir in the peas. Cover and cook over
very low heat for 10 minutes, or until the
rice is tender. Stir in the parmesan and
parsley and serve.

vegetable stock

Most dishes cooked with vegetable stock have
more flavour than those simply made with
water. When making stock, vegetables should be
cleaned, but do not need to be peeled. Aromatic
vegetables such as leeks, onions, carrots and
celery are those most commonly used. Starchy
vegetables such as peas and potatoes are
not as suitable as they can 'cloud' the stock.
Vegetables with a stronger flavour, such as
eggplants (aubergines), cabbages or turnips
should be avoided. The liquid remaining after
cooking mildly flavoured vegetables also makes a
nutritious stock. Vegetable stock can be used in
sauces, soups and casseroles.

spinach rice

✳

Preparation time: **10 minutes**
Cooking time: **40 minutes**
Serves **4–6**

90 g (3¼ oz) butter
200 g (7 oz/1 cup) long-grain white rice
500 ml (17 fl oz/2 cups) vegetable stock
2 tablespoons olive oil
2 large onions, finely chopped
250 g (9 oz) frozen chopped spinach, thawed
4 spring onions (scallions), chopped

1 Melt the butter in a heavy-based saucepan over low heat. Add the rice and cook, stirring, for 10 minutes, or until the rice is lightly golden.
2 Pour in the stock and season with salt and freshly ground black pepper. Slowly bring to the boil, stirring constantly. Reduce the heat, then cover and simmer for 20 minutes.
3 Meanwhile, heat the oil in a small saucepan over medium heat. Add the onion and cook, stirring, for 5 minutes. Add the spinach, reduce the heat, then cover and simmer for 5–10 minutes, or until the spinach is hot. Add the spring onion and stir for 1 minute.
4 Add the spinach mixture to the rice and stir until just heated through. Serve hot.

crispy lentil balls

✳ ✳

Preparation time: **20 minutes**
Cooking time: **25 minutes**
Makes **about 30**

250 g (9 oz/1 cup) red lentils
4 spring onions (scallions), chopped
2 garlic cloves, crushed
1 teaspoon ground cumin
80 g (2¾ oz/1 cup) fresh breadcrumbs
125 g (4½ oz/1 cup) grated cheddar cheese
1 large zucchini (courgette), grated
145 g (5½ oz/¾ cup) polenta
vegetable oil, for deep-frying

1 Bring a large saucepan of water to the boil. Add the lentils and simmer, uncovered, for 10 minutes, or until tender. Drain and rinse well under cold water.
2 Place half the lentils in a food processor or blender with the spring onion and garlic. Process for 10 seconds, or until the mixture is pulpy. Transfer to a large bowl and add the remaining lentils, cumin, breadcrumbs, cheese and zucchini. Stir until combined.
3 Spread the polenta on a plate. Using your hands, roll level tablespoons of the lentil mixture into balls and toss lightly in the polenta.
4 Heat about 5 cm (2 inches) oil in a heavy-based saucepan over medium–high heat. Working in small batches, gently lower the balls into the oil and cook for 1 minute, or until golden brown and crisp. Carefully remove using tongs or a slotted spoon and drain on paper towels. Repeat with the remaining balls. Serve hot.

NOTE: These are delicious served with chutney or yoghurt for dipping.

vegetable pilaff

✳

Preparation time: **20 minutes**
Cooking time: **40 minutes**
Serves **4**

60 ml (2 fl oz/¼ cup) olive oil
1 onion, sliced
2 cloves garlic, crushed
2 teaspoons ground cumin
2 teaspoons paprika
½ teaspoon ground allspice

spinach rice

300 g (10½ oz/1½ cups) long-grain
    white rice
375 ml (13 fl oz/1½ cups) vegetable stock
185 ml (6 fl oz/¾ cup) white wine
3 tomatoes, peeled and chopped
150 g (5½ oz/1¾ cups) sliced button
    mushrooms
2 zucchini (courgettes), sliced
150 g (5½ oz) broccoli, cut into florets

1 Heat the oil in a large heavy-based
saucepan over medium heat. Add the
onion and cook, stirring, for 10 minutes,
or until golden brown. Add the garlic
and spices and cook for 1 minute, or
until aromatic.

2 Stir in the rice, stock, wine, tomato
and mushrooms. Bring to the boil, then
reduce the heat to low, cover and simmer
for 15 minutes.

3 Add the zucchini and broccoli. Cover
and cook for a further 5–7 minutes, or
until the vegetables are just tender.
Serve immediately.

indian dal with pitta toasts

❈

Preparation time: **15 minutes**
Cooking time: **25 minutes**
Serves 4–6

310 g (11 oz/1¼ cups) red lentils
2 tablespoons ghee (see Note)
1 onion, finely chopped
2 garlic cloves, crushed
1 teaspoon finely grated fresh ginger
1 teaspoon ground turmeric
1 teaspoon garam masala

PITTA TOASTS
4 pitta bread rounds
2–3 tablespoons olive oil

1 Put the lentils in a large bowl and
cover with water. Remove any floating
particles and drain the lentils well.

2 Heat the ghee in a saucepan over
medium heat. Add the onion and cook

lentils

When buying lentils, look for bright, shiny
pulses with no hint of dust, damp or mould.
Unless you cook them very often, avoid buying
them in bulk as lentils become harder and drier
with time — they then take longer to cook and
are more likely to break up during cooking.

Lentils make excellent purées and are popular
in soups, and of all the pulses are the easiest to
prepare: green lentils require only a few hours
soaking, and red lentils none at all. Pick over
lentils before cooking as they can easily conceal
small stones.

for 3 minutes, or until softened. Add
the garlic, ginger and spices and cook,
stirring, for 1 minute.

3 Add the lentils and 500 ml (17 fl oz/
2 cups) water and bring to the boil.
Reduce the heat and simmer, stirring
occasionally, for 15 minutes, or until
all the water has been absorbed. Watch
carefully towards the end of cooking time,
as the mixture could burn and stick to the
bottom of the pan.

4 Meanwhile, make the pitta toasts.
Preheat the oven to 180°C (350°F/Gas 4).
Cut the pitta bread into wedges and brush
lightly with the oil. Arrange on a baking
tray and cook for 5–7 minutes, or until
lightly browned and crisp.

5 Serve the dal warm or at room
temperature with the pitta toasts, or
with warm naan or pitta bread.

NOTE: Vegetable oil may be used instead
of ghee if ghee is difficult to obtain. To
make your own ghee, melt some butter,
skim away the white froth on the surface
and then pour the clear butter into
another container, discarding the
white residue.

polenta

There is some conjecture as to the origins of polenta: some say it dates back to Ancient Rome; others believe it was discovered in the New World. Ground from corn, and also called cornmeal, this flour-like staple has found a new home in the contemporary kitchen.

basic polenta

In a saucepan, bring 1 litre (35 fl oz/4 cups) water or stock to the boil. Reduce the heat to medium and slowly whisk in 145 g (5½ oz/¾ cup) coarse polenta. Continue whisking for 5 minutes. Replace the whisk with a wooden spoon and stir until the spoon can stand up in the polenta and the polenta comes away from the side of the pan. Stir in 2 tablespoons softened butter and season with sea salt and freshly ground black pepper.

mediterranean polenta frittata

Make the polenta as instructed in the Basic polenta recipe. Transfer the mixture to a bowl; stir in 50 g (1¾ oz/½ cup) grated parmesan cheese, 4 finely chopped marinated artichoke hearts, 90 g (3¼ oz/½ cup) chopped sun-dried tomatoes, 60 g (2¼ oz/½ cup) pitted, chopped niçoise olives and 1 tablespoon oregano. Spoon the mixture into a lightly greased 30 cm (12 inch) spring-form cake tin; spread the mixture evenly into the tin and press down with the back of a spoon. Set aside to cool. Release the frittata from the tin, brush lightly with olive oil and cook under a preheated grill (broiler) until just crisp and golden brown. Cut into wedges and serve hot or at room temperature. Serves 6–8.

chargrilled polenta

Make the polenta as directed in the Basic polenta recipe. Stir in 25 g (1 oz/¼ cup) grated parmesan cheese and 1 tablespoon chopped basil. Spread the mixture over a large pizza tray to form a circle about 2 cm (¾ inch) thick. Set aside to cool. Cut the polenta into wedges, brush lightly with olive oil and cook on a preheated chargrill or barbecue plate for 3 minutes on each side, or until the wedges are crisp. Serve warm as a finger food, perhaps accompanied by a large spoonful of mascarpone cheese, some rocket (arugula) leaves drizzled with balsamic vinegar, and chilli jam or your favourite spicy tomato relish. Serves 4–6.

polenta sticks with artichoke, feta and capsicum

Make the polenta as directed in the Basic polenta recipe. Spread the mixture into a lightly greased 18 cm (7 inch) square cake tin. Set aside to cool. Cut the polenta into batons 3 cm (1¼ inches) wide, brush them lightly with olive oil and cook under a preheated grill (broiler) until crisp and golden. Serve the polenta sticks with quartered marinated artichokes (with the stems still attached), marinated feta cheese, and strips of roasted red and yellow capsicum (pepper). Serves 4–6.

polenta pizza

Make the polenta as directed in the Basic polenta recipe. Stir in 50 g (1¾ oz/½ cup) grated parmesan cheese. Spoon the mixture evenly into a deep 30 cm (12 inch) pizza tray and press down with the back of a spoon. Set aside to cool. Brush the polenta with olive oil and bake in a preheated 200°C (400°F/Gas 6) oven for 10 minutes. Remove from the oven and spread 3 tablespoons ready-made pesto sauce over the top, leaving a 1 cm (½ inch) border. Top with some sliced button mushrooms, halved cherry and teardrop tomatoes and 1 sliced green capsicum (pepper). Sprinkle with 150 g (5½ oz/1 cup) grated mozzarella cheese and bake for 20 minutes, or until the cheese is golden. Serve hot. Serves 4.

tomato and cheese risotto cakes

tomato and cheese risotto cakes

✳ ✳

Preparation time: 20 minutes
  + 1 hour 15 minutes chilling time
Cooking time: 40 minutes
Serves 6

810 ml (28 fl oz/3¼ cups) vegetable
  stock
1 tablespoon olive oil
20 g (¾ oz) butter
1 small onion, finely chopped
275 g (9¾ oz/1¼ cups) arborio rice
35 g (1¼ oz/⅓ cup) grated parmesan
  cheese
30 g (1 oz/¼ cup) chopped sun-dried
  tomatoes
30 g (1 oz) mozzarella cheese, cut into
  1 cm (½ inch) cubes
vegetable oil, for deep-frying
75 g (2½ oz) mixed salad leaves,
  to serve

1 Bring the stock to the boil in a small saucepan. Reduce the heat, then cover and keep at a simmer.
2 Meanwhile, heat the oil and butter in a heavy-based saucepan over medium heat. Add the onion and cook for 3 minutes, or until golden. Reduce the heat to low, then add the rice and cook, stirring, for 3 minutes, or until the rice is lightly golden. Pour in one-quarter of the hot stock and stir constantly until the liquid has been absorbed. Repeat until all the stock has been added and the rice is almost tender; this will take about 20 minutes. Stir in the parmesan and remove from the heat. Transfer the mixture to a bowl, allow to cool, then refrigerate for 1 hour.
3 With wet hands, roll 2 tablespoons of the rice mixture into a ball. Make an indentation in the ball and press a cube of mozzarella and a few pieces of sun-dried tomato into it. Reshape into a ball, then flatten slightly. Repeat with the remaining rice mixture and refrigerate for a further 15 minutes.

4 Fill a deep-fryer or large heavy-based saucepan one-third full of oil and heat to 180°C (350°F), or until a cube of bread dropped in the oil browns in 15 seconds. Using a large spoon, gently lower the risotto cakes, a few at a time, into the oil. Cook for 1–2 minutes, or until golden brown. Remove with a slotted spoon and drain on paper towels.
5 Serve hot, with the salad leaves.

adzuki bean stir-fry

✳

Preparation time: 15 minutes +
  overnight soaking
Cooking time: 1 hour 15 minutes
Serves 4

220 g (7¾ oz/1 cup) adzuki beans (see Note)
1 teaspoon sesame oil
1 tablespoon vegetable oil
1 garlic clove, crushed
1 tablespoon finely grated fresh ginger
3 spring onions (scallions), sliced
185 g (6½ oz) firm tofu, cut into
  bite-sized pieces
125 g (4½ oz) shimeji mushrooms, separated
1 red capsicum (pepper), sliced
1 carrot, sliced
100 g (3½ oz) baby corn
500 g (1 lb 2 oz) baby bok choy (pak choy),
  leaves separated
1 tablespoon oyster sauce
1 tablespoon hoisin sauce
60 ml (2 fl oz/¼ cup) salt-reduced soy sauce
1 tablespoon sweet chilli sauce
1 tablespoon lime juice
2 tablespoons chopped coriander (cilantro)
steamed rice, to serve

1 Soak the beans overnight in cold water.
2 Rinse the beans and drain well. Place in a large, heavy-based saucepan, cover with water and bring to the boil. Reduce the heat and simmer for 1 hour, or until tender. Drain and set aside.
3 Heat the oils in a wok or large frying pan over high heat. Stir-fry the garlic, ginger and spring onion for 2 minutes. Add the tofu and stir-fry for 5 minutes,

or until golden brown. Add the mushrooms, capsicum, carrot, corn and bok choy and stir-fry for 3 minutes.
4 Stir in the drained beans and the remaining ingredients. Stir for 2 minutes until combined and heated through.
5 Serve with steamed rice.

NOTE: Popular in Japan, adzuki beans are related to soya beans and are also called red beans. Easily digested, they are used to make many Asian sweets.

lentil and chickpea burgers with coriander garlic cream

✳ ✳

Preparation time: 30 minutes
Cooking time: 30 minutes
Makes 10

250 g (9 oz/1 cup) red lentils
1 tablespoon vegetable oil
2 onions, sliced
1 tablespoon tandoori mix powder
400 g (14 oz) tin chickpeas, rinsed
    and drained
1 tablespoon finely grated fresh ginger
1 egg
3 tablespoons chopped flat-leaf
    (Italian) parsley
2 tablespoons chopped coriander (cilantro)
180 g (6½ oz/2¼ cups) stale breadcrumbs
flour, for dusting

CORIANDER GARLIC CREAM
125 g (4½ oz/½ cup) sour cream
125 ml (4 fl oz/½ cup) cream
1 garlic clove, crushed
2 tablespoons chopped coriander (cilantro)
2 tablespoons chopped flat-leaf (Italian)
    parsley

1 Bring a large saucepan of water to the boil. Add the lentils and simmer, uncovered, for 10 minutes, or until tender. Drain and rinse well under cold water.
2 Meanwhile, heat the oil in a frying pan over medium heat. Add the onion and cook for 3 minutes, or until soft. Add the tandoori powder and stir until fragrant. Allow the mixture to cool slightly.
3 Combine all the coriander garlic cream ingredients in a bowl and mix well. Cover and refrigerate until required.
4 Place the chickpeas, half the lentils, the ginger, egg and the onion mixture in a food processor and process for 20 seconds, or until smooth. Transfer to a bowl and stir in the remaining lentils, the parsley, coriander and the breadcrumbs. Divide the mixture into 10 portions.
5 Shape the portions into round patties. (If the mixture is too soft, refrigerate for 15 minutes, or until firm.) Toss them in flour to coat, shaking off any excess.
6 Heat a lightly greased barbecue grill or hotplate to medium. Cook the patties for 3–4 minutes on each side, or until browned, turning once. Serve with the coriander garlic cream.

NOTE: The patties can be prepared up to 2 days ahead and stored, covered, in the refrigerator. If you prefer, you can cook the patties in a frying pan brushed lightly with oil. The coriander garlic cream can be made up to 3 days in advance. Store in a covered container in the refrigerator.

filo risotto pie

filo risotto pie

✳ ✳ ✳

Preparation time: 45 minutes
Cooking time: 1 hour 45 minutes
Serves 8

2 large red capsicums (peppers),
    cut into flat pieces
250 ml (9 fl oz/1 cup) white wine
1 litre (35 fl oz/4 cups) vegetable
    stock
2 tablespoons olive oil
1 leek, white part only, sliced
1 garlic clove, crushed
1 fennel bulb, thinly sliced
440 g (15½ oz/2 cups) arborio rice
60 g (2¼ oz) grated parmesan cheese
10 sheets filo pastry
60 ml (2 fl oz/¼ cup) olive oil
500 g (1 lb 2 oz) English spinach, blanched
    and well drained
250 g (9 oz) feta cheese, crumbled
1 tablespoon sesame seeds

1   Preheat the grill (broiler) to medium–
high. Grill (broil) the capsicum until
the skin blackens and blisters. Place on
a cutting board, cover with a tea towel
(dish towel) and allow to cool. Peel, then
cut the flesh into small pieces.
2   Meanwhile, start making the risotto.
Bring the wine and stock to the boil in a
large saucepan. Reduce the heat, cover
and keep at a simmer.
3   Heat the oil in a large heavy-based
saucepan over medium heat. Add the
leek, garlic and fennel and cook, stirring,
for 5 minutes, or until the leek and fennel
are lightly browned. Add the rice and
cook, stirring, for 3 minutes, or until the
rice is translucent.
4   Pour in 250 ml (9 fl oz/1 cup) stock
and stir constantly until the liquid is
absorbed. Continue adding more stock,
125 ml (4 fl oz/½ cup) at a time, stirring
for 20–25 minutes, or until the rice is
creamy and tender. Remove from the
heat, stir in the parmesan and season to
taste. Set aside to cool slightly.
5   Preheat the oven to 180°C (350°F/
Gas 4). Lay the filo pastry on a work

surface and cover with a damp tea towel
(dish towel) to stop it drying out. Working
one at a time, brush each sheet with
oil and fold in half lengthways. Lay the
sheets in a 23 cm (9 inch) spring-form tin,
overlapping like spokes on a wheel, with
one side of the pastry hanging over the
side of the tin.
6   Spoon half the risotto mixture over the
pastry and top with half the capsicum,
half the spinach and half the feta. Repeat
with the remaining risotto, capsicum,
spinach and feta.
7   Fold the pastry over the filling, brush
lightly with oil and sprinkle with sesame
seeds. Bake for 50 minutes, or until the
pastry is crisp and golden and the pie is
heated through.

mediterranean
lentil salad

✳

Preparation time: 20 minutes
    + 4 hours chilling time
Cooking time: 20 minutes
Serves 8

1 large red capsicum (pepper),
    cut into flat pieces
1 large yellow capsicum (pepper),
    cut into flat pieces
250 g (9 oz/1 cup) red lentils
1 red onion, finely chopped
1 Lebanese (short) cucumber,
    chopped

rice for risotto

The rice variety that is
most commonly used for
making risotto is arborio —
a short-grain rice first grown
in the Piedmont region of Italy.
It is sold in supermarkets and
delicatessens. Arborio's large,
round, pearly grains have a
clearly defined hard white core,
which, when cooked, remains
visible and slightly resistant to
the teeth. Other short-grain
rices can be substituted, but the
result won't be nearly as good,
as risotto that is made with
arborio rice has a particularly
rich, creamy texture. Arborio
rice has a distinctive aroma and
flavour — it is in fact the rice,
and not the additions, that
make the northern Italian
risotto unique.

DRESSING
80 ml (2½ fl oz/⅓ cup) olive oil
2 tablespoons lemon juice
1 teaspoon ground cumin
2 garlic cloves, crushed

1   Preheat the grill (broiler) to medium–
high. Grill (broil) the capsicum until
the skin blackens and blisters. Place on
a cutting board, cover with a tea towel
(dish towel) and leave to cool. Peel, then
cut the flesh into 5 mm (¼ inch) strips.
2   Meanwhile, bring a large saucepan
of water to the boil. Add the lentils and
simmer, uncovered, for 10 minutes, or
until tender. Drain and rinse well under
cold water.
3   Place the lentils in a salad bowl with
the capsicum, onion and cucumber.
4   Whisk the dressing ingredients in a
small bowl until well combined. Season
to taste, then pour over the salad and toss
together well. Cover and refrigerate for
4 hours.
5   Allow the salad to return to room
temperature before serving.

brown rice

Brown rice has more vitamins and minerals than white rice, as it still has its bran layer. To retain the maximum nutrients, it is best to cook rice (white or brown) by the absorption method where possible, as most of the vitamins are water soluble and are lost if the rice is drained.

brown rice tart with fresh tomato filling

✳ ✳

Preparation time: 25 minutes
Cooking time: 1 hour 50 minutes
Serves 6

200 g (7 oz/1 cup) brown rice
60 g (2¼ oz/½ cup) grated cheddar cheese
1 egg, lightly beaten

FRESH TOMATO FILLING
6 roma (plum) tomatoes, halved
6 garlic cloves, unpeeled
1 tablespoon olive oil
8 lemon thyme sprigs
50 g (1¾ oz) goat's cheese, crumbled
3 eggs
60 ml (2 fl oz/¼ cup) milk

1 Cook the rice in a saucepan of boiling water for 35 minutes. Rinse and drain.
2 Meanwhile, preheat the oven to 200°C (400°F/Gas 6).
3 To make the tomato filling, put the tomatoes, cut side up, on a non-stick baking tray with the garlic. Brush the tomatoes and garlic with the oil and sprinkle with freshly ground black pepper. Bake for 30 minutes, then remove from the oven to cool slightly. Remove the garlic from the skins.
4 Put the rice, cheese and egg in a bowl and mix until well combined. Spread the mixture over the base and side of a lightly greased 25 cm (10 inch) flan tin or quiche dish. Bake for 15 minutes.
5 Turn the oven down to 180°C (350°F/Gas 4). Whisk the eggs and milk in a bowl, then pour over the rice crust.
6 Arrange the tomato halves, garlic, lemon thyme and goat's cheese in the centre of the tart.
7 Bake for 1 hour, or until set.

brown rice tart with fresh tomato filling

tex mex chilli beans

✳

Preparation time: 20 minutes
Cooking time: 20 minutes
Serves 4

1 tablespoon vegetable oil
2 garlic cloves, crushed
2 small red chillies, finely chopped
1 onion, finely chopped
1 green capsicum (pepper), chopped
400 g (14 oz) tin red kidney beans, rinsed and drained
400 g (14 oz) tin chopped tomatoes
125 g (4½ oz/½ cup) ready-made tomato salsa

chickpeas

Chickpeas contain dietary fibre, protein, iron, vitamin B1 and potassium. Dried chickpeas need to be soaked overnight before being cooked. Tinned chickpeas do not need soaking and do not require as much cooking time.

1 teaspoon soft brown sugar
sour cream, to serve
guacamole, to serve
corn chips, to serve

1   Heat the oil in a heavy-based saucepan over medium heat. Add the garlic, chilli and onion and cook for 3 minutes, or until the onion is golden.
2   Add the remaining ingredients and bring to the boil. Reduce the heat and simmer, uncovered, for 15 minutes, or until the sauce thickens.
3   Serve with sour cream, guacamole and corn chips.

NOTE: Red kidney beans originated in Mexico about 5000 years ago. They contain dietary fibre, iron, potassium, and several B vitamins. Tinned chickpeas, rinsed and drained, can be substituted for kidney beans in this recipe.

beetroot hummus

✳

Preparation time: 25 minutes
    + overnight soaking time
Cooking time: 1 hour
Serves 8

250 g (9 oz) dried chickpeas
1 large onion, chopped
500 g (1 lb 2 oz) beetroot
    (beets)
125 g (4 oz/½ cup) tahini
3 garlic cloves, crushed
60 ml (2 oz/¼ cup) lemon juice
1 tablespoon ground cumin
60 ml (2 oz/¼ cup) olive oil, plus extra,
    to serve
pitta bread, to serve

1   Soak the chickpeas in cold water overnight. Rinse and drain.

2   Put the chickpeas and onion in a large heavy-based saucepan, cover with cold water and bring to the boil. Cook for 1 hour, or until the chickpeas are very soft. Drain, reserving 250 ml (9 fl oz/1 cup) of the cooking liquid. Leave to cool.
3   Meanwhile, cook the beetroot in a large saucepan of boiling water until tender. Drain and leave to cool slightly, then remove the skins.
4   Chop the beetroot, place in a food processor and process (in batches if necessary) until roughly chopped. Add the chickpea and onion mixture, tahini, garlic, lemon juice and cumin and process until smooth. With the motor running, gradually add the reserved cooking liquid and the oil and process until the mixture is thoroughly combined.
5   Serve in a bowl drizzled with a little olive oil, with pitta bread on the side.

borlotti beans

Brown with speckled red markings, borlotti beans are also known as cranberry or roman beans. They have a distinctive chestnut flavour and a creamy texture. Fresh borlotti beans have a long, burgundy-speckled pod and are available in spring and summer.

borlotti bean moussaka

✳ ✳

Preparation time: 45 minutes + overnight soaking + 10 minutes resting time
Cooking time: 2 hours 30 minutes
Serves 6

250 g (9 oz/1¼ cups) dried borlotti (cranberry) beans
2 large eggplants (aubergines)
80 ml (2½ fl oz/⅓ cup) olive oil
1 garlic clove, crushed
1 onion, chopped
125 g (4½ oz) button mushrooms, sliced
2 x 400 g (14 oz) tins chopped tomatoes

250 ml (9 fl oz/1 cup) red wine
1 tablespoon tomato paste (concentrated purée)
1 tablespoon chopped oregano

TOPPING
250 g (9 oz/1 cup) plain yoghurt
4 eggs, lightly beaten
500 ml (17 fl oz/2 cups) milk
¼ teaspoon paprika
50 g (1¾ oz/½ cup) grated parmesan cheese
40 g (1½ oz/½ cup) fresh breadcrumbs

1 Soak the beans in cold water overnight. Rinse and drain.
2 Place the beans in a large heavy-based saucepan, cover with cold water and bring to the boil. Reduce the heat and simmer for 1½ hours, or until tender. Drain and rinse well under cold water. Set aside.
3 Meanwhile, slice the eggplant, sprinkle with salt and set aside for 30 minutes. Rinse and pat dry. Brush the eggplant slices with a little of the oil and cook under a preheated grill (broiler) for 3 minutes on each side, or until golden. Drain on paper towels.
4 While the beans are still simmering, heat the remaining oil in a large heavy-based saucepan over medium heat. Add the garlic and onion and cook for 3 minutes, or until the onion is golden. Add the mushrooms and cook for 3 minutes, or until browned. Stir in the tomato, wine, tomato paste and oregano. Bring to the boil, reduce the heat and simmer for 40 minutes, or until the sauce has thickened.
5 Spoon the borlotti beans into a large baking dish. Top with the tomato sauce, then the eggplant slices.
6 To make the topping, whisk the yoghurt, eggs, milk and paprika in a bowl until combined. Pour over the eggplant and set aside for 10 minutes.
7 Meanwhile, preheat the oven to 200°C (400°F/Gas 6). Combine the parmesan and breadcrumbs and sprinkle over the moussaka. Bake for 45–60 minutes, or until the moussaka is heated through and the top is golden. Serve hot.

braised lima beans with leeks and pears

※

Preparation time: 30 minutes
  + overnight soaking time
Cooking time: 1 hour 30 minutes
Serves 4

250 g (9 oz) dried large lima beans
  (butter beans)
2 tablespoons vegetable oil
2 garlic cloves, crushed
2 leeks, white part only, sliced
1 teaspoon soft brown sugar
2 pears, peeled and cut into thick slices
2 tomatoes, peeled, seeded and diced
1 teaspoon fennel seeds
250 ml (9 fl oz/1 cup) white wine
2 tablespoons white wine vinegar
155 g (5 oz) asparagus, woody ends
  trimmed, spears cut into 4 cm
  (1½ inch) lengths
8 sage leaves
2 tablespoons pine nuts, toasted

1 Soak the lima beans in cold water
overnight. Rinse and drain.
2 Place the beans in a large heavy-based
saucepan, cover with water and bring
to the boil. Reduce heat and simmer for
1 hour. Drain and rinse well under cold
water. Set aside.
3 Heat the oil in a large non-stick frying
pan over medium heat. Add the garlic,
leek and sugar and cook, stirring, for
10 minutes, or until the leek begins
to caramelise.
4 Add the pear, tomato, fennel seeds,
wine and vinegar and simmer for
10 minutes, or until the liquid has
reduced by one quarter.
5 Stir in the lima beans, asparagus
and sage and season to taste. Cook for
5 minutes, or until the asparagus is
tender. Sprinkle with pine nuts and serve.

NOTE: Lima beans have a light buttery
flavour and a creamy texture. The
smaller beans can be white or green, the
large ones are only white. To toast pine
nuts, spread them on a baking tray and
bake in a 180°C (350°F/Gas 4) oven for
5 minutes, or until golden.

chilli polenta cake

※

Preparation time: 30 minutes
Cooking time: 35 minutes
Serves 6

165 g (5¾ oz/1⅓ cups) plain
  (all purpose) flour
1½ teaspoons baking powder
1 teaspoon sea salt
190 g (6¾ oz/1 cup) polenta
125 g (4½ oz/1 cup) grated cheddar
  cheese
250 g (9 oz/1 cup) plain yoghurt
125 ml (4 fl oz/½ cup) milk
2 eggs
80 g (2¾ oz/½ cup) chopped red
  capsicum (pepper)
2 teaspoons chopped chilli
60 g (2¼ oz) unsalted butter

1 Preheat the oven to 200°C (400°F/
Gas 6).
2 Sift the flour, baking powder and salt
into a large bowl. Stir in the polenta
and cheese.
3 In a separate bowl, whisk together the
yoghurt, milk, eggs, capsicum and chilli.
4 Heat a 20 cm (8 inch) ovenproof frying
pan. Melt the butter in the pan, then
stir the butter into the yoghurt mixture.
Pour the yoghurt mixture into the dry
ingredients and mix well.
5 Pour the mixture back into the
frying pan. Transfer to the oven and bake
for 25–30 minutes, or until a skewer
inserted in the centre comes out clean.
6 Cut into wedges to serve.

chilli polenta cake

casseroles & bakes

These one-dish courses give new meaning to the idea of 'pot luck'.
No matter how many different ingredients go into making a savoury
casserole or bake, the finished product is always immensely satisfying,
either on its own, or eaten with a loaf of home-made bread. There's
little more one could ask for — except perhaps to invite a few friends
to share the indulgence.

baked fettucine

❋

Preparation time: **20 minutes**
Cooking time: **30 minutes**
Serves **4**

500 g (1 lb 2 oz) spinach fettucine
60 g (2¼ oz) butter or margarine
1 onion, finely chopped
300 g (10½ oz/1¼ cups) sour cream
250 ml (9 fl oz/1 cup) cream
¼ teaspoon ground nutmeg

50 g (1¾ oz/½ cup) grated
  parmesan cheese
150 g (5½ oz/1 cup) grated
  mozzarella cheese

1 Preheat the oven to 180°C (350°F/
Gas 4). Cook the pasta in a large saucepan
of rapidly boiling salted water until
al dente. Drain and return to the pan.
2 Meanwhile, melt the butter in a large
frying pan over low heat. Add the onion
and cook for 5 minutes, or until softened.
3 Add the onion mixture and sour cream
to the fettucine. Toss well, using a spoon
and a fork. Simmer, stirring, over medium
heat until the pasta is well coated. Stir in
the cream, nutmeg and half the parmesan
and season to taste.
4 Pour the mixture into a greased
casserole dish, then sprinkle with the
mozzarella and remaining parmesan.
Bake for 15 minutes, or until the cheese
is golden. Serve hot.

NOTE: You can vary this recipe by using
plain fettucine or adding chopped herbs
such as basil, parsley or thyme. Grated
carrot can also be stirred in. If you like
garlic, stir in a crushed clove or two just
before you finish frying the onion.

baked fettucine

carrot pesto bake

❋

Preparation time: **45 minutes**
  + 30 minutes standing time
Cooking time: **55 minutes**
Serves **4**

50 g (1¾ oz) butter
60 g (2 oz/½ cup) plain (all-purpose) flour
750 ml (26 fl oz/3 cups) milk
160 g (5¾ oz/⅔ cup) light sour cream
1 teaspoon freshly ground black pepper
150 g (5½ oz/1¼ cups) grated cheddar
  cheese
4 eggs, lightly beaten
2 tablespoons ready-made pesto
750 g (1 lb 10 oz) carrots, peeled and grated
250 g (9 oz) instant lasagne sheets

---

fast vegetable stew

Heat 1 tablespoon olive oil in a saucepan over medium heat. Add 1 chopped
onion and cook, stirring, for 5 minutes, or until soft. Add 2 chopped zucchini
(courgettes), 100 g (3½ oz) sliced button mushrooms, 1 chopped red capsicum
(pepper), 400 g (14 oz) tin chopped tomatoes and a splash of balsamic vinegar.
Cover and cook for 10 minutes, or until the vegetables are tender. Remove the lid
and cook for a further 5 minutes, or until the stew has thickened slightly. Season
to taste and serve over pasta or rice. Serves 4.
VARIATION: Mix the stew with 350 g (12 oz/2 cups) cooked short pasta shapes,
such as spirals or penne, and place in a baking dish. Sprinkle with grated cheese
and breadcrumbs and bake in a 210°C (415°F/Gas 6–7) oven for 10 minutes, or
until the topping is golden.

1 Melt the butter in a large saucepan over low heat. Add the flour and stir until the mixture is lightly golden, smooth and bubbling. Gradually add the combined milk, sour cream and pepper, stirring until the sauce is completely smooth.

2 Increase the heat to medium and stir constantly for 5 minutes, or until the mixture boils and thickens. Boil for another minute, then remove from the heat. Stir in two-thirds of the cheese and set aside to cool slightly. Gradually add the beaten eggs, stirring constantly.

3 Set aside one-third of the sauce for the topping. Add the pesto and carrot to the remaining sauce, stirring to combine.

4 Grease a 30 x 20 cm (12 x 8 inch) baking dish. Beginning with one-third of the carrot mixture, alternate layers of carrot mixture with sheets of lasagne in the baking dish. Use three layers of each, finishing with lasagne sheets. Spread the reserved sauce evenly over the top. Sprinkle with the remaining cheese, then set aside for 15 minutes before cooking to allow the pasta to soften.

5 Meanwhile, preheat the oven to 150°C (300°F/Gas 2). Put the baking dish in the oven and bake for 40 minutes, or until the sauce is golden.

6 Remove the bake from the oven, then cover and leave to rest for 15 minutes before serving, to make it easier to slice.

fast pumpkin gratin

Preheat the oven to 200°C (400°F/Gas 6). Put 400 g (14 oz) grated butternut pumpkin in a small, shallow baking dish; stir in 250 ml (9 fl oz/1 cup) cream. In a small bowl, combine 40 g (1½ oz/½ cup) fresh breadcrumbs, 4 tablespoons finely grated cheese and ½ teaspoon nutmeg. Sprinkle over the pumpkin mixture and bake for 20 minutes, or until the topping is golden. Serves 4.

carrot pesto bake

pesto

Pesto genovese is the classic basil pesto and is a simple combination of basil leaves, pine nuts, grated parmesan cheese, garlic cloves and olive oil, seasoned with a little salt and pepper. All pestos are highly flavoured and should be used sparingly, to complement rather than overwhelm the foods they accompany. In Italian the word pesto means 'pounded' — the traditional method of making pesto being to grind the ingredients using a mortar and pestle.

hungarian casserole

✳

Preparation time: 30 minutes
Cooking time: 30 minutes
Serves 4–6

1 tablespoon olive oil
30 g (1 oz) butter
4 large potatoes, peeled and cut into
    large chunks
1 onion, chopped
1 green capsicum (pepper), chopped
1 red capsicum (pepper), chopped
2 teaspoons paprika
2 teaspoons caraway seeds
400 g (14 oz) tin chopped tomatoes
250 ml (9 fl oz/1 cup) vegetable stock

CROUTONS
250 ml (9 fl oz/1 cup) vegetable oil
4 slices white bread, crusts removed,
    cut into small cubes

1   Heat the oil and butter in a large
heavy-based saucepan over medium
heat. Add the potato and cook, turning
regularly, for 10 minutes, or until crisp
on the edges.
2   Add the onion and capsicums and cook,
stirring, for 5 minutes. Stir in the paprika,
caraway seeds, tomato and stock. Season
to taste and simmer, uncovered, for
10 minutes, or until the potato is tender.
3   Meanwhile, make the croutons. Heat
the oil in a frying pan over medium heat.
Add the bread and cook, turning often,

for 2 minutes, or until golden brown and
crisp. Drain on paper towels.
4   Serve the casserole hot, sprinkled with
the croutons.

mexican tomato bake

✳

Preparation time: 25 minutes
Cooking time: 30 minutes
Serves 4–6

6 ripe tomatoes
2 tablespoons vegetable oil
2 red onions, chopped
2 garlic cloves, crushed
1 green capsicum (pepper), chopped

caraway seeds

Caraway seeds are renowned
for their digestive properties
and are rich in mineral salts and
proteins. When chewed, the
seeds help get rid of the smell
of garlic and are also said to
stimulate the appetite. Most
commonly seen in heavy rye
bread, caraway seeds are also
used in seed bread. A little bowl
of caraway seeds is a great
accompaniment for strongly
flavoured cheeses such as
munster or livarot.

hungarian casserole

1 tablespoon red wine vinegar
1 teaspoon sugar
½ teaspoon chilli powder
400 g (14 oz/2 cups) tin corn kernels,
   drained
125 g (4½ oz) plain corn chips
150 g (5½ oz/1¼ cups) grated cheddar
   cheese
250 g (9 oz/1 cup) sour cream
snipped chives, to garnish

1 Preheat the oven to 160°C (315°F/
Gas 2–3).
2 Score a cross in the base of the
tomatoes. Place in a heatproof bowl
and cover with boiling water. Leave for
30 seconds, then transfer to cold water
and peel the skin away from the cross.
Cut the tomatoes in half, scoop out the
seeds and chop the flesh. Set aside.
3 Heat the oil in a saucepan over
medium heat. Add the onion and
garlic and cook, stirring, for 3 minutes.
Add the tomato, capsicum, vinegar,
sugar and chilli powder and cook,
uncovered, for 6–7 minutes, or until
the tomato is soft and the liquid has
evaporated. Stir in the corn and heat
for 3 minutes.
4 Arrange layers of corn chips, the
tomato sauce and cheese in a baking
dish, finishing with a layer of cheese.
Spoon the sour cream over the top.
5 Bake, uncovered, for 15 minutes.
Serve hot, sprinkled with chives.

winter vegetable casserole

✳

Preparation time: 15 minutes
Cooking time: 45 minutes
Serves 4

200 g (7 oz) pumpkin (winter squash)
2 potatoes
1 parsnip
30 g (1 oz) butter
1 tablespoon plain (all-purpose) flour
375 ml (13 fl oz/1½ cups) milk

½ teaspoon ground nutmeg
cress leaves, to garnish (optional)

CRUMBLE TOPPING
80 g (2¾ oz/1 cup) fresh breadcrumbs
100 g (3½ oz) roasted unsalted cashew
   nuts, roughly chopped
30 g (1 oz) butter

1 Preheat the oven to 180°C (350°F/
Gas 4).
2 Cut the pumpkin into large bite-sized
pieces, and cut the potato and parsnip
into smaller pieces. Add the vegetables to
a saucepan of boiling water and cook for
8 minutes, or until just tender. Drain well,
then arrange in a large, deep baking dish.

3 Meanwhile, melt the butter in a
saucepan over low heat. Add the flour
and cook, stirring constantly, for 1 minute.
Remove from the heat and gradually
stir in the milk. Return the pan to the
heat and bring the mixture to the boil,
stirring constantly, until thickened. Boil
for 1 minute, then stir in the nutmeg
and season to taste. Pour the sauce over
the vegetables.
4 To make the crumble topping, combine
the breadcrumbs and cashews in a bowl
and sprinkle them over the vegetables.
Dot with the butter.
5 Bake for 30 minutes, or until the
crumble topping is golden. Serve
garnished with cress, if desired.

bay leaves

Also called laurel, the bay tree (Laurus nobilis) is an evergreen shrub native to the Mediterranean. The ancient Greeks gave bay or laurel wreaths to winners of Olympic Games, poets and heroes.

Bay leaves have an exquisite flavour, and their pungency increases with cooking. Burning a few leaves on a baking tray or saucer will help remove unwanted kitchen smells.

baked cheese and spinach cannelloni

1 To make the tomato sauce, heat the oil in a large frying pan over medium heat. Add onion and garlic and cook, stirring, for 5 minutes, or until onion is soft. Add tomato, herbs and tomato paste and mix thoroughly. Bring to the boil, reduce the heat and simmer for 25–30 minutes, or until the sauce is thick. Remove bay leaves and rosemary sprigs and season to taste.

2 Meanwhile, preheat the oven to 200°C (400°F/Gas 6).

3 Steam the spinach until just wilted, then drain and chop. Place in a bowl with ricotta, parmesan, mint, eggs and pine nuts and season to taste. Mix until combined. Using a small spoon or knife, carefully fill the cannelloni tubes with the mixture.

4 Spoon some tomato sauce into a large, shallow baking dish, spreading it evenly. Arrange the filled cannelloni tubes on top. Cover with the remaining tomato sauce and sprinkle with the mozzarella.

5 Bake for 30–40 minutes, or until the cheese is golden and bubbling and the pasta is tender.

roasted vegetable lasagne

❋ ❋ ❋

Preparation time: 50 minutes
Cooking time: 1 hour
Serves 6

1 red capsicum (pepper), cut into flat pieces
1 large eggplant (aubergine), sliced lengthways, salted, rinsed and well drained
2 large zucchini (courgettes), thinly sliced lengthways
400 g (14 oz) orange sweet potato, peeled and thinly sliced lengthways
6 egg (roma) tomatoes, quartered
375 g (13 oz) fresh lasagne sheets
90 g (3¼ oz/⅓ cup) good-quality ready-made pesto
300 g (10½ oz) bocconcini (fresh baby mozzarella cheese), thinly sliced
olive oil, for brushing
100 g (3½ oz/1 cup) grated parmesan cheese

baked cheese and spinach cannelloni

❋ ❋

Preparation time: 40 minutes
Cooking time: 1 hour 20 minutes
Serves 4

500 g (1 lb 2 oz) English spinach, washed and stems removed
150 g (5½ oz) feta cheese, crumbled
150 g (5½ oz) ricotta cheese
50 g (1¾ oz/½ cup) grated parmesan cheese

2 tablespoons finely chopped mint
2 eggs, lightly beaten
2 tablespoons pine nuts, toasted
16 instant cannelloni tubes
200 g (7 oz) mozzarella cheese, finely grated

TOMATO SAUCE
2 tablespoons olive oil
1 large onion, finely chopped
2 garlic cloves, finely chopped
3 x 400 g (14 oz) tins chopped tomatoes
2 rosemary sprigs
2 bay leaves
2 tablespoons tomato paste (concentrated purée)

MARINADE
125 ml (4 fl oz/½ cup) olive oil
2 tablespoons red wine vinegar
1 tablespoon finely chopped capers
1 tablespoon finely chopped parsley
1 garlic clove, finely chopped
1 teaspoon tomato paste (concentrated
   purée)

1 Preheat the oven to 200°C (400°F/ Gas 6). Heat the grill (broiler) to high.
2 Grill (broil) the capsicum until the skin blackens and blisters. Place on a cutting board, cover with a tea towel (dish towel) and allow to cool. Cut the flesh into thick strips and place in a large baking dish with the remaining vegetables.
3 Combine the marinade ingredients in a bowl and whisk thoroughly. Pour half the marinade over the vegetables and toss to coat. Bake for 15 minutes, then turn and coat again with the remaining marinade. Bake for a further 15 minutes.
4 Cut the pasta into 24 sheets, each measuring approximately 10 x 16 cm (4 x 6¼ inches). Make six individual lasagne stacks by assembling the ingredients in the following order: a layer of pasta, zucchini, sweet potato, 2 teaspoons pesto and bocconcini slices; pasta, eggplant and capsicum; pasta, tomato, 2 teaspoons pesto and bocconcini slices. Top with a final sheet of pasta.
5 Transfer the stacks to a greased baking dish. Brush the tops with olive oil and sprinkle with the parmesan.
6 Bake for 15–20 minutes, or until the vegetables are heated through and tender.

potato cake

✳

Preparation time: 20 minutes
Cooking time: 1 hour
Serves 4–6

30 g (1 oz) butter
2 tablespoons olive oil
1 garlic clove, crushed
200 g (7 oz/2 cups) dry breadcrumbs
125 g (4½ oz/1 cup) grated cheddar cheese

50 g (1¾ oz/½ cup) grated parmesan
   cheese
8 roasting potatoes, thinly sliced

1 Preheat the oven to 180°C (350°F/ Gas 4). Grease a deep, 20 cm (8 inch) spring-form tin and line the base and side with baking paper.
2 Heat the butter and oil in a frying pan, then stir in the garlic and season well with freshly ground black pepper. Remove from the heat.

3 In a bowl, combine the breadcrumbs, cheddar and parmesan.
4 Overlap a layer of potato slices in the spring-form tin, then brush with some of the garlic butter mixture. Sprinkle with the breadcrumb mixture and continue layering, ending with a layer of breadcrumbs and cheese. Press the mixture down firmly into the tin.
5 Bake for 1 hour, or until golden. Allow to cool slightly, then cut into wedges to serve.

potato cake

flavoured vinegars

Wine vinegars are, in general, the mildest and most versatile of the vinegar family. The name derives from the French 'vinaigre', meaning soured wine. Wine vinegars can be flavoured with herbs such as tarragon, basil, mint and thyme. Put a few sprigs of your chosen herb in a sterilised bottle, pour in the vinegar, seal and leave for three weeks. Strain the vinegar and return to a sterilised bottle with one small fresh sprig of the herb for identification.

layered potato and apple bake

✳

Preparation time: **30 minutes**
Cooking time: **45 minutes**
Serves **4–6**

2 all-purpose potatoes, thinly sliced
3 green apples, peeled, cored and thinly
   sliced
1 onion, thinly sliced into rings
60 g (2¼ oz/½ cup) grated cheddar cheese
250 ml (9 fl oz/1 cup) cream
¼ teaspoon freshly grated nutmeg

1 Preheat the oven to 180°C (350°F/
Gas 4). Grease a large shallow baking dish.
2 Layer the potato, apple and onion in
the baking dish, ending with a layer of
potato. Sprinkle evenly with the cheddar.
Pour the cream evenly over the top and
sprinkle with the nutmeg and some
freshly ground black pepper.
3 Bake for 45 minutes, or until golden
brown. Remove from the oven and allow
to stand for 5 minutes before serving.

fast eggplant bake

Slice 6 baby eggplants (aubergines)
lengthways, dust lightly with plain
(all-purpose) flour, then fry in a little
olive oil over medium heat until
golden brown. Drain on paper
towels. Lay the eggplant in a shallow
baking dish and spread with 125 ml
(4 fl oz/½ cup) ready-made tomato
pasta sauce. Sprinkle with 150 g
(5½ oz/1 cup) grated mozzarella
cheese and 25 g (1 oz/¼ cup)
grated parmesan cheese. Season
with freshly ground black pepper
and bake in a preheated 180°C
(350°F/Gas 4) oven for 15 minutes,
or until the cheese is golden and
bubbling. Serve with a rocket
(arugula) salad dressed with olive
oil and lemon juice. Serves 2.

spicy chickpea and vegetable casserole

✳

Preparation time: 25 minutes +
   overnight soaking time
Cooking time: 1 hour 30 minutes
Serves 4

335 g (11¾ oz/1½ cups) dried
   chickpeas (see Note)
2 tablespoons olive oil
1 large onion, chopped
1 garlic clove, crushed
3 teaspoons ground cumin
½ teaspoon chilli powder
½ teaspoon ground allspice

400 g (14 oz) tin chopped
   tomatoes
375 ml (13 fl oz/1½ cups) vegetable
   stock
300 g (10½ oz) pumpkin (winter
   squash), cubed
150 g (5½ oz) green beans, topped
   and tailed
200 g (7 oz) button squash, quartered
2 tablespoons tomato paste
   (concentrated purée)
1 teaspoon dried oregano

1   Soak the chickpeas in cold water
overnight. Rinse and drain.
2   Heat the oil in a large saucepan over
medium heat. Add the onion and garlic
and cook, stirring, for 2 minutes, then
add the cumin, chilli powder and allspice
and cook for 1 minute. Add the chickpeas,
tomato and stock. Bring to the boil, then
reduce the heat and simmer, covered, for
1 hour, stirring occasionally.
3   Stir in the pumpkin, beans, squash,
tomato paste and oregano. Simmer, covered,
for 15 minutes, then remove the lid and
simmer for a final 10 minutes, or until the
sauce has reduced and thickened slightly.

NOTE: To reduce the soaking time for
chickpeas, place them in a large saucepan
and cover with cold water. Bring to the
boil, then remove from the heat and
soak for two hours. If you are in a hurry,
substitute tinned chickpeas; drain and
rinse thoroughly before use.

cumin

Cumin is a small seed with
an earthy, warm flavour,
commonly used in curries
and in Middle Eastern and
Mediterranean dishes. In Spain
it is the traditional seasoning
for chickpeas and is also used
in vegetable and rice dishes.
Cumin is usually sold ground
as a powder, which preserves
the flavour and makes it easy
to add the right amount. The
flavour is quite pungent.

cauliflower and pasta bake with crouton topping

✹

Preparation time: 25 minutes
Cooking time: 1 hour
Serves 6

150 g (5½ oz) short pasta (such as penne)
600 g (1 lb 5 oz) cauliflower, cut into florets
2 tablespoons olive oil
2 red onions, chopped
2 garlic cloves, finely chopped
80 g (2¾ oz) butter
40 g (1½ oz/⅓ cup) plain (all-purpose) flour
1 litre (35 fl oz/4 cups) milk
1 large handful shredded basil
200 g (7 oz/2 cups) grated parmesan cheese

CROUTON TOPPING
5 slices day-old bread, crusts removed,
   cut into large cubes
50 g (1¾ oz) butter, melted

1 Preheat the oven to 180°C (350°F/Gas 4).
2 Cook the pasta in a saucepan of rapidly boiling salted water until al dente. Drain and set aside.
3 Meanwhile, steam the cauliflower until just tender, then place in a bowl.
4 Heat the olive oil in a frying pan over medium heat. Add the onion and garlic and cook for 3 minutes, or until the onion is soft. Add the mixture to the cauliflower.
5 Melt the butter in a large saucepan over medium heat. Blend in the flour and cook, stirring constantly, for 1 minute. Gradually whisk in the milk, stirring constantly until the mixture boils and thickens. Remove from the heat and stir in the basil and 125 g (4½ oz/1¼ cups) of the parmesan. Add the cauliflower mixture and the pasta and mix thoroughly. Spoon the mixture into a large baking dish.
6 To make the crouton topping, toss the bread cubes in the melted butter, then scatter them over the pasta mixture.

7 Sprinkle with the remaining parmesan and bake for 35–40 minutes, or until the topping is golden.

stuffed pumpkins

✹

Preparation time: 25 minutes
Cooking time: 50 minutes
Serves 4

4 golden nugget pumpkins (squash)
95 g (3¼ oz/½ cup) cooked rice
2 teaspoons curry paste
1 tablespoon finely chopped coriander (cilantro)
1 green apple, cored and finely chopped
1 zucchini (courgette), finely chopped
1 carrot, finely chopped
65 g (2¼ oz/¾ cup) button mushrooms, thinly sliced
155 g (5½ oz) asparagus spears, woody ends trimmed, spears chopped
2 teaspoons currants
¼ teaspoon garam masala
60 g (2¼ oz) butter, melted

1 Preheat the oven to 210°C (415°F/Gas 6–7). Cut the top off each pumpkin and reserve. Scoop out the seeds and discard. Arrange the pumpkins in a baking dish and replace the tops. Add 60 ml (2 fl oz/¼ cup) water to the baking

cauliflower and pasta bake with crouton topping

fast couscous

Couscous is a simple and delicious bed for serving casseroles on. Put 185 g (6½ oz/1 cup) instant couscous in a large heatproof bowl and add 185 ml (6 fl oz/¾ cup) boiling water. Cover and leave to stand for 3–5 minutes. Stir through 30 g (1 oz) butter with a fork, until the butter has melted and the grains have fluffed up. Season to taste. For extra flavour, stir through a little crushed garlic that has been sautéed in some butter or oil. Serves 2.

dish and cover firmly with foil. Bake the pumpkins for 30 minutes.

2   Remove the baking dish from the oven. Remove the pumpkins from the dish and drain the water out. Grease the baking dish.

3   In a bowl, combine the remaining ingredients and mix together well. Spoon the mixture into the pumpkin cavities and top with the reserved lids. Return the pumpkins to the dish and cover with foil.

4   Bake for 20 minutes, or until the pumpkins are just cooked. Serve hot.

fennel crumble

❋

Preparation time: 25 minutes
Cooking time: 40 minutes
Serves 6

2 fennel bulbs, trimmed and sliced
60 ml (2 fl oz/¼ cup) lemon juice, plus
    2 tablespoons extra
1 tablespoon honey
1 tablespoon plain (all-purpose) flour
315 ml (10¾ fl oz/1¼ cups) cream

CRUMBLE TOPPING
75 g (2½ oz/¾ cup) rolled (porridge)
    oats
60 g (2 oz/½ cup) plain (all-purpose)
    flour
110 g (3¾ oz/1 cup) black rye breadcrumbs
    (made from 3 slices bread)
60 g (2¼ oz) butter
1 garlic clove, crushed

1   Preheat the oven to 180°C (350°F/ Gas 4). Grease a large baking dish.

2   Add the fennel and the 60 ml (2 fl oz/¼ cup) lemon juice to a saucepan of boiling water. Cook for 3 minutes, then rinse and drain.

3   Place the fennel in a large bowl. Stir in the extra lemon juice and honey and season to taste. Sprinkle with the flour, then spoon the mixture into the baking dish and pour the cream over the top.

4   To make the crumble topping, combine the oats, flour and breadcrumbs in a bowl.

Melt the butter in a small frying pan over medium heat. Add the garlic and cook for 30 seconds, then pour the butter over the breadcrumb mixture and mix well.

5   Sprinkle the topping mixture over the fennel. Bake for 20–30 minutes, or until the fennel is tender and the crumble topping has browned.

NOTE: White or wholemeal (whole-wheat) breadcrumbs can be used in place of rye bread. Blanching the fennel before baking it softens the texture slightly and reduces its strong aniseed flavour.

fennel

Fennel adds a light aniseed flavour to soups, sauces and roasted or marinated vegetables. The leaves can be used in salads and stuffings, and the raw bulb can be cooked as a vegetable, or served thinly sliced as part of an antipasto platter.

eggplant

When buying eggplants (aubergines), look for firm, glossy fruit that are neither wrinkled nor patchy and that feel heavy and solid. If the eggplant is soft, it is old and will be bitter; if it is hard, it is under-ripe; if it yields slightly to pressure, it is perfect. Eggplants can be stored for 4–5 days in a plastic bag in the refrigerator.

eggplant and asparagus sandwich

eggplant and asparagus sandwich

☀

Preparation time: 30 minutes
  + 30 minutes resting time
Cooking time: 40 minutes
Serves 6

2 eggplants (aubergines)
1 tablespoon olive oil
155 g (5½ oz) asparagus, woody ends trimmed
50 g (1¾ oz) butter
40 g (1½ oz/⅓ cup) finely chopped spring onions (scallions)
60 g (2 oz/½ cup) plain (all-purpose) flour
250 ml (9 fl oz/1 cup) milk
3 tablespoons grated romano cheese
1 tablespoon lemon juice
1 egg yolk

SOUFFLÉ TOPPING
1 egg white
3 tablespoons grated romano cheese

1 Cut each eggplant into 6 slices lengthways. Sprinkle with salt and leave

to stand for 30 minutes. Rinse under cold water, then pat dry with paper towels.

2 Meanwhile, preheat the grill (broiler) to medium–high. Brush the eggplant slices with oil and grill (broil) for 5 minutes, or until golden brown on each side, turning once. Drain on paper towels.

3 Steam or microwave the asparagus until just tender. Cut six spears into 5 cm (2 inch) lengths and set aside; finely chop the remaining asparagus.

4 Melt the butter in a saucepan over medium–high heat. Add the spring onion and cook for 1 minute. Stir in the flour until smooth. Gradually add the milk, stirring constantly over medium heat for 5 minutes, or until the mixture boils and thickens. Cook for 1 minute longer, then add the cheese, lemon juice, egg yolk and chopped asparagus. Mix well, season to taste and remove from the heat.

5 Meanwhile, preheat the oven to 180°C (350°F/Gas 4). Line a baking tray with foil and brush with oil. Place six eggplant slices on the baking tray and spread the asparagus mixture evenly over each. Top with the remaining eggplant slices.

6 To make the soufflé topping, beat the egg white in a small, clean bowl, using electric beaters, until stiff peaks form. Spread the egg white evenly over each sandwich, then sprinkle with the cheese and decorate with the remaining asparagus.

7 Bake for 15 minutes, or until the cheese has melted and the topping has set.

eggplant and tomato bake

☀

Preparation time: 20 minutes
  + 20 minutes standing time
Cooking time: 1 hour 15 minutes
Serves 6

2 eggplants (aubergines)
60 ml (2 fl oz/¼ cup) olive oil
2 large onions, chopped
1 teaspoon ground cumin
250 ml (9 fl oz/1 cup) good-quality white wine
800 g (1 lb 12 oz) tin chopped tomatoes

2 garlic cloves, crushed
2 red chillies, finely chopped
(optional)
75 g (2½ oz/½ cup) currants
3 tablespoons chopped coriander (cilantro)

1 Preheat the oven to 210°C (415°F/
Gas 6–7). Cut the eggplants into rounds
2 cm (¾ inch) thick. Sprinkle with salt
and leave to stand for 30 minutes. Rinse
under cold water, then pat dry with
paper towels.
2 Meanwhile, heat 2 tablespoons of the
oil in a large saucepan over medium heat.
Add the onion and cook for 5 minutes, or
until softened. Add the cumin and cook,
stirring for 1 minute, then pour in the
wine. Bring to the boil, reduce the heat
and simmer for 10 minutes, or until the
mixture has reduced by three-quarters.
Add the tomato and bring to the boil,
then reduce the heat and simmer for
10 minutes. Stir in the garlic, chilli and
currants and simmer for a final 5 minutes,
then remove from the heat.
3 Heat the remaining oil in a large frying
pan over medium heat. Cook the eggplant
in batches for 3–4 minutes, or until
golden brown, turning once. Drain on
paper towels.
4 Layer the eggplant and tomato
mixture in a large baking dish, sprinkling
coriander between each layer. Finish with
a layer of eggplant.
5 Bake for 30 minutes, or until the
eggplant is tender.

NOTE: This dish is delicious served with
cooked pasta.

fast oven fries

Preheat the oven to 230°C (450°F/
Gas 8). Leave the skins on desiree
potatoes and cut them into thin
chips. Lightly grease a baking tray,
then spread the chips on the tray
and drizzle with olive oil. Bake
for 20–25 minutes, or until crisp,
turning only once. Serve hot.

mushroom lasagne

✳

Preparation time: 20 minutes
Cooking time: 1 hour
Serves 6

250 g (9 oz) packet instant lasagne
sheets
310 ml (10¾ fl oz/1¼ cups) ready-made
pasta sauce
2 tablespoons olive oil
2 garlic cloves, crushed
4 spring onions (scallions), sliced
500 g (1 lb 2 oz) button mushrooms
2 tablespoons chopped basil
250 g (9 oz/1 cup) ricotta cheese, crumbled
50 g (1¾ oz/½ cup) grated parmesan
cheese
½ teaspoon ground nutmeg
150 g (5½ oz) rocket (arugula)
60 g (2¼ oz/½ cup) grated cheddar cheese
75 g (2¾ oz/½ cup) grated mozzarella
cheese

1 Preheat the oven to 200°C (400°F/
Gas 6). Divide the lasagne sheets into
three equal portions. Pour about 60 ml
(2 fl oz/¼ cup) of the pasta sauce evenly
into a large, rectangular baking dish.
Top with a layer of lasagne sheets.
2 Heat the oil in a frying pan over medium
heat. Add the garlic and spring onion and
cook for 3 minutes. Add the mushrooms
and cook for a futher 5 minutes. Remove
from the heat and stir in the basil.
3 Spread half the mushroom mixture
evenly over the pasta sheets, then top
with half the ricotta. Sprinkle with half
the parmesan, the nutmeg and the rocket.
Layer the second portion of lasagne
sheets on top, then half the remaining
pasta sauce.
4 Repeat the top layer using the
remaining ingredients, finishing with
the pasta sauce. Scatter the cheddar and
mozzarella over the top and bake for
45 minutes, or until the pasta is tender
and the cheese is golden and bubbling.

mushroom lasagne

salads

If your idea of a salad is a few chopped lettuce leaves topped with slices of cucumber and tomato wedges, then read on. Vegetarian food really comes into its own with the salad. Vegetables either raw, roasted, blanched or even steamed, partnered with nuts, grains or pulses, and either splashily dressed or simply drizzled with good extra virgin olive oil — the scope for innovation is vast indeed.

pasta salad with sun-dried tomatoes and spinach

✳

Preparation time: **20 minutes**
Cooking time: **15 minutes**
Serves **4–6**

500 g (1 lb) farfalle or spiral pasta
3 spring onions (scallions),
    finely chopped
60 g (2¼ oz/½ cup) sun-dried tomatoes,
    cut into thin strips
500 g (1 lb) English spinach, stalks
    trimmed, leaves shredded
50 g (1¾ oz/⅓ cup) toasted pine nuts
1 tablespoon chopped oregano

DRESSING
60 ml (2 fl oz/¼ cup) olive oil
1 teaspoon chopped red chilli
1 garlic clove, crushed

1 Cook the pasta in a large saucepan of rapidly boiling salted water until al dente. Drain and rinse well under cold water.
2 Transfer the pasta to a large salad bowl. Add the spring onion, tomato, spinach, pine nuts and oregano.
3 Whisk the dressing ingredients in a small bowl until well combined. Season with sea salt and freshly ground black pepper.
4 Pour the dressing over the salad. Toss well and serve.

capsicum salad

✳

Preparation time: **15 minutes**
Cooking time: **10 minutes**
Serves **4–6**

1 red capsicum (pepper)
1 green capsicum (pepper)
1 yellow capsicum (pepper)
1 tablespoon olive oil
2 tablespoons tinned green peppercorns,
    rinsed and drained
155 g (5½ oz/1 cup) kalamata
    olives
2 tablespoons mint
1 tablespoon raspberry vinegar
rocket (arugula) leaves, to serve

1 Preheat the grill (broiler) to medium–high. Cut the capsicums into flat pieces and remove the seeds and membranes. Grill (broil) the capsicums until the skin blackens and blisters. Place on a cutting board, cover with a tea towel (dish towel) and allow to cool before peeling.
2 Cut the capsicums into thick strips and place in a bowl with the oil, peppercorns and olives.
3 Gently stir the mint and vinegar through. Serve on a bed of rocket.

pasta salad with sun-dried
tomatoes and spinach

mixed herbed tabouleh

✳

Preparation time: 20 minutes
  + 15 minutes soaking
Cooking time: nil
Serves 8

130 g (4½ oz/¾ cup) burghul
  (bulgur)
150 g (5½ oz/1 bunch) flat-leaf
  (Italian) parsley, chopped
30 g (1 oz/1 bunch) chives, chopped
2 large handfuls basil, chopped
1 handful mint, chopped
4 spring onions (scallions),
  finely chopped
3 tomatoes, chopped
80 ml (2½ fl oz/⅓ cup) lemon juice
60 ml (2 fl oz/¼ cup) olive oil

1 Put the burghul in a bowl with
185 ml (6 fl oz/¾ cup) water. Leave to
soak for 15 minutes, or until the water
has been absorbed.
2 Put the burghul and the remaining
ingredients in a serving bowl and toss
well to combine. Cover and refrigerate
until required.

herbed feta salad

herbed feta salad

✳

Preparation time: 20 minutes
  + at least 30 minutes marinating
Cooking time: 10 minutes
Serves 6–8

2 slices thick white bread
200 g (7 oz) feta cheese
1 garlic clove, crushed
1 tablespoon finely chopped
  marjoram
1 tablespoon finely snipped chives
1 tablespoon finely chopped basil
2 tablespoons white wine vinegar
80 ml (2½ fl oz/⅓ cup) olive oil
1 red coral lettuce
1 butter, coral or oak-leaf lettuce

1 Preheat the oven to 180°C (350°F/
Gas 4). Remove the crusts from the bread
and cut the bread into cubes. Place on
a baking tray in a single layer and bake
for 10 minutes, or until crisp and lightly
golden. Remove from the oven and leave
to cool completely.
2 Cut the feta into small cubes and
place in a bowl. Mix together the garlic,
marjoram, chives, basil, vinegar and oil.
Pour over the feta and cover with plastic
wrap, then leave to marinate for at least
30 minutes, stirring occasionally.
3 Wash and dry the lettuces. Tear the
leaves into pieces and place in a bowl.
Add the dressed feta and toasted bread
cubes. Toss well and serve.

burghul

Burghul, also known as bulgur,
is cracked wheat that has been
hulled, steamed and dried, a
process that makes the grain
softer and easier to cook
and gives it a lighter texture.
Burghul has a nutty flavour
and is a key ingredient in the
Lebanese salad, tabouleh.

garden salad

garden salad

❉

Preparation time: **15 minutes**
Cooking time: **nil**
Serves **6–8**

1 green oak-leaf lettuce
150 g (5½ oz) rocket (arugula)
1 small radicchio lettuce
1 large green capsicum (pepper),
    cut into thin strips
finely grated zest of 1 lemon

DRESSING
2 tablespoons roughly chopped
    coriander (cilantro) leaves
60 ml (2 fl oz/¼ cup) lemon juice
2 teaspoons soft brown sugar
2 tablespoons olive oil
1 garlic clove, crushed
    (optional)

1 Tear the salad greens and radicchio into bite-sized pieces and place in a large serving bowl. Add the capsicum and lemon zest.

2 Whisk the dressing ingredients in a small bowl until well combined. Drizzle over the salad, toss well and serve.

NOTE: Make the dressing and salad just before serving. Choose a selection of your favourite salad greens for this recipe. This is delicious served on a summer table with a chilled frascati or a light red wine.

warm lentil and rice salad

❉ ❉

Preparation time: **15 minutes**
Cooking time: **40 minutes**
Serves **6**

185 g (6½ oz/1 cup) green lentils
200 g (7 oz/1 cup) basmati rice
250 ml (9 fl oz/1 cup) olive oil
45 g (1½ oz) butter
4 large red onions, thinly sliced
4 garlic cloves, crushed
2 teaspoons ground cinnamon
2 teaspoons sweet paprika
2 teaspoons ground cumin
2 teaspoons ground coriander
3 spring onions (scallions),
    chopped

1 Cook the lentils and rice in separate saucepans of water until just tender. Drain well, then place in a bowl.
2 Meanwhile, heat the oil and butter over low heat. Add the onion and garlic and cook for 30 minutes, or until very soft. Stir in the ground spices and cook for 2–3 minutes, or until aromatic.
3 Add the onion mixture to the rice and lentils and mix until well combined. Stir in the spring onion and season to taste.
4 Serve warm.

NOTE: Don't use red lentils for this recipe as they become mushy very quickly and will not retain their shape. It isn't necessary to soak the green lentils prior to cooking, but they should be rinsed thoroughly before using.

greek salad

✳

Preparation time: 15 minutes
Cooking time: nil
Serves 4

1 tomato, chopped
1 Lebanese (short) cucumber,
   cut into rounds
2 radishes, thinly sliced
1 small onion, thinly sliced
100 g (3½ oz) feta cheese, cut into cubes
45 g (1½ oz/⅓ cup) pitted black olives

DRESSING
2 tablespoons lemon juice
60 ml (2 fl oz/¼ cup) olive oil
½ teaspoon dried oregano

1 Combine the tomato, cucumber, radish, onion, feta and olives in a serving bowl.
2 Whisk the dressing ingredients in a small bowl until well combined. Drizzle over the salad and serve.

cabbage with crisp-fried onion

✳

Preparation time: 20 minutes
Cooking time: nil
Serves 4–6

½ Chinese or savoy cabbage, shredded
35 g (1¼ oz/½ cup) crisp-fried onion
25 g (1 oz/¼ cup) crisp-fried garlic
½ red capsicum (pepper), cut into very
   fine strips
3 tablespoons shredded mint, plus extra
   whole leaves, to garnish
80 ml (2½ fl oz/⅓ cup) coconut milk
1 tablespoon fish sauce (optional)
1 teaspoon soft brown sugar
2 red chillies, thinly sliced
lime wedges, to serve

1 Arrange the cabbage on a serving platter and scatter the onion, garlic, capsicum and mint over.

2 Whisk the coconut milk, fish sauce (if using) and sugar in a small bowl until well combined. Pour over the salad.
3 Garnish with the chilli slices and a few whole mint leaves. Serve immediately, with lime wedges.

NOTE: Crisp-fried onion and crisp-fried garlic are available in jars from Asian food stores. They are commonly used in Thai cooking as a garnish for salads, soups and noodle dishes. You can make your own at home by finely slicing peeled onion and garlic and cooking over low heat in a little vegetable oil, stirring regularly until crisp and golden brown. Drain on paper towels and allow to cool. Just before using, season with salt.

cabbage with crisp-fried onion

pears

Buy pears when they are slightly underripe and allow them to ripen at room temperature until there is a little 'give' at the stalk end. Beware of an oozing softness at the blossom end as this indicates trouble within. Once ripe, they will keep for a day or two in the refrigerator. If you are serving pears on a fruit platter or as a dessert, allow them to return to room temperature so that their full flavour can be appreciated. Asian pears such as the Chinese and the tientsin ya add a crisp texture to fruit and vegetable salads — they should be used while firm. Williams and comice pears are best suited to desserts.

sprout and pear salad with sesame dressing

sprout and pear salad with sesame dressing

✳

Preparation time: 30 minutes
Cooking time: nil
Serves 6

250 g (9 oz) snow pea (mangetout) sprouts
250 g (9 oz) bean sprouts
30 g (1 oz/1 bunch) chives
100 g (3½ oz) snow peas (mangetout)
1 celery stalk
2 firm ripe pears
1 small handful coriander (cilantro) sprigs
sesame seeds, to garnish

SESAME DRESSING
2 tablespoons soy sauce
1 teaspoon sesame oil
1 tablespoon soft brown sugar
2 tablespoons peanut oil
1 tablespoon rice vinegar

1 Wash and drain the snow pea sprouts. Remove the brown ends from the bean sprouts. Snip the chives into 4 cm (1½ inch) lengths and cut the snow peas and celery into thin strips.
2 Peel and core the pears, then slice into thin strips, slightly wider than the celery and snow peas. Place in a bowl and cover with water to prevent discolouration.
3 Whisk the sesame dressing ingredients in a small bowl until well combined.
4 Drain the pears and place in a large serving bowl with the other salad ingredients. Pour the dressing over and toss lightly.
5 Sprinkle with sesame seeds and serve.

spinach and avocado salad with warm mustard vinaigrette

✳

Preparation time: 15 minutes
Cooking time: 5 minutes
Serves 8

watercress salad

30 English spinach leaves (about 90 g/3¼ oz)
1 red or green curly-leafed lettuce
2 avocados
60 ml (2 fl oz/¼ cup) olive oil
2 teaspoons sesame seeds
1 tablespoon lemon juice
2 teaspoons wholegrain mustard

1 Wash and dry the spinach and lettuce leaves. Tear the leaves into bite-sized pieces and place in a large serving bowl.
2 Peel the avocados and cut the flesh into thin slices. Scatter over the leaves.
3 Heat 1 tablespoon of the oil in a small frying pan over low heat. Add the sesame seeds and cook until they just start to turn golden. Remove from the heat and allow to cool slightly.
4 Add the lemon juice, remaining oil and mustard to the pan and stir to combine. While still warm, pour over the salad and toss gently to coat the leaves.
5 Serve immediately.

watercress salad

✳

Preparation time: 35 minutes
Cooking time: nil
Serves 4–6

500 g (1 lb 2 oz) watercress
3 celery stalks
1 cucumber
3 oranges
1 red onion, thinly sliced
30 g (1 oz/1 bunch) chives, snipped
60 g (2¼ oz/½ cup) chopped pecans
    or walnuts

DRESSING
60 ml (2 fl oz/¼ cup) olive oil
60 ml (2 fl oz/¼ cup) lemon juice
2 teaspoons finely grated orange zest
1 teaspoon wholegrain mustard
1 tablespoon honey

1 Break the watercress into small sprigs, discarding the coarser stems. Cut the celery into thin sticks about 5 cm (2 inch) long. Peel, halve and seed the cucumber and cut into thin slices. Peel the oranges, remove the white pith and cut the oranges into segments between the membrane. Refrigerate all the ingredients until required.
2 In a bowl, whisk together the dressing ingredients until well combined. Season with freshly ground black pepper.
3 Combine all the salad ingredients except the nuts in a serving bowl. Pour the dressing over and toss.
4 Sprinkle with the nuts and serve.

olives

Round or rectangular, plump or wrinkled, black, green
or brown, marinated with chillies and herbs, puréed
into a luscious tapenade, or simply eaten on their own,
olives capture the very essence of the Mediterranean.

marinated lemon and garlic olives

Rinse and drain 500 g (1 lb 2 oz) brined kalamata olives.
Make a small incision in the side of each olive to allow the
marinade to penetrate thoroughly. Layer the olives in a
sterilised jar with fine strips of lemon zest, 3 thinly sliced garlic
cloves, 1 tablespoon coriander seeds and 2 bay leaves. Pour
60 ml (2 fl oz/¼ cup) balsamic vinegar over the olives, then
cover with extra virgin olive oil. Seal the jar and set aside in
a cool, dark place to marinate for 1 week. Serve as part of an
antipasto platter.

chilli-spiced baby olives with herbs

Rinse and drain 500 g (1 lb 2 oz) brined niçoise olives. Layer
in a sterilised jar with 4 halved small red chillies, a few thinly
cut slices of lime, 1 teaspoon chilli flakes, 2 thinly sliced garlic
cloves and a few sprigs of your favourite herbs. Whisk together
2 tablespoons lime juice, 2 tablespoons tarragon vinegar,
250 ml (9 fl oz/1 cup) extra virgin olive oil and a few crushed
peppercorns, then pour over the olives. Add extra oil to cover
the olives if needed. Seal the jar and and set aside in a cool,
dark place to marinate for 1 week.

olive and tomato tapenade

Place 155 g (5½ oz/1 cup) pitted and roughly chopped
marinated niçoise olives in a food processor. Add 2 finely
chopped spring onions (scallions), 60 g (2¼ oz/⅓ cup) drained
capers, 60 g (2¼ oz/½ cup) chopped sun-dried tomatoes and
60 g (2¼ oz/½ cup) chopped sun-dried capsicums (peppers).

Process for 10 seconds, or until the ingredients are roughly
chopped — do not overprocess or the mixture will turn to a
paste. Transfer the mixture to a bowl, fold in 2 finely chopped
egg (roma) tomatoes, 1 tablespoon chopped parsley and
1 tablespoon extra virgin olive oil. Season to taste and serve
with crackers or toast.

olive salsa

Put 250 g (9 oz/1¼ cup) chopped marinated green olives and
90 g (3¼ oz/⅔ cup) chopped marinated black olives in a bowl.
Add 1 finely chopped red onion, 1 chopped yellow capsicum
(pepper), 4 chopped egg (roma) tomatoes and 3 tablespoons
chopped basil. In a bowl, whisk together 1 crushed garlic
clove, 2 finely chopped red chillies, 1 tablespoon orange juice,
1 tablespoon lemon juice and 60 ml (2 fl oz/¼ cup) extra virgin
olive oil. Pour the dressing over the olive mixture and toss.
Cover and refrigerate until required. Serve at room temperature.

bruschetta with olives, bocconcini and tomato

Cut wood-fired bread into slices 1 cm (½ inch) thick. Brush
each slice lightly with olive oil and toast under a preheated grill
(broiler), turning once, until golden on both sides. Top with a
thick slice of egg (roma) tomato, thin slices of bocconcini (fresh
baby mozzarella cheese), a slice of gherkin (pickle), a basil leaf,
and some finely chopped marinated black olives. Drizzle with
extra virgin olive oil, sprinkle with freshly ground black pepper
and serve.

snow pea salad

✳

Preparation time: 25 minutes
Cooking time: 5 minutes
Serves 4–6

200 g (7 oz) snow peas (mangetout),
  sliced diagonally
1 red capsicum (pepper), sliced

4 oak leaf lettuce leaves, torn
5 green coral lettuce leaves, torn
250 g (9 oz) cherry tomatoes, halved
60 g (2¼ oz/2 cups) watercress sprigs
parmesan cheese shavings, to serve

GARLIC CROUTONS
3 slices white bread, crusts removed
60 ml (2 fl oz/¼ cup) olive oil
1 garlic clove, crushed

DRESSING
2 tablespoons olive oil
1 tablespoon whole-egg
  mayonnaise
1 tablespoon sour cream
2 tablespoons lemon juice
1 teaspoon soft brown sugar

1 Combine the snow peas, capsicum,
lettuce, tomatoes and watercress in a
large salad bowl.
2 To make the croutons, cut the bread
into 1 cm (½ inch) squares. Heat the oil
in a small, heavy-based frying pan over
medium heat. Add the garlic and cook
briefly, then stir in the bread cubes and
cook until golden and crisp. Remove
from the heat and drain on paper towels.
3 Whisk the dressing ingredients in a
small bowl with some freshly ground
black pepper until well combined.
4 Just before serving, top the salad with
the croutons and parmesan shavings,
then pour the dressing over. Toss well
and serve.

snow pea salad

To 'top and tail' snow peas, pull
any threads from the tails, then
snap off the tops.

Pull the tops down to remove the
string from the side.

fast spinach salad

✳

Preparation time: 15 minutes
Cooking time: nil
Serves 2–4

2 tablespoons olive oil
1 garlic clove, crushed
2 teaspoons white wine vinegar
100 g (3½ oz) mushrooms,
  thinly sliced
300 g (10½ oz) English spinach
  leaves, torn
2 hard-boiled eggs, sliced
100 g (3½ oz) feta cheese

1 In a large bowl, combine the olive oil,
garlic, vinegar and a little freshly ground
black pepper. Add the mushrooms and stir
to coat well.
2 Put the spinach in a salad bowl. Add
the mushroom mixture and the egg and
gently toss together.
3 Crumble the feta over and serve.

warm bean salad

☀

Preparation time: 10 minutes
Cooking time: 10 minutes
Serves 4

2 tablespoons olive oil
1 onion, finely chopped
1 garlic clove, crushed
1 red capsicum (pepper), cut into strips
90 g (3¼ oz) green beans, trimmed
60 g (2¼ oz/⅔ cup) sliced button
   mushrooms
1 tablespoon balsamic vinegar
420 g (14¾ oz) tin mixed beans, rinsed
   and drained
chopped flat-leaf (Italian) parsley, to serve

1 Heat half the oil in a frying pan over medium heat. Add the onion and cook for 2 minutes. Add the garlic, capsicum, green beans, mushrooms and vinegar and cook for another 5 minutes, stirring occasionally.
2 Add the beans to the vegetable mixture with the remaining oil and stir until just warmed through.
3 Serve warm, sprinkled with the parsley.

pears with brie and pecans

☀

Preparation time: 15 minutes
Cooking time: nil
Serves 4

1 butter or mignonette lettuce
4 tablespoons finely chopped pecans
200 g (7 oz) brie cheese (see Note)
3 pears, cored and quartered

DRESSING
3 tablespoons extra virgin olive oil
1 tablespoon tarragon vinegar

1 Wash and dry the lettuce thoroughly, then separate the leaves and arrange on individual serving plates. Cut the brie into thin wedges, slice the pears thinly, then arrange over the lettuce.
2 Whisk the dressing ingredients in a small bowl until well combined. Drizzle over the salad.
3 Sprinkle with the pecans and serve.

NOTE: Camembert can be used instead of brie. Ripe cheese gives the best flavour. Serve at room temperature.

warm bean salad

brie

At the Congress of Vienna in 1815, when the boundaries of Europe were being established after the Battle of Waterloo, brie was decreed 'the king of cheeses'. Since then it has gained a worldwide following. When brie is perfectly ripe it will ooze slightly at room temperature. It has a lovely warm, creamy flavour, best experienced from the whole cheese, rather than from a packaged wedge.

red cabbage salad

☀

Preparation time: 10 minutes
Cooking time: nil
Serves 6

150 g (5½ oz/2 cups) finely shredded
    red cabbage
125 g (4½ oz/1½ cups) finely shredded
    green cabbage
2 spring onions (scallions), finely chopped

DRESSING
3 tablespoons olive oil
2 teaspoons white wine vinegar
½ teaspoon dijon mustard
1 teaspoon caraway seeds

1   Combine the cabbage and spring onion
in a serving bowl.

2   Whisk the dressing ingredients in a
small bowl until well combined.
3   Pour the dressing over the salad. Toss
well and serve.

curly endive and
blue cheese salad

☀

Preparation time: 15 minutes
Cooking time: 5 minutes
Serves 6

1 curly endive
125 g (4½ oz) blue cheese
2 tablespoons olive oil
3 teaspoons white wine vinegar
2 tablespoons snipped chives

CROUTONS
3 slices bread, crusts removed
60 ml (2 fl oz/¼ cup) olive oil
30 g (1 oz) butter

1   To make the croutons, cut the
bread into small squares. Heat the oil
and butter in a frying pan over medium
heat until bubbling. Add the bread and
cook, tossing frequently, for 3 minutes,
or until golden. Drain on paper towels.
2   Wash and dry the endive thoroughly.
Place the leaves in a serving bowl and
crumble the blue cheese over the top.
3   In a small bowl, whisk together the oil
and vinegar. Drizzle over the salad, then
add the chives and croutons. Toss well
and serve immediately.

blue cheese

Blue cheeses happened first
by accident, but the penicillin
moulds that give cheese blue
veins have since been identified
and isolated, and blue varieties
are now manufactured by most
cheese-producing countries.
The colour of blue cheese
can be anything from golden
yellow to chalky white, but
should be flecked with blue
mould throughout. A blue
cheese should never be brown
and clouded.

red cabbage salad

spinach and nut salad

✳

Preparation time: 15 minutes
Cooking time: nil
Serves 4

250 g (9 oz) young green beans,
   trimmed and chopped
30 English spinach leaves (about
   90 g/3¼ oz)
½ onion, thinly sliced
90 g (3¼ oz/⅓ cup) plain yoghurt
1 tablespoon lemon juice
1 tablespoon shredded mint
40 g (1½ oz/⅓ cup) chopped walnuts,
   toasted (see Note)
mint leaves, to serve
thinly sliced red capsicum (pepper),
   to serve

1   Put the beans in a heatproof bowl,
cover with boiling water and leave for
2 minutes. Drain, allow to cool, then pat
dry with paper towels.
2   Rinse the spinach leaves in cold water
and pat dry with paper towels.
3   Arrange the spinach, beans and onion
on a serving plate.
4   In a bowl, mix together the yoghurt,
lemon juice and mint. Pour over the salad.
5   Sprinkle with the walnuts, garnish with
mint and capsicum and serve.

NOTE: Toast the walnuts in a dry frying
pan over medium heat, stirring constantly,
until they are golden brown and fragrant.
Watch carefully as they will burn easily.

green bean salad

✳

Preparation time: 15 minutes
Cooking time: 15 minutes
Serves 4

1 tablespoon pine nuts
300 g (10½ oz) green beans, topped
   and tailed

green bean salad

1 tablespoon olive oil
2 teaspoons lemon juice
80 ml (2½ fl oz/⅓ cup) tomato juice
1 garlic clove, crushed
a few drops of Tabasco sauce

1   Preheat the oven to 180°C (350°F/
Gas 4). Spread the pine nuts on a
foil-covered baking tray and bake for
5 minutes, or until golden — do not let
them burn.
2   Meanwhile, add the beans to a
saucepan of boiling water and cook for
1 minute. Drain and plunge into iced
water. Drain again.
3   Put the beans in a bowl and toss
with the oil and lemon juice.
4   In a small saucepan, bring the
tomato juice, garlic and Tabasco to the
boil. Reduce the heat, then simmer,
uncovered, for 8 minutes, or until the
liquid has reduced by half. Remove from
the heat and allow to cool.
5   Arrange the beans on a serving plate
and pour the tomato sauce over. Sprinkle
with the pine nuts and serve.

peanuts

The peanut is native to South America and is not actually a nut but a legume. Raw peanuts taste faintly like green beans. Peanuts can be tossed in a little hot oil and salt, then toasted in a moderate oven.

herbed potato salad

herbed potato salad

❄

Preparation time: 15 minutes
Cooking time: 15 minutes
Serves 4

650 g (1 lb 7 oz) red-skinned potatoes
1 red onion, thinly sliced
1 tablespoon chopped mint
1 tablespoon chopped flat-leaf (Italian) parsley
1 tablespoon snipped chives
90 g (3¼ oz/⅓ cup) whole-egg mayonnaise
90 g (3¼ oz/⅓ cup) plain yoghurt

1 Scrub the potatoes and cut into cubes. Add to a large saucepan of boiling water and cook until just tender. Drain and allow to cool completely.

2 Put the potato, onion and herbs in a large bowl.
3 Combine the mayonnaise and yoghurt, then gently mix through the potato to coat, taking care not to break it up too much. Serve at room temperature.

cucumber salad with peanuts and chilli

❄

Preparation time: 25 minutes
  + 45 minutes marinating
Cooking time: nil
Serves 4–6

3 Lebanese (short) cucumbers
½ red onion, chopped
1 large handful coriander (cilantro) leaves

2 tablespoons white vinegar
2 teaspoons sugar
1–2 tablespoons chilli sauce
160 g (5¾ oz/1 cup) unsalted roasted peanuts, chopped
2 tablespoons crisp-fried garlic
½ teaspoon chopped chilli
1 tablespoon fish sauce, optional

1 Peel the cucumbers and slice in half lengthways. Scoop out the seeds, slice the flesh thinly and place in a large bowl. Add the onion and coriander.
2 Mix the vinegar and sugar in a cup or small bowl until the sugar dissolves. Add to the cucumber mixture with the chilli sauce and toss well. Cover and set aside to marinate for 45 minutes.
3 Just before serving, add the peanuts, garlic, chilli and fish sauce, if using. Toss lightly and serve.

tofu salad

✻

Preparation time: 25 minutes
+ 1 hour marinating time
Cooking time: nil
Serves 4

2 teaspoons sweet chilli sauce
½ teaspoon finely grated fresh ginger
1 garlic clove, crushed
2 teaspoons soy sauce
2 tablespoons vegetable oil
250 g (9 oz) firm tofu, cut into 2 cm
   (¾ inch) cubes
100 g (3½ oz) snow peas (mangetout),
   sliced in half on the diagonal
2 carrots, cut into thin batons
100 g (3½ oz/1⅓ cups) finely shredded
   red cabbage
2 tablespoons chopped peanuts

1 Whisk the chilli sauce, ginger, garlic, soy sauce and oil in a bowl until well combined. Add the tofu and toss to coat. Cover and marinate in the refrigerator for 1 hour.
2 Put the snow peas in a small heatproof bowl. Pour boiling water over and leave to stand for 1 minute. Drain, then plunge the peas into iced water. Drain and pat dry with paper towels.
3 Add the snow peas to the tofu with the carrot and cabbage. Toss lightly to combine.
4 Transfer the salad to a serving bowl or individual plates, sprinkle with peanuts and serve.

chickpea and olive salad

✻

Preparation time: 20 minutes
+ overnight soaking time
Cooking time: 50 minutes
Serves 6

330 g (11¾ oz/1½ cups) dried chickpeas
1 small Lebanese (short) cucumber
2 tomatoes
1 small red onion, finely chopped
3 tablespoons chopped flat-leaf
   (Italian) parsley
60 g (2¼ oz/½ cup) pitted black olives

DRESSING
1 tablespoon lemon juice
60 ml (2 fl oz/¼ cup) olive oil
1 garlic clove, crushed
1 teaspoon honey

1 Soak the chickpeas in cold water overnight. Rinse and drain.
2 Place the chickpeas in a large heavy-based saucepan, cover with cold water and bring to the boil. Cook for 45 minutes, or until just tender. Drain and leave to cool.
3 Cut the cucumber in half lengthways and scoop out the seeds. Cut the flesh into 1 cm (½ inch) slices and place in a serving bowl.
4 Cut the tomatoes into cubes the same size as the chickpeas. Add to the serving bowl with the chickpeas, onion, parsley and olives.
5 Whisk the dressing ingredients in a small bowl until well combined. Drizzle over the salad and toss lightly to combine.
6 Serve at room temperature.

chickpea and olive salad

cottage cheese

Cottage cheese originated in the United States and is made from the curds of skimmed milk. Its low fat content makes it a popular dieter's choice. Cottage cheese goes well with fruit salad, while creamed cottage cheese is excellent in cooking.

penne salad with sun-dried tomatoes

☀

Preparation time: **15 minutes**
Cooking time: **15 minutes**
Serves **6**

500 g (1 lb 2 oz) penne
60 ml (2 fl oz/¼ cup) extra virgin olive oil
150 g (5½ oz) sun-dried tomatoes, drained and thinly sliced
1 handful basil
70 g (2½ oz/½ cup) pitted black olives, halved
2 teaspoons white wine vinegar
1 garlic clove, halved
60 g (2¼ oz/⅔ cup) shaved parmesan cheese

penne salad with sun-dried tomatoes

1 Cook the pasta in a large saucepan of rapidly boiling salted water until al dente. Drain and rinse under cold water, then drain again.
2 Transfer the pasta to a large serving bowl and mix with 1 tablespoon of the oil to prevent sticking. Add the tomatoes, basil and olives and lightly toss.
3 In a small bowl, whisk together the remaining oil, vinegar and garlic. Leave for 5 minutes, then discard the garlic.
4 Whisk the dressing again, then pour over the salad. Stir gently to combine. Garnish with the parmesan and serve.

cottage cheese salad

☀

Preparation time: **20 minutes**
Cooking time: **5 minutes**
Serves **4**

1 sheet lavash or other unleavened bread
2 teaspoons vegetable oil
mild paprika, to sprinkle
2 tablespoons snipped chives
500 g (1 lb 2 oz/2 cups) cottage cheese
16 red oak leaf lettuce leaves, washed and dried
200 g (7 oz) red grapes
1 carrot, grated
3 tablespoons alfalfa sprouts

1 Preheat the oven to 180°C (350°F/ Gas 4). Brush the bread with the oil and sprinkle lightly with the paprika. Cut in half lengthways, then across into 16 strips. Place on a baking tray and bake for 5 minutes, or until golden. Remove from the oven and cool on a wire rack.
2 Mix the chives through the cottage cheese until combined.
3 Arrange the lettuce, cheese mixture and other ingredients on individual plates. Serve immediately, with four lavash crisps on the side.

NOTE: Lavash is rectangular flat bread. It is available from most supermarkets. In some countries it is known as soft Armenian cracker bread.

nachos salad

☀

Preparation time: **15 minutes**
Cooking time: **nil**
Serves **4**

400 g (14 oz) tin red kidney beans,
    rinsed and drained
1 tomato, cubed
125 g (4½ oz/½ cup) mild ready-made
    tomato salsa
280 g (10 oz) plain corn chips
8 lettuce leaves, shredded
1 avocado, sliced
20 g (¾ oz) cheddar cheese, grated

1 Combine the beans, tomato and
salsa in a bowl.
2 Arrange a bed of corn chips on each
plate. Top with the lettuce, the bean
mixture and the avocado.
3 Sprinkle with the cheese and serve.

spicy potato salad

☀

Preparation time: **15 minutes**
Cooking time: **20 minutes**
Serves **6**

500 g (1 lb 2 oz) baby new potatoes,
    halved
250 g (9 oz) green beans, topped and
    tailed, then halved diagonally

DRESSING
60 ml (2 fl oz/¼ cup) olive oil
2 red chillies, seeded and sliced
1 garlic clove, crushed
1 large handful coriander (cilantro) leaves,
    chopped
1 tablespoon red wine vinegar
½ teaspoon caraway seeds

1 Add the potatoes to a large saucepan
of gently simmering water and cook for
20 minutes, or until tender but still firm.
Drain and set aside.
2 Meanwhile, blanch the beans in a
saucepan of boiling water for 2 minutes,

citrus walnut salad

or until bright green and just tender.
Plunge into iced water, then drain and
pat dry with paper towels.
3 Combine the potatoes and beans in a
large serving bowl.
4 Whisk the dressing ingredients in a
small bowl until well combined. Pour the
dressing over the salad and serve.

citrus walnut salad

☀

Preparation time: **20 minutes**
Cooking time: **nil**
Serves **8**

2 oranges
2 grapefruit
125 g (4½ oz) sugar snap peas
75 g (2½ oz) rocket (arugula), leaves torn
½ oak leaf lettuce, leaves torn
1 large Lebanese (short) cucumber, sliced
40 g (1½ oz/⅓ cup) walnut pieces

WALNUT DRESSING
2 tablespoons walnut oil
2 tablespoons vegetable oil
2 teaspoons tarragon vinegar
2 teaspoons wholegrain mustard
1 teaspoon sweet chilli sauce

1 Peel the oranges and grapefruit,
removing the white pith. Working over a
large serving bowl to capture the juices,
cut the fruit into segments between the
membranes, removing the seeds.
2 Put the sugar snap peas in a small
heatproof bowl. Pour boiling water over
and leave to stand for 2 minutes. Drain,
then plunge the peas into iced water.
Drain and pat dry with paper towels.
3 Add the peas to the citrus segments,
along with the rocket, lettuce, cucumber
and walnut pieces.
4 Whisk the walnut dressing ingredients
in a small bowl until well combined. Pour
the dressing over the salad, toss lightly
and serve.

vegetables on the side

Accompaniments they may be — but good-quality, well-prepared vegetables take on a special identity when counterpointing a main course and complementing the theme of the meal. With a plethora now available, in so many colours, shapes and tastes, the only dilemma you'll have at the greengrocer is deciding which to choose.

ghee

Ghee is simply clarified butter. It is the fat most commonly used in Indian cooking and in many Arab countries, where it is known as samna. Its strong, sweet flavour is produced by melting butter, then clarifying it by discarding the white froth and whey. Flavourings are also often added: in India, cumin seeds, bay leaves, cloves and ginger; and in the Middle East, oregano, thyme and other herbs.

potato and pea curry

potato and pea curry

❋

Preparation time: 20 minutes
Cooking time: 35 minutes
Serves 4

2 teaspoons brown mustard seeds
2 tablespoons ghee or oil
2 onions, sliced
2 garlic cloves, crushed
2 teaspoons finely grated fresh ginger
1 teaspoon ground turmeric
½ teaspoon chilli powder
1 teaspoon ground cumin
1 teaspoon garam masala
750 g (1 lb 10 oz) potatoes, peeled
    and cubed
110 g (3¾ oz/⅔ cup) fresh or frozen peas
2 tablespoons chopped mint

1   Fry the mustard seeds in a large dry saucepan over medium heat until they start to pop. Add the ghee, onion, garlic and ginger and cook, stirring, for 5 minutes, or until the onion is soft. Add the turmeric, chilli, cumin, garam masala and potato and stir until the potatoes are coated. Season to taste.
2   Add 125 ml (4 fl oz/½ cup) water and bring to the boil. Reduce the heat, cover and simmer for 15–20 minutes, or until the potato is just tender.
3   Stir in the peas, then cover and simmer for 3–5 minutes, or until the potato is cooked and the liquid is absorbed. Stir in the mint. Serve hot or warm.

eggplant with tomato herb sauce

❋

Preparation time: 30 minutes
Cooking time: 40 minutes
Serves 4

olive oil, for pan-frying
6–8 slender eggplants (aubergines),
    cut in half lengthways
2 garlic cloves, crushed

eggplant with tomato herb sauce

thyme

Thyme is one of the essential herbs of Mediterranean cooking. It has its best flavour when in flower and, though it dries well, it is best to cook with fresh thyme whenever possible. When buying dried thyme, be aware that powdery leaves indicate the herb is older and will have less flavour and fragrance. Buy dried thyme in small quantities, as stale herbs will spoil a dish.

1 onion, chopped
1 red capsicum (pepper), chopped
2 ripe tomatoes, chopped
125 ml (4 fl oz/½ cup) vegetable stock
1 teaspoon finely chopped thyme
1 teaspoon finely chopped marjoram
2 teaspoons finely chopped oregano
1 teaspoon sugar
3–4 teaspoons white wine vinegar
3 tablespoons small black olives
1 handful basil leaves, shredded

1 Pour enough oil into a large frying pan to cover the base. Heat over medium–high heat until the oil is almost smoking. Fry the eggplant in batches for 2–3 minutes on each side, or until golden brown, adding more oil as needed. Drain on paper towels, cover and keep warm.
2 Heat another 2 tablespoons oil in a frying pan over medium heat. Add the onion and garlic and cook, stirring, for 2–3 minutes. Add the capsicum and tomato and cook for 1–2 minutes, or until just softened.

3 Pour in the stock and bring to the boil. Reduce the heat and simmer, stirring occasionally, for 5–10 minutes, or until the liquid has reduced and thickened.
4 Stir in the thyme, marjoram, oregano, sugar and vinegar. Cook for 3–4 minutes, then stir in the olives and season to taste.
5 Serve the eggplant topped with the tomato sauce and garnished with basil.

NOTE: The tomato mixture can be made a day ahead, without the herbs. Add the herbs when reheating; this helps retain the colour and will ensure the flavour does not become bitter.

rösti

☀

Preparation time: **10 minutes**
  + overnight chilling time
Cooking time: **45 minutes**
Serves **4**

6 potatoes (about 750 g/1 lb 10 oz)
60 g (2 oz) butter

1 Boil the potatoes in a saucepan of water until they are just tender. Drain and allow to cool, then peel. Cover and refrigerate overnight.
2 Grate the potatoes into a bowl and season to taste.
3 Melt half the butter in a heavy-based frying pan over medium–low heat. When the butter is sizzling, add the grated potato and press down firmly to form a thin, even layer. Cook for 15–20 minutes, or until the potato is crusty and golden brown underneath, taking care it doesn't burn, and shaking the pan regularly to prevent sticking. Place a large plate over the pan, then invert the rösti onto it.
4 Melt the remaining butter in the pan. Slide the rösti back into the pan and cook for another 15–20 minutes, or until the other side is crisp and golden.
5 Cut into wedges and serve hot.

stuffed zucchini flowers

2 Cut the mozzarella into 20 even pieces. Insert a piece of mozzarella, half an anchovy fillet and some basil into each zucchini blossom. Press the petals closed.
3 Heat 2.5 cm (1 inch) oil in a heavy-based frying pan to 180°C (350°F), or until a cube of bread dropped into the oil browns in 15 seconds.
4 Dip one zucchini flower at a time into the batter, shaking off the excess. Working in batches, gently lower the flowers into the oil and cook for 3 minutes, or until crisp and golden. Drain on paper towels.
5 Season well and serve immediately, with lemon wedges.

NOTE: Zucchini flowers are available in the male or female form (the male flower has a stalk; the female flower has a baby zucchini attached). They are sold in speciality fruit and vegetable shops. Wash them thoroughly before use and make sure there are no insects hidden inside.

baked root vegetables with sweet ginger glaze

☀

Preparation time: **25 minutes**
Cooking time: **1 hour 5 minutes**
Serves **4–6**

150 g (5½ oz) orange sweet potato
1 potato
1 carrot
1 parsnip
1 turnip
2 tablespoons olive oil
60 g (2¼ oz) butter
2 tablespoons caster (superfine) sugar
1 tablespoon finely grated
 fresh ginger

1 Preheat the oven to 210°C (415°F/ Gas 6–7). Grease a large baking tray.
2 Peel all the root vegetables and cut into batons about 5 cm (2 inches) long and 1 cm (½ inch) thick. Place in a single layer on the baking tray and brush all

basil

Basil (*Ocymum basilicum*) has a unique spiciness and aroma and in most recipes it is best used in its fresh form. It should be added to dishes at the end of cooking time, to preserve its flavour. If the leaves are to be chopped, shredded or torn, do so at the last possible minute, as they will blacken when cut.

stuffed zucchini flowers

☀ ☀

Preparation time: **20 minutes**
Cooking time: **15 minutes**
Makes **20**

75 g (2½ oz) plain (all-purpose) flour
100 g (3½ oz) mozzarella cheese
10 anchovy fillets, halved lengthways
 and patted dry
10 basil leaves, torn
20 zucchini (courgette) flowers, stems
 and pistils removed (see Note)
olive oil, for pan-frying
2 lemon wedges, to serve

1 Put the flour and 250 ml (9 fl oz/ 1 cup) water in a bowl. Add a pinch of salt and mix to a smooth batter.

over with the oil. Bake for 1 hour, or until golden.

3 Near serving time, melt the butter in a small saucepan over low heat. Add the sugar and stir until the sugar has dissolved. Add the ginger and 60 ml (2 fl oz/¼ cup) water and stir to combine. Bring to the boil, reduce the heat to low and simmer for 5 minutes, or until the mixture has reduced and thickened slightly.

4 Pour the glaze over the baked vegetables and toss to coat. Bake for a final 5 minutes and serve.

sautéed rosemary potatoes

✺

Preparation time: **15–20 minutes**
Cooking time: **35 minutes**
Serves **4–6**

750 g (1 lb 10 oz) small new potatoes, unpeeled
2 tablespoons olive oil
30 g (1 oz) butter
2 garlic cloves, crushed
1 tablespoon finely chopped rosemary
1 teaspoon coarse rock salt or sea salt
½ teaspoon freshly ground black pepper

1 Wash the potatoes, pat dry with paper towels, then cut in half. Lightly boil or steam until just tender, then drain and allow to cool slightly.

2 Heat the oil and butter in a large heavy-based frying pan over medium heat. When the mixture is foaming, add the potatoes and cook for 5–10 minutes, or until golden and crisp, tossing regularly to ensure even colouring.

3 Sprinkle the potatoes with the garlic, rosemary and salt. Cook, tossing, for 1 minute, or until well coated. Stir in the pepper and mix well. Serve hot or warm.

salt
Salt, or sodium chloride, has been used as a food preservative and seasoning since ancient times. One of its most valuable properties is its ability to draw the moisture from foods. This is why we often chop up eggplant (aubergine) and leave it covered in salt before cooking — the salt draws out the bitter juice.

fast pan-fried asparagus
Trim the ends from 155 g (5½ oz) young, slim asparagus spears. Heat 1 tablespoon olive oil and 20 g (¾ oz) butter in a frying pan over medium heat. Add the asparagus and cook for 3–4 minutes, turning frequently — the asparagus will turn bright green, then begin to brown in patches. Add 2 teaspoons lemon juice, toss well and serve immediately. Serves 2–4.

sugar snap peas and carrots in lime butter

☀

Preparation time: **15 minutes**
Cooking time: **5 minutes**
Serves **4**

60 g (2¼ oz) butter
2 garlic cloves, crushed
1 tablespoon lime juice

½ teaspoon soft brown sugar
125 g (4½ oz) carrots, cut diagonally
  into thin slices
125 g (4½ oz) sugar snap peas,
  strings removed
lime zest strips, to garnish

1 Melt the butter in a large, heavy-based frying pan over low heat. Add the garlic and cook for 1 minute. Add the lime juice and sugar and cook until the sugar has dissolved.

2 Increase the heat to medium, add the carrot and peas and cook for 2–3 minutes, or until just tender.
3 Serve immediately, garnished with the lime zest.

NOTE: Snow peas (mangetout) or green beans can be used instead of peas. Baby carrots also make an attractive addition to this recipe — leave a portion of the green tops on. If limes are unavailable, substitute lemon juice and zest.

potato cakes with apple sauce

☀

Preparation time: **20 minutes**
Cooking time: **30 minutes**
Serves **4**

620 g (1 lb 6 oz/4 cups) finely
  grated potato
1 onion, finely chopped
2 teaspoons celery or fennel seeds
3 tablespoons plain (all-purpose) flour
2 eggs, beaten
vegetable oil, for pan-frying
ready-made apple sauce, to serve

1 Squeeze the excess liquid from the potatoes. Place in a large bowl with the onion, celery seeds, flour and egg. Season well and stir until just combined.
2 Heat 2 cm (¾ inch) oil in a large heavy-based frying pan over medium heat. Form two heaped tablespoons of mixture at a time into flat cakes and fry in batches for 3 minutes on each side, or until golden brown and cooked through.
3 Serve immediately, with apple sauce.

NOTE: Squeezing the excess liquid from the grated potato helps stop the oil spitting during frying.

sugar snap peas and
carrots in lime butter

spring onion and celery bundles

☀

Preparation time: 20 minutes
Cooking time: 10 minutes
Serves 6

4 celery stalks
24 spring onions (scallions)
30 g (1 oz) butter
1 teaspoon celery seeds
1 tablespoon honey
125 ml (4 fl oz/½ cup) vegetable stock
1 teaspoon soy sauce
1 teaspoon cornflour (cornstarch), blended
    with 1 teaspoon water

1 Cut the celery into 10 cm (4 inch) lengths, then into strips the same thickness as the spring onions. Trim the root from the spring onions, then cut the spring onions into 10 cm (4 inch) lengths. Reserve the spring onion tops for ties.
2 Plunge the spring onion tops into a saucepan of boiling water for 30 seconds, or until bright green. Plunge immediately into iced water, then drain and pat dry with paper towels.
3 Combine the spring onion and celery strips, then divide evenly into six bundles. Tie each bundle firmly with a blanched spring onion top.
4 Melt the butter in a frying pan over medium–high heat. Fry the bundles for 1 minute on each side, then remove from the pan.
5 Add the celery seeds to the pan and cook for 30 seconds. Stir in the honey, stock, soy sauce and cornflour. Bring to the boil, then reduce the heat, stirring continuously.
6 Add the spring onion and celery bundles and simmer gently for 7 minutes, or until just tender. Serve immediately, with the cooking juices.

potato curry with sesame seeds

☀

Preparation time: 20 minutes
Cooking time: 20 minutes
Serves 4

4 large potatoes
1 tablespoon oil
1 teaspoon cumin seeds
1 teaspoon coriander seeds
2 teaspoons mustard seeds
2 tablespoons sesame seeds
1/2 teaspoon ground turmeric
1 teaspoon chopped chilli
2 teaspoons finely grated lemon zest
2 tablespoons lemon juice

1 Boil, steam or microwave the potatoes until tender, then drain well and leave to cool. Peel and chop the potatoes and set aside.
2 Heat the oil in a large heavy-based frying pan over medium heat. Add the cumin, coriander and mustard seeds and cook for 1 minute, stirring constantly.
3 Add the sesame seeds and cook for 1–2 minutes, stirring until golden.
4 Add the turmeric, chilli, potato, lemon zest and juice. Stir until well combined and heated through.
5 Season to taste and serve.

mexican-style vegetables

the polenta and cook, stirring constantly, for 10 minutes, or until very thick. (The polenta must be stirred constantly or it will be gritty.) Remove from the heat and stir in the parmesan. Spread the mixture into the cake tin and smooth the surface. Refrigerate for 2 hours.

3 Heat the oil in a large saucepan over medium heat. Cook the onion for 5 minutes, or until soft. Stir in the cumin and chilli powder and cook for 1 minute, then add the vegetables. Bring to the boil, reduce the heat and simmer, covered, for 30 minutes, or until the vegetables are tender, stirring occasionally.

4 Just before serving, preheat the grill (broiler) to medium–high. Turn the polenta out of the tin and cut into six wedges. Brush one side with half the oil and grill (broil) for 5 minutes, or until the edges are browned. Repeat with the other side.

5 Stir the coriander through the vegetable mixture and season to taste. Serve spooned over the polenta wedges.

NOTE: The vegetables and polenta can be cooked up to a day ahead. Grill (broil) the polenta just before serving; a little crushed garlic can be added to the olive oil before brushing.

mexican-style vegetables

☀

Preparation time: 30 minutes
+ 2 hours chilling time
Cooking time: 50 minutes
Serves 4–6

1 tablespoon vegetable oil
1 onion, sliced
1 tablespoon ground cumin
½ teaspoon chilli powder
1 corn cob, cut into 2 cm (¾ inch) slices, then into quarters
1 green capsicum (pepper), chopped
1 red capsicum (pepper), chopped

3 tomatoes, chopped
6 green button squash, quartered
6 yellow button squash, quartered
2 tablespoons chopped coriander (cilantro)

POLENTA
350 ml (12 fl oz) vegetable stock
145 g (5½ oz/¾ cup) polenta (cornmeal)
50 g (1¾ oz/½ cup) grated parmesan cheese
2 tablespoons olive oil

1 Grease a 20 cm (8 inch) round spring-form cake tin.

2 To make the polenta, pour the stock and 250 ml (9 fl oz/1 cup) water into a saucepan and bring to the boil. Stir in

vegetable curry

☀

Preparation time: 25 minutes
Cooking time: 20–25 minutes
Serves 4–6

1 tablespoon brown mustard seeds
2 tablespoons ghee or oil
2 onions, chopped
4 tablespoons mild curry paste
400 g (14 oz) tin chopped tomatoes
125 g (4½ oz/½ cup) plain yoghurt
250 ml (9 fl oz/1 cup) coconut milk
2 carrots, sliced
225 g (8 oz/1¾ cups) cauliflower florets
2 slender eggplants (aubergines), sliced

225 g (8 oz) green beans, halved
150 g (5½ oz/2½ cups) broccoli florets
2 zucchini (courgettes), sliced
90 g (3¼ oz oz) baby button mushrooms, halved
steamed rice, to serve

1 Fry the mustard seeds in a dry frying pan over medium heat until they start to pop. Add the ghee and onion and cook, stirring, for 3 minutes, or until the onion is just soft. Add the curry paste and stir for 1 minute, or until fragrant.
2 Reduce the heat to low and add the tomato, yoghurt and coconut milk. Stir to combine, then add the carrot and simmer, uncovered, for 5 minutes.
3 Add the cauliflower and eggplant and simmer for 5 minutes. Stir in the remaining ingredients and simmer, uncovered, for 10–12 minutes. Serve hot, with steamed rice.

pumpkin with chilli and avocado

☀

Preparation time: **20 minutes**
Cooking time: **10 minutes**
Serves **6**

750 g (1 lb 10 oz) pumpkin (winter squash), peeled and cut into thin slices
1 avocado

DRESSING
1 red onion, finely chopped
2 tablespoons olive oil
1 tablespoon chopped coriander (cilantro) leaves
1 tablespoon chopped mint
2 teaspoons sweet chilli sauce
2 teaspoons balsamic vinegar
1 teaspoon soft brown sugar

1 Cook the pumpkin in a large saucepan of simmering water until tender but still firm. Remove from the heat and drain well.
2 Whisk the dressing ingredients in a small bowl until well combined.
3 Cut the avocado in half. Remove the stone and skin, then cut the flesh into thin slices.
4 Arrange the warm pumpkin and avocado in a serving bowl. Drizzle with the dressing and serve.

NOTE: Assemble this dish just before serving. The dressing can be made several hours ahead — cover and refrigerate until required. For a spicier flavour, add a finely chopped red chilli to the dressing.

pumpkin with chilli and avocado

To cut an avocado in half, insert a knife in until it is just touching the stone and cut all the way around. Twist the two halves in opposite directions and gently pull apart.

Embed the knife into the stone, twist and pull out.

vegetable purées

These versatile mixtures can double as dips and pasta sauces, and are fabulous as fillings for pancakes and omelettes — but never forget how great they are on their own.

jerusalem artichoke purée

Place 1 kg (2 lb 4 oz) peeled Jerusalem artichokes and 2 sliced garlic cloves in a saucepan. Cover with cold water, bring to the boil and cook until the artichokes are tender. Remove the artichokes and garlic using a slotted spoon; place in a food processor with 60 g (2¼ oz) butter. Process until smooth, gradually adding 60 ml (2 fl oz/¼ cup) extra virgin olive oil. Season to taste. Remove to a bowl, drizzle with olive oil and serve sprinkled with sweet paprika.

parsnip and leek purée

Cook 1 thinly sliced leek (white part only) and 3 large peeled, chopped parsnips in a saucepan of boiling salted water until tender. Drain well, then purée in food processor. Place the purée in a saucepan with 2 tablespoons snipped chives and 30 g (1 oz) butter. Cook, stirring, until the purée is heated through, then remove from the heat and stir in 3 tablespoons crème fraîche or sour cream. Season to taste and serve.

asparagus purée

Heat 30 g (1 oz) butter and 1 tablespoon vegetable oil in a saucepan over medium heat. Add 3 chopped spring onions (scallions) and 300 g (10 ½ oz) young, thin chopped asparagus and cook for 3 minutes. Pour in 125 ml (4 fl oz/½ cup) vegetable stock and 125 ml (4 fl oz/½ cup) cream, then cover and simmer until tender. Remove the vegetables from the liquid using tongs and process until smooth. Bring the liquid to the boil and reduce by one-quarter, then return the purée to the pan and stir in 1 tablespoon grated parmesan cheese. Cook over medium heat for 5 minutes, or until the purée thickens slightly. Season to taste. If the asparagus is stringy, pass the purée through a sieve before serving.

red capsicum purée

Cut 3 red capsicums (peppers) into flat pieces, removing the seeds and membranes. Grill (broil) until the skin blisters and blackens. Place on a cutting board and cover with a tea towel (dish towel) to cool slightly, then peel and roughly chop the flesh. Place in a food processor with 4 chopped spring onions (scallions), 2 crushed garlic cloves and 2 finely chopped red chillies. Process until smooth, then transfer to a saucepan. Stir in 2 tablespoons fish sauce (optional), 2 tablespoons lime juice and 2 tablespoons chopped coriander (cilantro). Cook over medium heat for 5 minutes, or until thickened slightly. Serve warm.

roast tomato and chickpea purée

Soak 250 g (9 oz) dried chickpeas in cold water overnight. Rinse and drain, then place in a saucepan and cover with cold water. Add 1 chopped onion and 1 bay leaf, bring to the boil, then reduce to a rapid simmer and cook for 1 hour 30 minutes, or until tender. Remove the bay leaf and drain, reserving 60 ml (2 fl oz/¼ cup) of the liquid. Meanwhile, cut 4 egg (roma) tomatoes in half, sprinkle with sea salt and drizzle with olive oil. Bake in a preheated 200°C (400°F/Gas 6) oven for 30–40 minutes, or until the tomato is very tender. Allow the tomato and chickpeas to cool a little, then place in a food processor with 2 crushed garlic cloves, 2 tablespoons lime juice, 1 teaspoon sugar, 60 ml (2 fl oz/¼ cup) olive oil and the reserved cooking liquid. Process until smooth. Transfer to a bowl, stir in 2 tablespoons chopped basil and 1 tablespoon grated parmesan cheese and serve.

To roast capsicum, discard the seeds and membrane from the capsicum and cut the flesh into large, flattish pieces.

Put under a hot grill, skin-side-up, until the skin is black and blistered. Cover with a tea towel (or put in a plastic bag) and set aside.

When the capsicum pieces are cool enough to handle, peel away and discard the skins. The roasted flesh will be sweeter than the raw.

marinated barbecued vegetables

hasselback potatoes

✳

Preparation time: 20 minutes
Cooking time: 50 minutes
Serves 4

8 all-purpose potatoes (such as spunta,
    sebago, russet, desiree, pontiac)
20 g (¾ oz) butter, melted
2 teaspoons dry breadcrumbs
2 teaspoons grated parmesan
    cheese (optional)

1 Preheat the oven to 180°C (350°F/
Gas 4). Cut a slice off the base of each
potato so the potatoes will sit flat. Place
on a board, cut side down, and make thin,
evenly spaced cuts about two-thirds of the
way through each potato.
2 Place the potatoes on a lightly greased
baking tray and brush with the butter.
Combine the breadcrumbs and parmesan,
then sprinkle over the potatoes.
3 Roast for 40–50 minutes, or
until golden brown and tender.
Serve immediately.

quick steamed cabbage with basil

Finely shred 440 g (15½ oz) red
or green cabbage. Melt 30 g (1 oz)
butter in a saucepan over low
heat. Add the cabbage and toss to
combine with the butter. Cover and
'steam' for 5 minutes, or until the
cabbage is tender — remove the
lid and lift the cabbage with tongs
from time to time to cook it evenly.
Stir 4 tablespoons finely shredded
basil through and season to taste.
Serves 2.

marinated barbecued vegetables

✳

Preparation time: 40 minutes
    + 20 minutes standing time
    + 1 hour chilling time
Cooking time: 5 minutes
Serves 4–6

3 slender eggplants (aubergines)
6 button mushrooms
2 red capsicums (peppers), cut into
    thick pieces
3 zucchini (courgettes), sliced
    diagonally

MARINADE
60 ml (2 fl oz/¼ cup) olive oil
60 ml (2 fl oz/¼ cup) lemon juice
2 tablespoons torn basil
1 garlic clove, crushed

1 Cut the eggplants into diagonal slices.
Place on a tray in a single layer, sprinkle
with salt and set aside for 20 minutes.
Rinse thoroughly and pat dry with
paper towels.
2 Trim each mushroom stalk so it is level
with the cap. Place all the vegetables in a
large, shallow non-metallic dish.
3 Combine the marinade ingredients in a
bowl and whisk well. Pour the marinade
over the vegetables and stir gently. Cover
with plastic wrap and refrigerate for
1 hour, stirring occasionally.
4 Grease and heat a barbecue grill. Place
the vegetables on the hottest part of
the barbecue and cook for 2 minutes on
each side, brushing frequently with any
remaining marinade.
5 Transfer to a serving dish. Serve warm
or at room temperature.

NOTE: The vegetables can be marinated
for up to 2 hours; take the vegetables
out of the refrigerator 15 minutes before
cooking. Other herbs such as parsley,
rosemary or thyme can be added to the
marinade. Serve any leftovers with crusty
bread or bread rolls.

fast herbed potatoes

Cook 12 small new potatoes in a
saucepan of boiling water until just
tender. Drain and return to the pan.
Add 30 g (1 oz) butter, 1 tablespoon
snipped chives and 1 tablespoon
lemon thyme. Cover and shake over
low heat until the butter has melted.
Season to taste. Serves 4.

wrinkled potatoes with mojo sauce

✳

Preparation time: 20 minutes
Cooking time: 25 minutes
Serves 4–6

18 baby potatoes
1 tablespoon olive oil
2 teaspoons salt

MOJO SAUCE
2 garlic cloves
1 teaspoon cumin seeds
1 teaspoon sweet paprika
80 ml (2½ fl oz/⅓ cup) olive oil
2 tablespoons white wine vinegar

1 Preheat the oven to 210°C (415°F/
Gas 6–7). Place the potatoes in a single
layer in a baking dish. Drizzle with the oil
and shake the pan to distribute it evenly.
Sprinkle the salt evenly over the potatoes.
2 Bake for 20–25 minutes, or until the
potatoes are golden brown and slightly
wrinkled. During cooking, shake the pan
twice so they brown evenly.
3 Meanwhile, make the mojo sauce.
Place the garlic, cumin and paprika in a
food processor and blend for 1 minute.
With the motor running, gradually add
the oil in a thin stream, blending until
all the oil is added. Add the vinegar and
1 tablespoon hot water and blend for
1 minute.
4 Serve the potatoes hot, drizzled with
the mojo sauce.

ratatouille

✳

Preparation time: 25 minutes
Cooking time: 40 minutes
Serves 4–6

6 vine-ripened tomatoes
500 g (1 lb 2 oz) eggplants (aubergines)
375 g (13 oz) zucchini (courgettes)
1 green capsicum (pepper)
1 red onion
100 ml (3½ fl oz) olive oil
3 garlic cloves, finely chopped
¼ teaspoon cayenne pepper
2 teaspoons chopped thyme
2 bay leaves
1 tablespoon red wine vinegar
1 teaspoon caster (superfine) sugar
3 tablespoons shredded basil

1   Score a cross in the base of each tomato. Place in a heatproof bowl and cover with boiling water. Leave for 30 seconds, then transfer to cold water, drain and peel the skin away from the cross. Cut the tomatoes in half, scoop out the seeds and chop the flesh.
2   Cut the eggplants and zucchini into 2 cm (¾ inch) cubes, and the capsicum into 2 cm (¾ inch) squares. Cut the onion into 2 cm (¾ inch) wedges.
3   Heat 2 tablespoons oil in a large saucepan over medium heat. Cook the eggplant, stirring, for 4–5 minutes, or until softened. Transfer to a bowl.

4   Heat 2 tablespoons oil in the pan. Add the zucchini and cook for 3–4 minutes, or until softened. Remove from the pan. Add the capsicum and cook for 2 minutes, then add to the eggplant.
5   Heat the remaining oil in the pan. Add the onion and cook for 2–3 minutes, or until softened. Add the garlic, cayenne pepper, thyme and bay leaves and cook, stirring, for 1 minute.
6   Return the vegetables to the pan and add the tomato, vinegar and sugar. Simmer, uncovered, for 20 minutes, stirring occasionally. Stir in the basil and season. Serve hot or at room temperature.

NOTE: You can also serve ratatouille as a starter with bread.

red vegetable curry

✳

Preparation time: 25 minutes
Cooking time: 25 minutes
Serves 4

1 tablespoon vegetable oil
1 onion, chopped
1–2 tablespoons red curry paste
375 ml (13 fl oz/1½ cups) coconut milk
2 potatoes, chopped
225 g (8 oz/1¾ cups) cauliflower florets
6 kaffir lime leaves
150 g (5½ oz) snake beans, cut into
    short pieces
½ red capsicum (pepper), cut into strips
10 fresh baby corn, halved
    lengthways
1 tablespoon green peppercorns, drained
    and roughly chopped
3 tablespoons chopped basil leaves
2 tablespoons fish sauce (optional)
1 tablespoon lime juice
2 teaspoons soft brown sugar
1 handful coriander (cilantro) leaves
steamed rice, to serve

1   Heat the oil in a large wok or frying pan over medium heat. Add the onion and curry paste and cook, stirring, for 4 minutes.

ratatouille

2 Pour in the coconut milk and 250 ml (9 fl oz/1 cup) water and bring to the boil. Reduce the heat and simmer, uncovered, for 5 minutes.

3 Add the potato, cauliflower and lime leaves and simmer for 7 minutes, then add the snake beans, capsicum, corn and peppercorns and simmer for a further 5 minutes, or until all the vegetables are tender.

4 Stir in the basil, fish sauce (if using), lime juice and sugar. Sprinkle with the coriander and serve with steamed rice.

NOTE: If fresh baby corn is not available, use tinned baby corn instead. Drain well and add just before serving.

kaffir lime leaves

Both the fruit and the leaves of this South-East Asian citrus tree are highly aromatic. The leaves are used in Asian cooking in much the same way as bay leaves are in European dishes. Fresh leaves are available from greengrocers and supermarkets; dried leaves, which still have quite a strong flavour, can be found in Asian grocery stores.

fennel, tomato and white bean stew

☀

Preparation time: **25 minutes**
Cooking time: **1 hour 15 minutes**
Serves **4**

5 tomatoes
2 leeks, white part only, washed and
    sliced
2 garlic cloves, finely chopped
1 large fennel bulb, washed, halved,
    cored and sliced
60 ml (2 fl oz/¼ cup) extra virgin olive oil
60 ml (2 fl oz/¼ cup) Pernod
2 bay leaves
5 thyme sprigs
500 g (1 lb 2 oz) all-purpose potatoes,
    peeled and cut into large chunks
400 g (14 oz) tin cannellini beans,
    rinsed and drained
250 ml (9 fl oz/1 cup) vegetable stock
250 ml (9 fl oz/1 cup) dry white wine
ready-made pesto, to serve

1 Preheat the oven to 180°C (350°F/ Gas 4). Score a cross in the base of each tomato. Place in a heatproof bowl and cover with boiling water. Leave for 30 seconds, then transfer to cold water, drain and peel the skin away from the cross. Cut the tomatoes in half, scoop out the seeds and chop the flesh.

2 Place the tomato in a large baking dish with the leek, garlic, fennel, oil, Pernod, bay leaves and thyme. Toss well.

3 Cover the dish with a lid or foil and bake for 30 minutes.

4 Remove the dish from the oven and add the potato, beans, stock and wine. Mix well, cover and bake for a further 35–45 minutes, or until the potato is cooked through.

5 Discard the bay leaves and thyme. Serve topped with pesto.

NOTE: If possible, prepare the dish to the end of step 2 well ahead of time to allow the flavours to develop. The mixture can be left to marinate, covered, for several hours.

sweet potato

Sweet potato, sometimes known as kumera and often erroneously as yam, is not a potato at all. It is actually a tuber, although it is starchy, like potato. Sweet potato can be cooked in any way you would cook an ordinary potato.

candied sweet potato

candied sweet potato

❋

Preparation time: 10 minutes
Cooking time: 1 hour
Serves 6

800 g (1 lb 12 oz) orange sweet potato
90 g (3¼ oz) butter, melted
1 tablespoon lemon juice
125 ml (4 fl oz/½ cup) orange juice
95 g (3¼ oz/½ cup) soft brown sugar
1 cinnamon stick
2 teaspoons finely grated lemon zest

1 Preheat the oven to 180°C (350°F/ Gas 4). Peel the sweet potatoes and cut into thick rounds. Arrange in a baking dish, then drizzle with the melted butter and the lemon and orange juice. Sprinkle with the sugar, add the cinnamon stick and toss until combined.
2 Cover with a lid or foil and bake for 30 minutes.

3 Remove the lid and cinnamon stick. Gently stir the mixture, then sprinkle the lemon zest over the top. Bake, uncovered, for a further 15–30 minutes, or until slightly crisp on top.

NOTE: Candied sweet potato is traditionally served at Thanksgiving in North America as an accompaniment.

combination vegetable stew

❋

Preparation time: 15 minutes
Cooking time: 15 minutes
Serves 4–6

2 teaspoons olive oil
1 onion, sliced
60 g (2¼ oz/¼ cup) tomato paste (concentrated purée)
¼ teaspoon chilli powder
1 teaspoon cumin seeds
125 ml (4 fl oz/½ cup) tomato juice
250 ml (9 fl oz/1 cup) vegetable stock
400 g (14 oz) tin chopped tomatoes
2 carrots, sliced
2 zucchini (courgettes), cut into chunks
350 g (12 oz) cauliflower, cut into florets
20 green beans, topped and tailed
warmed tortillas, to serve

1 Heat the oil in a large saucepan over medium heat. Add the onion, tomato paste, chilli powder, cumin and tomato juice and stir until combined.
2 Stir in the stock and tomato and bring to the boil. Reduce the heat and add the remaining vegetables. Simmer, uncovered, for 10–15 minutes, or until the vegetables are soft.
3 Serve with warm tortillas.

broad beans with peas and artichokes

✳

Preparation time: **15 minutes**
Cooking time: **15 minutes**
Serves **4–6**

60 ml (2 fl oz/¼ cup) olive oil
2 onions, sliced into rings
250 g (9 oz/1⅔ cups) frozen broad
   (fava) beans
2 tablespoons lemon juice
250 g (9 oz/2 cups) frozen peas
400 g (14 oz) tin artichoke hearts,
   drained and halved
2 tablespoons chopped dill
1 tablespoon chopped mint
4 spring onions (scallions), chopped

1 Heat the oil in a large saucepan
over low heat. Add the onion and cook,
stirring, for 5 minutes, or until soft
and golden.
2 Add the beans, lemon juice and
125 ml (4 fl oz/½ cup) water. Bring to
the boil, then reduce the heat, cover and
simmer for 5 minutes.
3 Stir in the peas, artichoke and herbs.
Simmer, covered, for 5 minutes, or until
the peas are just tender, but not soft.
4 Remove from the heat, stir in the
spring onion and season to taste. Serve
warm or at room temperature.

beans with tomatoes

✳

Preparation time: **15 minutes**
Cooking time: **20 minutes**
Serves **6**

500 g (1 lb 2 oz) green beans,
   topped, tailed and cut in half
2 tablespoons olive oil
1 large onion, chopped
1 garlic clove, crushed
2 teaspoons sugar
2 tablespoons red wine vinegar
400 g (14 oz) tin chopped tomatoes

1 tablespoon chopped basil
3 tablespoons snipped olives (optional)
basil leaves, to garnish

1 Add the beans to a saucepan of boiling
water and cook for 3 minutes. Drain and
plunge into iced water. Drain again and
set aside.
2 Meanwhile, heat the oil in a frying pan
over medium heat. Add the onion and
garlic and cook, stirring, for 2 minutes,
or until the onion starts to brown.
Sprinkle the sugar over the onion and
cook for a further 10 minutes, or until
it caramelises.
3 Stir in the vinegar and cook for
1 minute, then add the tomato, basil
and olives. Season to taste, then simmer,
uncovered, for 5 minutes.
4 Add the beans and simmer until
warmed through. Serve garnished
with basil.

broad beans with peas
and artichokes

organic vegetables

Some people may find the
label 'organic' on foods quite
confusing. It means that the
fruit or vegetables are grown
without the use of any chemical
fertilisers or pesticides.
There are strict regulations
governing the labelling of such
produce for sale, so you can
be assured that they really
are chemical-free. They may
be slightly more expensive, as
organic vegetables are more
labour intensive for the grower,
but are preferred by people
concerned about the possible
ill effects of chemicals on their
health and the environment.

home-made yoghurt

Pour 500 ml (17 fl oz/2 cups) skim or full-cream milk into a saucepan and bring to the boil until the froth rises. Reduce the heat and simmer gently for at least 2 minutes, then leave to cool until lukewarm. Blend 2 tablespoons plain yoghurt with a little of the warm milk, then stir the mixture into the rest of the milk. Pour the mixture into either a warmed ovenproof bowl or sterilised jars and seal tightly. If the air temperature is cold, stand the bowl or jars in a saucepan of hot tap water and wrap a blanket or towel around the pan. Leave in a warm place for at least 6 hours, or until the yoghurt has set. Refrigerate the yoghurt for about 2 hours before using. For a thicker, creamier yoghurt, blend 1–2 tablespoons milk powder with the milk before heating.

spicy eggplant slices

spicy eggplant slices

✸

Preparation time: 15 minutes
 + 15 minutes standing time
Cooking time: 15 minutes
Serves 4–6

2 eggplants (aubergines)
40 g (1½ oz/⅓ cup) plain (all-purpose) flour
2 teaspoons ground cumin
2 teaspoons ground coriander
1 teaspoon chilli powder
vegetable oil, for pan-frying
125 g (4½ oz/½ cup) plain yoghurt
1 tablespoon chopped mint

1 Cut the eggplants into 1 cm (½ inch) slices. Sprinkle with salt and leave to stand for 15 minutes. Rinse under cold water, then pat dry with paper towels.
2 Sift the flour and spices onto a plate. Dust the eggplant slices with the flour mixture, shaking off any excess.
3 Heat about 2 cm (¾ inch) oil in a heavy-based frying pan over medium heat. Cook the eggplant slices a few at a time, for 2–3 minutes on each side, or until golden. Drain on paper towels.
4 Combine the yoghurt and mint in a bowl. Serve with the warm eggplant.

golden roast vegetables

☀

Preparation time: 15 minutes
Cooking time: 1 hour
Serves 6

6 potatoes, peeled and cut in half
90 g (3¼ oz) butter, melted
60 ml (2 fl oz/¼ cup) olive oil
6 small onions
750 g (1 lb 10 oz) pumpkin (winter squash), peeled
6 baby carrots

1 Preheat oven to 210°C (415°F/Gas 6–7). Add the potatoes to a saucepan of boiling water and cook for 5 minutes. Drain, allow to cool slightly, then pat dry with paper towels. Using the prongs of a fork, scrape the potatoes to roughen the surface.

2 Place potatoes in a shallow baking dish. Combine melted butter and oil and brush over potatoes. Bake for 20 minutes.

3 Meanwhile, peel the onions and trim the bases so they sit flat. Peel the pumpkin, then cut into six even pieces. Trim the tops of the carrots.

4 Add the onions, pumpkin and carrots to the potatoes and brush them with the butter mixture from the baking dish. Bake for 20 minutes.

5 Brush all the vegetables again with the butter mixture. Bake for a final 15 minutes, or until tender. Serve hot.

garlic cream mushrooms

vegetables in coconut milk

✸

Preparation time: **20 minutes**
Cooking time: **15 minutes**
Serves **4**

2 tablespoons vegetable oil
2 garlic cloves, chopped
5 cm (2 inch) knob of ginger, finely grated
2 teaspoons tinned green peppercorns, rinsed and drained (optional)
1 eggplant (aubergine), diced
1 orange sweet potato, diced
100 g (3½ oz) green beans, topped, tailed and cut into 5 cm (2 inch) lengths
750 g (1 lb 10 oz) asparagus, cut into 5 cm (2 inch) lengths
125 ml (4 fl oz/½ cup) coconut milk
2 teaspoons fish sauce (optional)
100 g (3½ oz/2 cups) baby English spinach leaves
1 handful basil

1 Heat oil in a wok or heavy-based frying pan over medium heat. Add the garlic, ginger and peppercorns and cook for 30 seconds. Add the eggplant, sweet potato and 2 teaspoons water and cook for 5 minutes, stirring frequently.

2 Add the beans, then cover and steam for 4 minutes, shaking the pan frequently to prevent sticking.

3 Stir in the asparagus and coconut milk and cook for 3 minutes, or until the asparagus is just tender.

4 Add the fish sauce (if using), spinach and basil and toss until the spinach and basil soften slightly. Serve hot.

fast grilled mushrooms

Remove the stems from large flat field mushrooms (allow one per person) and wipe the caps with paper towels. Place, upturned, on a foil-lined grill (broiling) tray and brush with olive oil (or an oil infused with herbs, garlic or chilli). Grill (broil) under low heat for 5 minutes, or until tender and juicy, brushing occasionally with more oil. Season to taste and serve.

garlic cream mushrooms

✸

Preparation time: **10 minutes**
Cooking time: **10 minutes**
Serves **4**

30 g (1 oz) butter
250 g (9 oz) button mushrooms, sliced
2 garlic cloves, crushed
250 ml (9 fl oz/1 cup) cream
1 tablespoon chopped flat-leaf (Italian) parsley

1 Melt the butter in a saucepan over medium heat. Add the mushroom and garlic and cook, stirring, for 3–5 minutes, or until the mushroom is soft.

2 Increase the heat to high, stir in the cream and bring to the boil. Reduce the heat and simmer for 3 minutes, or until the cream has thickened slightly.

3 Stir in the parsley, season to taste and serve.

stir-fries

Stir-frying means dinner in a snap. Quick and easy, it's one of the best ways to ensure that vegetables, once cooked, retain their natural colour, full flavour and crisp texture. Very little nutritional value is lost when you stir-fry, and it's a brilliant solution to the age-old quandary of what to do with those few random vegetables in the crisper. It's so easy to transform a selection of vegetables and a few other ingredients into a fabulous meal.

To trim asparagus, bend the stem end of each spear. They will snap where any woodiness begins.

To blanch asparagus, tie the spears into a bundle. Place the asparagus, tips upwards, into a pan of boiling water. Cook for 2–3 minutes, then lift out with tongs. Dip the tips briefly into the boiling water.

peppered stir-fried snake beans

peppered stir-fried snake beans

❋

Preparation time: 20 minutes
Cooking time: 5 minutes
Serves 4

1 tablespoon tinned green peppercorns, rinsed, drained and crushed
1 handful coriander (cilantro) leaves and stems, chopped
1 tablespoon vegetable oil
2 garlic cloves, chopped
225 g (8 oz) snake beans, cut into 4 cm (1½ inch) lengths
150 g (5½ oz) asparagus, woody ends trimmed, cut into 4 cm (1½ inch) lengths

1 teaspoon soft brown sugar
long red or green chilli strips, to garnish (optional)

1 Combine the peppercorns and coriander in a bowl.
2 Heat the oil in a wok or large heavy-based frying pan over medium heat, swirling to coat the base and side. Add the peppercorn mixture, the garlic, beans, asparagus and sugar and stir-fry for 30 seconds.
3 Add 2 teaspoons water, then cover and steam for 2 minutes, or until the vegetables are just tender. Sprinkle with the chilli and serve.

NOTE: Snake beans have a delicious crisp texture. If they are not available, green beans may be substituted.

vegetable stir-fry

❋

Preparation time: 15 minutes
Cooking time: 10 minutes
Serves 4

1 tablespoon sesame seeds
1 tablespoon vegetable oil
1 teaspoon sesame oil
1 garlic clove, crushed
2 teaspoons finely grated fresh ginger
2 spring onions (scallions), thinly sliced
250 g (9 oz) broccoli, cut into florets
1 red capsicum (pepper), cut into thin strips
1 yellow capsicum (pepper), cut into thin strips
150 g (5½ oz) button mushrooms, halved
45 g (1½ oz/¼ cup) black olives

1 tablespoon soy sauce
1 tablespoon honey
1 tablespoon sweet chilli sauce

1 Spread the sesame seeds on a baking tray and briefly toast under a hot grill (broiler) until golden. Set aside.
2 Heat the oils in a wok or large heavy-based frying pan over medium heat, swirling to coat the base and side. Add the garlic, ginger and spring onion and stir-fry for 1 minute.
3 Add the broccoli, capsicum, mushroom and olives and stir-fry for another 2 minutes, or until the vegetables are brightly coloured and just tender.
4 Combine the soy sauce, honey and chilli sauce in a bowl and mix well. Pour the sauce over the vegetables and toss lightly to combine.
5 Sprinkle with the sesame seeds and serve immediately.

golden fried eggplant and cabbage

✳

Preparation time: **20 minutes**
Cooking time: **5 minutes**
Serves **4**

2 tablespoons vegetable oil
3 spring onions (scallions), chopped
3 garlic cloves, chopped
1 tablespoon soft brown sugar
2 eggplants (aubergines), cut
 into wedges (see Note)
2 teaspoons soy sauce
¼ Chinese cabbage, shredded
2 tablespoons lime juice
1 red chilli, thinly sliced

1 Heat the oil in a wok or large heavy-based frying pan over medium heat, swirling to coat the base and side. Add the spring onion and garlic and stir-fry for 1 minute.
2 Add the sugar and eggplant and stir-fry for 3 minutes, or until the eggplant is golden brown.

3 Add the soy sauce, cabbage and lime juice. Toss well, then cover and steam for 30 seconds, or until the cabbage softens slightly.
4 Sprinkle with the chilli and serve.

NOTE: If you can obtain them, you can use Thai eggplants in this dish. Thai eggplants are purple or have purple and white stripes, and come in a range of sizes. Some may be as small as a tiny pea, others the size of a golf ball or shaped like a small zucchini (courgette). Any of these may be used for this recipe — just alter the cooking time to suit the size of the eggplant.

fast spiced corn

Spicy corn is so quick to make, it is an excellent last-minute accompaniment to a meal where a little added zest is needed. Drain 425 g (15 oz) canned baby corn and pat dry with paper towels. Heat 1 tablespoon of oil in a wok. Add a crushed clove of garlic, 1 teaspoon of chopped red chilli and ½ teaspoon ground cumin; stir-fry for 30 seconds. Add the corn and stir-fry for 3 minutes or until heated through. Serve immediately. Serves 2–4.

tofu & tempeh

Rich in protein and carbohydrates, these soya bean products have been a vital part of the Oriental diet for centuries, contributing substance to vegetable dishes.

spicy tempeh salad (pictured)

Preheat the oven to 200°C (400°F/Gas 6). Cut 250 g (9 oz) spicy tempeh into fine strips and place on a non-stick baking tray. Brush lightly with sesame oil and bake for 20 minutes. Put the tempeh in a bowl with 400 g (14 oz/4 cups) julienned vegetables, such as carrots, snow peas (mangetout), red capsicum (pepper) and spring onions (scallions). Add 150 g (5½ oz/2 cups) shredded red cabbage, 2 tablespoons toasted sesame seeds and 125 g (4½ oz) crispy fried Chinese noodles. In a small bowl, whisk together 2 crushed garlic cloves, 1 tablespoon sweet chilli sauce, 2 tablespoons lime juice and 60 ml (2 fl oz/¼ cup) vegetable oil. Pour the dressing over the salad and toss to combine. Serves 4–6.

steamed tempeh with asian greens

Line a large bamboo steamer with a combination of Asian greens, such as bok choy (pak choy), cabbage and coriander (cilantro) leaves. Top with carrot strips, thinly sliced oyster mushrooms and 250 g (9 oz) spicy tempeh, cut into bite-sized pieces. Fill a wok one-quarter full of water and bring to the boil. Cover the steamer and place in the wok. Steam the vegetables for 7 minutes, then add a few snow peas (mangetout) and steam for another 3 minutes, or until the greens are tender and the tempeh is heated through. In a small bowl, whisk together 125 ml (4 fl oz/½ cup) sweet chilli sauce and 60 ml (2 fl oz/¼ cup) soy sauce. Serve the vegetables and tempeh drizzled with the sauce. Serves 4–6.

sesame tofu bites

Rinse 500 g (1 lb 2 oz) firm tofu and cut into 2.5 cm (1 inch) cubes. Place in a shallow dish with 2 crushed garlic cloves, 2 tablespoons finely grated fresh ginger, 1 tablespoon soft brown sugar and 80 ml (2½ fl oz/⅓ cup) salt-reduced soy sauce. Cover and refrigerate for 2 hours, then drain well. In a large mixing bowl, combine 150 g (5½ oz/1 cup) sesame seeds, 1 tablespoon cornflour (cornstarch) and 2 tablespoons wholemeal (whole-wheat) flour. Add the tofu cubes and toss to coat. Heat 60 ml (2 fl oz/¼ cup) vegetable oil in a wok or frying pan. Add the tofu in batches and stir-fry until golden; drain on paper towels. In a small bowl, whisk together 2 tablespoons sweet chilli sauce, 2 tablespoons lime juice, 2 tablespoons chopped coriander (cilantro) and 200 g (7 oz) Greek-style yoghurt. Serve the chilli dipping sauce with the warm tofu bites. Serves 4.

vegetable tofu kebabs

Rinse 375 g (13 oz) firm tofu and cut into cubes. Thread onto metal skewers with some cherry tomatoes, button mushrooms, bay leaves and green capsicum (pepper) chunks. In a small bowl, whisk together 60 ml (2 fl oz/¼ cup) pineapple juice, 1 tablespoon teriyaki marinade and 1 tablespoon chopped mint, then brush the mixture lightly over the kebabs. Cook on a preheated chargrill or barbecue, basting frequently, until the vegetables are tender. Serves 4.

tofu and vegetables

✳

Preparation time: 20 minutes
Cooking time: 15 minutes
Serves 4–6

185 ml (6 fl oz/¾ cup) vegetable oil,
   plus 1 tablespoon, extra
125 g (4½ oz) dried rice vermicelli,
   broken into short lengths
1 tablespoon soy sauce
1 tablespoon sherry
1 tablespoon oyster sauce
125 ml (4 fl oz/½ cup) vegetable
   stock
2 teaspoons cornflour (cornstarch)
1 garlic clove, crushed

1 teaspoon finely grated fresh ginger
375 g (13 oz) firm tofu, cut into
   small cubes
2 carrots, cut into matchsticks
250 g (9 oz) snow peas (mangetout),
   trimmed
4 spring onions (scallions),
   thinly sliced
425 g (15 oz) tinned straw mushrooms,
   drained

1   Heat half the oil in a wok or large
heavy-based frying pan over medium
heat. Cook the vermicelli in batches
until crisp, adding the remaining oil as
necessary. Drain on paper towels.
2   Combine the soy sauce, sherry, oyster
sauce and stock in a small bowl. Blend

the cornflour with 2 teaspoons water in
another small bowl.
3   Heat the extra 1 tablespoon oil in the
wok over high heat, swirling to coat the
base and side. Add the garlic and ginger
and stir-fry for 1 minute. Add the tofu and
stir-fry for 3 minutes, then remove the
tofu from the wok and set aside.
4   Add the carrot and snow peas to the
wok and stir-fry for 1 minute. Add the soy
sauce mixture, then cover and cook for a
further 3 minutes, or until the vegetables
are just cooked.
5   Return the tofu to the wok. Add the
spring onion, mushrooms and cornflour
mixture. Stir until the sauce has
thickened, then remove from the heat.
Serve with the crisp vermicelli.

ginger

Ginger is a rhizome (an
underground stem). Buy firm
pieces without any soft spots,
and make sure it isn't spongy
when squeezed. The longer
ginger has been growing before
harvesting, the more fibrous it
is — this can make it difficult to
cut finely, but it will be hotter
and more flavoursome. Ginger
can be kept for a week on
the kitchen bench; for longer
storage, wrap it in paper towels
to absorb any moisture, then
place in a plastic bag and keep
in the refrigerator.

snow peas with capsicum

✳

Preparation time: **15 minutes**
Cooking time: **10 minutes**
Serves **4**

1 tablespoon vegetable oil
1 onion, sliced into rings
1 tablespoon finely grated fresh ginger
1 capsicum (red pepper), cut
     into strips
1 garlic clove, crushed
185 g (6½ oz) snow peas (mangetout),
     trimmed
1 teaspoon sugar

1 Heat the oil in a wok or large heavy-based frying pan over high heat, swirling to coat the base and side. Add the onion, ginger and capsicum and stir-fry 4–5 minutes, or until the vegetables are just tender.
2 Add the garlic and snow peas and stir-fry for 2 minutes, or until the snow peas turn bright green.
3 Add the sugar, a pinch of sea salt and 1 tablespoon water. Toss well and serve.

thai coconut vegetables

✳

Preparation time: **15–20 minutes**
Cooking time: **15 minutes**
Serves **4–6**

1 tablespoon vegetable oil
2 onions, cut into wedges
1 teaspoon ground cumin
150 g (5½ oz/1¼ cups) cauliflower
     florets
1 red capsicum (pepper), chopped
2 celery stalks, sliced diagonally
185 g (6½ oz/1½ cups) grated pumpkin
     (winter squash)
250 ml (9 fl oz/1 cup) coconut milk
250 ml (9 fl oz/1 cup) vegetable stock

tempeh

Like tofu, tempeh is made from soya beans. However, unlike tofu it is a fermented product, like miso paste and soy sauce. Tempeh is made by adding a culture to the cooked soya beans, then compressing it into firm blocks. Tempeh is often available marinated in a spice mixture, as it is very bland on its own. Being less processed than tofu, it has a higher content of nutrients.

thai coconut vegetables

1 tablespoon sweet chilli sauce
150 g (5½ oz) green beans, topped,
     tailed and halved
1 tablespoon finely chopped coriander
     (cilantro)
steamed rice, to serve

1 Heat the oil in a wok or large heavy-based frying pan over medium heat, swirling to coat the base and side. Add the onion and cumin and stir-fry for 2 minutes, or until the onion is golden.
2 Increase the heat to high, add the cauliflower and stir-fry for 2 minutes. Add the capsicum, celery and pumpkin and stir-fry for a further 2 minutes, or until the vegetables have begun to soften.
3 Add the coconut milk, stock and sweet chilli sauce and bring to the boil. Reduce the heat and stir-fry for 8 minutes, or until the vegetables are almost tender.
4 Add the beans and coriander and cook, tossing, for 2 minutes, or until the beans are just tender. Serve with steamed rice.

sesame oil

Sesame oil not only lends its uniquely nutty flavour to dishes, but enlivens the other flavours as well. There are various types of sesame oil, which range from the thick, brown oil made from roasted sesame seeds and used by the Chinese for seasoning rather than frying, to the pale yellowish oil used in Indian and Middle Eastern dishes.

chinese vegetables with ginger

chinese vegetables with ginger

✳

Preparation time: 15 minutes
Cooking time: 5 minutes
Serves 4

1 tablespoon vegetable oil
3 teaspoons finely grated fresh ginger
4 spring onions (scallions), sliced
225 g (8 oz) tin water chestnuts, drained and sliced
410 g (14½ oz) tin baby corn, drained
45 g (1½ oz/1 cup) finely shredded Chinese cabbage (wong bok)
125 g (4½ oz) bean sprouts, tails trimmed
1 tablespoon soy sauce
1–2 tablespoons vegetarian oyster sauce (see Note)
2 teaspoons sesame oil

1   Heat the oil in a wok or large heavy-based frying pan over high heat, swirling to coat the base and side. Add the ginger and spring onion and stir-fry for 1 minute. Add the water chestnuts and baby corn and stir-fry for 30 seconds.
2   Add the cabbage, bean sprouts, soy sauce and vegetarian oyster sauce and stir-fry for 1 minute.
3   Stir in the sesame oil, toss well and serve immediately.

NOTE: Vegetarian oyster sauce is available from Asian food stores.

almond and broccoli stir-fry

✳

Preparation time: 10 minutes
Cooking time: 5 minutes
Serves 4

60 ml (2 fl oz/¼ cup) vegetable oil
1 teaspoon coriander seeds, crushed
2 tablespoons slivered almonds
1 garlic clove, crushed
1 teaspoon finely shredded ginger
500 g (1 lb 2 oz) broccoli, cut into florets
2 tablespoons red wine vinegar
1 tablespoon soy sauce
2 teaspoons sesame oil
1 teaspoon toasted sesame seeds (see Note)

1   Heat the oil in a wok or large heavy-based frying pan over medium heat, swirling to coat the base and side. Add the coriander seeds and almonds and stir-fry for 1 minute, or until the almonds are golden.
2   Increase the heat to high, add the garlic, ginger and broccoli and stir-fry for 2 minutes. Remove the pan from the heat.
3   In a small bowl, whisk together the vinegar, soy sauce and sesame oil. Add to the wok and toss until the broccoli is well coated.
4   Serve sprinkled with the sesame seeds.

NOTE: Toast the sesame seeds in a dry frying pan over medium heat, stirring constantly, until lightly golden. Watch carefully as they will burn easily.

stir-fried asparagus with sesame seeds

❄

Preparation time: 10 minutes
Cooking time: 6 minutes
Serves 4

1 tablespoon sesame seeds
2 tablespoons vegetable oil
1 garlic clove, finely chopped
1 teaspoon finely grated fresh ginger
750 g (1 lb 10 oz) asparagus, woody ends
    trimmed, cut into 5cm (2 inch) lengths
½ teaspoon freshly ground black pepper
½ teaspoon sugar
2 teaspoons sesame oil
1 tablespoon soy sauce

1 Heat a wok or large heavy-based frying pan over high heat. Add the sesame seeds and cook, stirring often, for 2 minutes, or until golden. Remove from the wok and set aside.
2 Heat the oil in the wok over high heat, swirling to coat the base and side. Add the garlic, ginger and asparagus and stir-fry for 3 minutes, or until almost tender.
3 Sprinkle with the pepper and sugar and stir-fry for 1 minute.
4 Drizzle with the sesame oil and soy sauce, sprinkle with the sesame seeds and serve.

stir-fried mushrooms

❄

Preparation time: 15 minutes
Cooking time: 5 minutes
Serves 4

1 tablespoon vegetable oil
2.5 cm (1 inch) piece of galangal,
    thinly sliced
2 garlic cloves, chopped
2 red chillies, thinly sliced
200 g (7 oz) button mushrooms, halved
100 g (3½ oz) oyster mushrooms, halved
1 teaspoon soy sauce
2 handfuls basil, chopped

fast stir-fried asian greens

Chinese green vegetables cooked in this manner turn bright green — they look irresistible and are very nutritious. Cut 500 g (1 lb 2 oz) bok choy (pak choy) or choy sum, or a combination of both, into 5 cm (2 inch) pieces. Heat 1 tablespoon peanut oil in a wok or large heavy-based frying pan over medium–high heat, swirling to coat the base and side. Add 1 crushed garlic clove and 1 teaspoon finely grated fresh ginger and cook for a few seconds. Add the greens and stir-fry for 1–2 minutes, or until just tender. Add 2 teaspoons soy sauce (and 1 teaspoon sesame oil, if you like), toss to combine and serve. Serves 4.

stir-fried mushrooms

1 Heat the oil in a wok or large heavy-based frying pan over medium–high heat, swirling to coat the base and side. Add the galangal, garlic and chilli and stir-fry for 2 minutes.
2 Add the button mushrooms and stir-fry for 2 minutes, then add the oyster mushrooms and stir-fry for 30 seconds, tossing constantly until the mushrooms begin to soften.
3 Add the soy sauce and basil and toss lightly until well combined. Serve as a side dish.

NOTE: Other varieties of mushroom may be used in this recipe.

lemongrass

Lemongrass gives dishes a balm-like flavour. It is easily grown and can be bought fresh from greengrocers. Usually only the pale, bulb-like base of its fibrous woody stalk is used. Dried lemongrass is a good substitute and can be used to make a refreshing herbal tea.

chinese-style stir-fried vegetables

☀

Preparation time: **15 minutes**
Cooking time: **10 minutes**
Serves **4**

2 tablespoons vegetable oil
2 garlic cloves, crushed
2 teaspoons finely grated fresh ginger
100 g (3½ oz) snake beans, cut into 5 cm (2 inch) lengths
2 spring onions (scallions), sliced
150 g (5½ oz) broccoli, cut into florets
1 red capsicum (pepper), cut into diamonds
300 g (10½ oz) baby bok choy (pak choy), chopped
1 tablespoon sesame oil
2 teaspoons soy sauce

1 Heat the oil in a wok or large heavy-based frying pan over medium heat, swirling to coat the base and side. Add the garlic and ginger and stir-fry for 30 seconds. Add the beans, spring onion and broccoli and stir-fry for 3 minutes.
2 Add the capsicum and stir-fry for 2 minutes, then add the bok choy and stir-fry for 1 minute.
3 Stir in the sesame oil and soy sauce and toss until well combined. Serve immediately.

NOTE: It is important not to overcook vegetables when stir-frying. Use the minimum amount of oil and cook over medium–high heat, stirring and tossing the vegetables constantly. They will soften slightly, but should never be cooked to a limp and greasy state. Add leafy green vegetables last when stir-frying, and cook only until the leaves have just softened. Cutting vegetables into thin, evenly sized pieces on the diagonal helps them cook more quickly.

thai stir-fried vegetables

☀

Preparation time: **25 minutes**
Cooking time: **5 minutes**
Serves **4**

1 tablespoon vegetable oil
4 garlic cloves, chopped
3 lemongrass stems, white part only, finely chopped
2 teaspoons chopped red chillies
2 celery stalks, cut into short lengths
100 g (3½ oz) beans, cut into short lengths
150 g (5½ oz) asparagus, cut into short lengths

thai stir-fried vegetables

½ red capsicum (pepper), cut into thin,
   short pieces
1 tablespoon sweet chilli sauce, or to taste
1 teaspoon soy sauce
100 g (3½ oz) bean sprouts, tails trimmed
80 g (2¾ oz/½ cup) unsalted roasted
   peanuts, chopped (optional)
1 handful coriander (cilantro) leaves

1 Heat the oil in a wok or large heavy-
based frying pan over medium–high heat,
swirling to coat the base and side. Add
the garlic and lemongrass and stir-fry for
1 minute. Add the chilli, celery and beans
and stir-fry for 1 minute.
2 Add the asparagus and capsicum and
toss well. Cover and steam for 1 minute.
Stir in the chilli sauce, soy sauce and bean
sprouts and toss well.
3 Arrange the vegetables on a platter.
Scatter with the peanuts and coriander
and serve.

NOTE: You can use any vegetable in
season, such as broccoli, baby corn or
snow peas (mangetout).

oriental mushrooms
with hokkein noodles

※

Preparation time: **25 minutes**
Cooking time: **10 minutes**
Serves **4**

250 g (9 oz) hokkein (egg) noodles
1 teaspoon sesame oil
1 tablespoon peanut oil
2 garlic cloves, crushed
2 tablespoons finely grated fresh ginger
8 spring onions (scallions), sliced
1 red capsicum (pepper), sliced
200 g (7 oz) oyster mushrooms, halved
200 g (7 oz) shiitake mushrooms, sliced
125 g (4½ oz/1 bunch) garlic chives,
   snipped
40 g (1½ oz/¼ cup) cashew nuts
2 tablespoons kecap manis (see Note)
60 ml (2 fl oz/¼ cup) salt-reduced
   soy sauce

1 Soak the noodles in boiling water for
2 minutes. Drain and set aside.
2 Heat the oils in a wok or large heavy-
based frying pan over high heat, swirling
to coat the base and side. Add the garlic,
ginger and spring onion and stir-fry for
2 minutes.
3 Add the capsicum and mushrooms
and stir-fry for 3 minutes, or until the
mushrooms are golden brown.
4 Add the drained noodles, chives,
cashews, kecap manis and soy sauce and
toss well. Stir-fry for 3 minutes, or until
the noodles are well coated. Serve hot.

NOTE: Kecap manis is an Indonesian
sweet soy sauce. If you are unable to
obtain it, use soy sauce sweetened with a
little soft brown sugar.

fast stir-fried vegetables
with sweet soy

Heat 1–2 teaspoons sesame oil and
2 teaspoons vegetable oil in a wok
or large heavy-based frying pan
over medium–high heat, swirling to
coat the base and side. Add 200 g
(7 oz/3 cups) broccoli florets and
stir-fry for 2 minutes. Add 150 g
(5½ oz/2 cups) finely shredded
cabbage and 100 g (3½ oz)
sugar snap peas and stir-fry for
2–3 minutes, or until the vegetables
are just cooked. Drizzle with a little
kecap manis (or some soy sauce
mixed with honey), then toss well
and serve. Serves 2–4.

savoury breads, muffins & scones

Few can resist a piping-hot tray of freshly baked goods plucked straight from the oven. Serve warm onion and parmesan scones with a stockpot of soup on a cold winter's night, or a golden focaccia for lunch on a sunny patio. These savoury breads fulfil their aromatic promise for any occasion, compelling everyone who bites into them to have the same response: 'More, please!'

sourdough rye bread

✹ ✹

Preparation time: 30 minutes
+ overnight souring time
+ 1 hour 30 minutes proving time
Cooking time: 40 minutes
Makes 2 loaves

SOURDOUGH STARTER
2 teaspoons dried yeast
1 teaspoon caster (superfine) sugar
200 g (7 oz/2 cups) rye flour

BREAD DOUGH
100 g (3½ oz/1 cup) rye flour, plus extra,
for sprinkling

550 g (1 lb 4 oz/4½ cups) unbleached
plain (all-purpose) flour
45 g (1½ oz/¼ cup) soft brown sugar
3 teaspoons caraway seeds
2 teaspoons sea salt
2 teaspoons dried yeast
60 ml (2 fl oz/¼ cup) vegetable or olive oil

1 To make the sourdough starter, combine the yeast, sugar, flour and 435 ml (15¼ fl oz/1¾ cups) warm water in a bowl. Cover with plastic wrap and set aside overnight at room temperature to sour. For a stronger flavour, leave for up to 3 days.

2 To make the bread dough, combine the rye flour, 525 g (1 lb 2 oz/3½ cups) of the plain flour, the sugar, caraway seeds and salt in a large bowl. Make a well in the centre. Dissolve the yeast in 250 ml (9 fl oz/1 cup) warm water, then add to the flour mixture with the sourdough starter and oil. Mix using a wooden spoon, and then your hands, until the dough forms a rough, slightly sticky ball that leaves the side of the bowl. Add some of the remaining flour, if necessary — you may not need to use it all.

3 Turn the dough out onto a lightly floured surface and knead for 10 minutes, or until tdough is smooth and springs back when pressed. Place in a large, lightly oiled bowl, cover with plastic wrap and leave in a warm, draught-free place for 45 minutes, or until the dough is well risen.

4 Turn the dough out onto a lightly floured surface. Gently punch down and knead for 1 minute. Divide the dough in half, then shape each portion into a round or oblong loaf. Sprinkle with extra rye flour. Make three slashes in the top of each, or use the end of a wooden spoon handle to press holes 2 cm (¾ inch) deep in the top. Cover with plastic wrap and leave in a warm place for 45 minutes, or until the loaves are well risen.

5 Preheat the oven to 180°C (350°F/ Gas 4). Brush a large baking tray with oil or melted butter. Sprinkle the loaves with more rye flour and place on the baking tray. Bake for 40 minutes, or until a skewer inserted in the centre of the loaves comes out clean. Cool on a wire rack.

sourdough

Historically, sourdough was made in areas where fresh yeast was scarce. Its wonderful flavour is produced by a starter combination of flour and water (or milk) that has been left to ferment before being added to a bread dough. The character of the starter differs depending on the climate of the region in which it is made. Traditionally, a portion of the starter is retained; flour and water are then added to it and the sourdough starter is kept to leaven more batches of dough.

malt bread

✻

Preparation time: 30 minutes +
    1 hour 40 minutes proving time
Cooking time: 40 minutes
Makes 1 loaf

2 teaspoons dried yeast
1 teaspoon sugar
300 g (9⅔ oz/2 cups) plain wholemeal
    (whole-wheat) flour
125 g (4 oz/1 cup) plain (all-purpose) flour
2 teaspoons ground cinnamon
60 g (2¼ oz/½ cup) raisins
30 g (1 oz) butter, melted
1 tablespoon treacle
1 tablespoon liquid malt extract,
    plus ½ teaspoon extra
1 tablespoon hot milk

1 Combine the yeast, sugar and 250 ml
(9 fl oz/1 cup) lukewarm water in a
small bowl. Cover with plastic wrap and
leave in a warm place for 10 minutes, or
until foamy.

2 Sift the flours and cinnamon into a
large bowl. Stir in the raisins and make a
well in the centre. Add the butter, treacle,
the 1 tablespoon of malt extract and the
yeast mixture. Mix with a flat-bladed
knife, using a cutting action, until the
mixture forms a soft dough. Turn out onto
a lightly floured surface and knead for
10 minutes, or until the dough is smooth
and springs back when pressed. Place in a
large, lightly oiled bowl, cover with plastic
wrap and leave in a warm, draught-free
place for 1 hour, or until well risen.

3 Grease a 21 x 14 x 7 cm (8½ x 5½ x
2¾ inch) loaf (bar) tin and line the base
with baking paper. Turn the dough out
onto a lightly floured surface. Gently
punch down and knead for 3 minutes,
or until smooth. Roll the dough out into
a 20 cm (8 inch) square, then roll it
up. Place in the loaf tin, with the seam
underneath. Cover with plastic wrap and
leave in a warm place for 40 minutes, or
until well risen.

4 Preheat the oven to 180°C (350°F/
Gas 4). Brush the loaf with the combined
milk and remaining malt extract. Bake
for 40 minutes, or until a skewer inserted
into the centre of the loaf comes out
clean. Remove from the oven and leave in
the tin for 3 minutes before transferring
to a wire rack to cool.

traditional corn bread

✻

Preparation time: 15 minutes
Cooking time: 25 minutes
Makes 1 loaf

145 g (5½ oz/¾ cup) polenta
2 tablespoons caster (superfine) sugar
125 g (4½ oz/1 cup) plain (all-purpose)
    flour
2 teaspoons baking powder
½ teaspoon bicarbonate of soda
    (baking soda)
½ teaspoon sea salt
1 egg
250 ml (9 fl oz/1 cup) buttermilk
60 g (2¼ oz) butter, melted

1 Preheat the oven to 210°C (425°F/
Gas 6–7). Brush a 20 cm (8 inch) square
cake tin with oil or melted butter and line
the base with baking paper.

2 Combine the polenta and sugar in a
large bowl. Sift the flour, baking powder,
bicarbonate of soda and salt over the top
and mix thoroughly.

3 In a separate bowl, whisk together
the egg, buttermilk and butter. Stir the
mixture into the dry ingredients until they
are just moistened.

4 Pour into the cake tin and smooth the
surface. Bake for 20–25 minutes, or until
a skewer inserted into the centre of the
bread comes out clean.

5 Place on a wire rack and leave to cool
for 10 minutes before turning out. Cut
into squares and serve warm.

traditional corn bread

lemon pepper bread

☀

Preparation time: 20 minutes
Cooking time: 25 minutes
Makes 2 loaves

250 g (9 oz/2 cups) self-raising flour, plus
    extra, for dusting
1 teaspoon sea salt
2 teaspoons lemon pepper, or 1 teaspoon
    finely grated lemon zest and 2 teaspoons
    freshly ground black pepper
50 g (1¾ oz) butter, chopped
1 tablespoon snipped chives
90 g (3¼ oz/¾ cup) grated
    cheddar cheese
2 teaspoons white vinegar
185 ml (6 fl oz/¾ cup) milk

1 Preheat the oven to 210°C (425°F/
Gas 6–7). Grease two baking trays.
2 Sift the flour and salt into a large bowl
and stir in the lemon pepper. Using your
fingertips, rub in the butter until the
mixture resembles coarse breadcrumbs.
Stir in the chives and cheese.
3 In a separate bowl, stir the vinegar into
the milk (it should look slightly curdled).
Add to the flour mixture and mix with a
flat-bladed knife, using a cutting action,
until the mixture forms a soft dough,
adding more milk if the dough is too stiff.
4 Turn the dough out onto a lightly
floured surface and knead until smooth.
Divide the dough in half. Place one on
each baking tray and press each portion
out to a circle about 2.5 cm (1 inch) thick.
Using a knife, score each loaf into eight

wedges, cutting lightly into the top of
the bread. Dust lightly with extra flour.
5 Bake for 20–25 minutes, or until the
loaves are a deep golden colour and
sound hollow when tapped on the base.
Serve warm.

grissini

☀

Preparation time: 40 minutes +
    1 hour proving time
Cooking time: 15 minutes
Makes 24

2 teaspoons dried yeast
1 teaspoon sugar
500 g (1 lb 2 oz/4 cups) strong white flour
1 teaspoon sea salt
60 ml (2 fl oz/¼ cup) olive oil
4 tablespoons chopped basil
4 garlic cloves, crushed
50 g (1¾ oz/½ cup) finely grated parmesan
    cheese, plus 2 tablespoons extra, for
    sprinkling
2 teaspoons sea salt flakes

1 Combine the yeast, sugar and 310 ml
(10¾ fl oz/1¼ cups) lukewarm water in
a small bowl. Cover with plastic wrap and
leave in a warm, draught-free place for
10 minutes, or until foamy.
2 Sift the flour and salt into a bowl
and make a well in the centre. Add the
yeast mixture and oil and mix with a
flat-bladed knife, using a cutting action,
until combined, adding a little water if the
dough is dry.
3 Turn out onto a lightly floured surface
and knead for 10 minutes, or until the
dough is soft and elastic. Divide the
dough in half. Add the basil and garlic
to one portion, and the parmesan to the
other. Knead for a few minutes. Place
in large, lightly oiled bowls, cover with
plastic wrap and leave in a warm place for
1 hour, or until doubled in size.
4 Preheat the oven to 230°C (450°F/
Gas 8). Lightly grease two baking trays.
5 Working with one portion at a time,
turn the dough out onto a lightly floured

lemon pepper bread

surface. Gently punch down and knead for 1 minute. Divide each piece into 12 portions, then roll each one into a thin rope about 30 cm (12 inches) long and 5 mm (¼ inch) across. Place on the baking trays and brush with water.

6 Sprinkle the basil and garlic dough with the sea salt flakes, and the cheese dough with the extra parmesan.

7 Bake for 15 minutes, or until crisp and golden brown.

focaccia

❋ ❋

Preparation time: 30 minutes +
1 hour 50 minutes proving time
Cooking time: 25 minutes
Makes 1 loaf

2 teaspoons dried yeast
1 teaspoon caster (superfine) sugar
2 tablespoons olive oil
405 g (14¼ oz/3¼ cups) white strong flour
1 tablespoon full-cream milk powder
½ teaspoon sea salt

TOPPING
1 tablespoon olive oil
1–2 garlic cloves, crushed
20 black olives
rosemary sprigs or leaves, for scattering
1 teaspoon dried oregano
1–2 teaspoons coarse sea salt

1 Combine the yeast, sugar and 250 ml (9 fl oz/1 cup) lukewarm water in a small bowl. Cover with plastic wrap and leave in a warm place for 10 minutes, or until foamy. Add the oil.

2 Sift 375 g (13 oz/3 cups) of the flour, the milk powder and salt into a large bowl. Make a well in the centre and add the yeast mixture. Beat with a wooden spoon until the mixture is well combined, then add enough of the remaining flour to form a soft dough.

3 Turn out onto a lightly floured surface and knead for 10 minutes, or until the dough is soft and elastic. Place in a large, lightly oiled bowl, cover with plastic wrap

olive oil

The best — and also the most expensive — olive oil is cold-pressed extra virgin olive oil. This is produced from the first pressing of high-grade fruit at a low temperature. The oil from the next pressing is called 'virgin' olive oil. Subsequent pressings will produce a blander oil (labelled 'light' olive oil), with a less distinct flavour and a paler colour. 'Light' refers to the colour and flavour of the olive oil, not to the amount of fat or kilojoules it contains, as these remain the same.

and leave in a warm, draught-free place for 1 hour, or until the dough is well risen.

4 Grease an 18 x 28 cm (7 x 11 inch) baking tin. Turn the dough out onto a lightly floured surface. Gently punch down and knead for 1 minute. Roll into an 18 x 28 cm (7 x 11 inch) rectangle, then place in the baking tin. Cover with plastic wrap and leave to rise in a warm place for 20 minutes.

5 Using the handle of a wooden spoon, make indents 1 cm (½ inch) deep all over the dough at regular intervals. Cover the dough again with plastic wrap and set aside for a final 30 minutes, or until well risen.

6 Preheat the oven to 180°C (350°F/ Gas 4). To make the topping, mix together the oil and garlic and brush over the top of the dough. Scatter with the olives and rosemary, then sprinkle with the oregano and salt.

7 Bake for 20–25 minutes, or until golden and crisp. Cut into large squares and serve warm.

NOTE: Focaccia is best eaten on the day of baking. It can be reheated if necessary.

beer

Beer is sometimes added to bread and batter, not only to add a subtle flavour, but to help aerate the mixture. Being a carbonated liquid, beer acts as a gentle leavening agent, helping bread to rise and making batters light and puffy when cooked. Using a stout or dark beer will impart a deeper flavour.

beer bread rolls

☀

Preparation time: 15 minutes
Cooking time: 20 minutes
Makes 4

405 g (14¼ oz/3¼ cups) plain
  (all-purpose) flour
3 teaspoons baking powder
1 tablespoon sugar
50 g (1¾ oz) butter, chopped
1 teaspoon sea salt
375 ml (13 fl oz/1½ cups) beer

1 Preheat the oven to 210°C (425°F/ Gas 6–7). Grease two baking trays.
2 Put the flour, baking powder, sugar, butter and salt in a food processor and blend until crumbly. Add the beer and process in bursts to form a soft dough.
3 Turn the dough out onto a well-floured surface and knead until smooth, adding extra flour if needed. Divide the dough into four evenly sized portions, then shape into balls. Place on the baking trays and flatten slightly. Brush with a little water and slash the tops with a knife. Bake for 10 minutes.

4 Turn the oven down to 180°C (350°F/Gas 4) and bake for a further 10 minutes, or until the rolls are golden brown and sound hollow when tapped on the base.
5 Cool slightly on a wire rack and serve.

chapattis

✳ ✳

Preparation time: 40 minutes +
    at least 2 hours standing time
Cooking time: 40 minutes
Makes 20

310 g (9¾ oz/2½ cups) fine
    wholemeal (whole-wheat) flour
    (see Note), plus 60 g (2 oz/½ cup),
    extra
1 teaspoon sea salt
1 tablespoon vegetable oil
250 ml (9 fl oz/1 cup) warm water

1 In a large mixing bowl, combine the 310 g (9¾ oz/2½ cups) flour and the salt. Make a well in the centre. Add the oil and water all at once and use a wooden spoon, then your hands, to mix to a firm dough.
2 Turn out onto a lightly floured surface and knead for 15 minutes — do not incorporate the extra flour at this stage. Gather the dough into a smooth ball. Place in a large, lightly oiled bowl, cover with plastic wrap and leave for 2 hours, or overnight if desired.
3 Divide the dough into 20 evenly sized portions. Form each portion into a smooth ball. Working one at a time, roll each ball into a thin, pancake-sized circle, using the extra flour to stop them sticking. Cover each chapatti with floured plastic wrap and leave to rest while rolling the remaining dough.
4 Heat a heavy-based frying pan until hot. Cook the chapatti one at a time. Cook the first side for 1 minute, pressing the edges with a folded tea towel (dish towel) to help bubbles to form, which will make the chapatti lighter. Turn and cook the other side for another minute, again pressing the edges with the tea towel.

During cooking, adjust the heat so that the chapattis brown but do not burn. As you cook each chapatti, stack and wrap them in a clean tea towel to keep them warm and soft.
5 Serve immediately, with curry and vegetable dishes.

NOTE: Fine wholemeal (whole-wheat) flour, often referred to as atta or roti flour, is available from most health food shops. Plain wholemeal flour can be used instead, but the chapattis may be a little denser.

tortillas

✳

Preparation time: 30 minutes
Cooking time: 20 minutes
Makes 16

185 g (6 oz/1½ cups) plain (all-purpose)
    flour
150 g (4¾ oz/1 cup) finely ground
    maize meal (see Note)

1 Sift the flour and maize meal into a large bowl and make a well in the centre. Gradually add 250 ml (9 fl oz/1 cup) warm water and mix with a flat-bladed knife, using a cutting action, until the mixture forms a firm dough. Turn out onto a lightly floured surface and knead for 3 minutes, or until smooth.
2 Divide the dough into 16 evenly sized portions. Roll out one portion on a lightly floured surface to a 20 cm (8 inch) round. Set aside and cover with plastic wrap.

Repeat with the remaining dough to make 16 rounds.
3 Heat a dry, heavy-based frying pan over medium–high heat. Place one tortilla in the pan. When the edges begin to curl slightly, turn and cook the other side — a few seconds each side should be ample. If residual flour begins to burn in the pan, wipe the pan clean with paper towels.
4 Use the tortillas warm, in Mexican-style dishes.

NOTE: Maize meal is a flour made from corn kernels. The texture varies and this recipe requires a finely ground one. It is not to be confused with polenta or cornmeal, which will not work in this recipe. Tortillas (pronounced tor-tee-yah) can also be cooked on a hot barbecue flatplate and will remain fresh for a week in an airtight container. Warm them quickly in the oven or microwave before using. Stale tortillas can be torn into bite-sized pieces and fried in oil until crisp.

chapattis

Widely enjoyed in India, chapattis are an unleavened bread made from a finely ground wholemeal (whole-wheat) flour called atta. Traditionally chapattis are cooked in two stages: first the dough is browned in a frying pan, and then it is toasted directly over a fire, the steam creating moist, puffed pockets in the centre. Chapattis are eaten hot with Indian savoury dishes and curries.

cheese

Everyone loves cheese, and the creative touches added to this selection of popular fresh cheeses helps dress them up just enough to turn a nearly perfect natural food into a perfectly delectable course on its own.

ashed herb goat's cheese

Place 4 sprigs each of sage, rosemary, thyme and marjoram in a small saucepan. Cover and cook the herbs over medium heat for 20 minutes without removing the lid. Transfer the blackened herbs to a food processor and blend until finely chopped. Pat four 100 g (3½ oz) goat's cheese logs or rounds dry with paper towels. Coat the cheeses in the ashed herbs. Cover each separately with fresh plastic wrap and refrigerate overnight before using.

marinated grilled garlic haloumi

Pat 500 g (1 lb 2 oz) haloumi cheese dry with paper towels. Cut the haloumi into thick slices and place in a shallow dish. Add 2 thinly sliced garlic cloves, 2 tablespoons chopped basil, 1 teaspoon lime juice, 60 g (2¼ oz/⅓ cup) sliced sun-dried tomatoes and 250 ml (9 fl oz/1 cup) olive oil. Turn the haloumi until well coated, then cover and marinate in the refrigerator overnight. Remove the haloumi and tomatoes from the marinade and arrange on top of slices of wood-fired bread. Cook under a grill (broiler) preheated to high until the cheese is soft and golden brown. Drizzle with lime juice, sprinkle with freshly ground black pepper and serve.

feta and sun-dried tomatoes in oil (pictured)

Pat 350 g (12 oz) feta cheese dry with paper towels, then cut into cubes. Place 1 tablespoon freshly cracked black pepper, 1 tablespoon dried oregano and 1 teaspoon coriander seeds in a sterilised 750 ml (26 fl oz/3 cup) jar. Arrange the feta, 4 small red chillies, several rosemary sprigs and 125 g (4½ oz/¾ cup) sun-dried tomatoes in a jar. Cover with olive oil, seal tightly and refrigerate. The mixture can be refrigerated for 1–2 months.

baked ricotta

Wrap 500 g (1 lb 2 oz/2 cups) ricotta cheese in a piece of muslin (cheesecloth). Tie the ends together, suspend over a bowl, then leave to drain for 3 hours. Place the ricotta in a bowl and mix in 3 lightly beaten egg whites. Spoon into a loaf (bar) tin and press down firmly. Drizzle with 125 ml (4 fl oz/½ cup) olive oil, then sprinkle with 1 tablespoon sweet paprika, 1 teaspoon ground cumin and some freshly ground black pepper. Bake in a preheated 180°C (350°F/Gas 4) oven for 40 minutes, or until the surface is golden brown. Leave to cool slightly, the remove from the tin and spoon the pan juices over. Serve sliced, with an antipasto platter and wood-fired bread.

pesto herb spread

Place 500 g (1 lb 2 oz/2 cups) cream cheese and 1 tablespoon ready-made pesto in a food processor and blend until smooth. Add 30 g (1 oz/1 bunch) snipped chives and 3 tablespoons chopped coriander (cilantro) and blend until combined. Spoon the mixture into a 20 cm (8 inch) round cake tin lined with plastic wrap. Cover and refrigerate for 3 hours, or until firm. Remove from the tin and coat with chopped smoked almonds. Serve with crackers, sun-dried tomatoes and olives.

almond ricotta cream with fruits and berries

In a bowl, mix 250 g (9 oz/1 cup) ricotta cheese, 200 g (7 oz) vanilla fromage frais, 1 tablespoon thick (double/heavy) cream, 80 g (2¾ oz/⅓ cup) caster (superfine) sugar, 100 g (3½ oz/1 cup) ground almonds and 1 teaspoon natural vanilla extract. Spoon into a double layer of muslin (cheesecloth), tie the ends together and suspend over a bowl. Leave to drain in a cool place overnight. Invert onto a plate and serve with fresh fruits and berries.

capsicum and corn muffins

✳

Preparation time: 15 minutes
Cooking time: 20 minutes
Makes 12

125 g (4½ oz/1 cup) plain (all-purpose) flour
1 tablespoon baking powder
¼ teaspoon sea salt
145 g (5½ oz/¾ cup) fine polenta
1 tablespoon caster (superfine) sugar
1 egg
170 ml (5½ fl oz/⅔ cup) milk
¼ teaspoon Tabasco sauce (optional)
60 ml (2 fl oz/¼ cup) olive oil
½ red capsicum (pepper), chopped
420 g (14¾ oz) tin corn kernels, drained
3 tablespoons finely chopped flat-leaf
    (Italian) parsley

1 Preheat the oven to 210°C (425°F/ Gas 6–7). Lightly grease a 12-hole standard muffin tin.
2 Sift the flour, baking powder and salt into a large bowl. Add the polenta and sugar and stir until thoroughly mixed. Make a well in the centre.
3 In a separate bowl, whisk together the egg, milk, Tabasco sauce and oil. In a third bowl, combine the corn, capsicum and parsley.
4 Add the egg mixture and the corn mixture all at once to the flour mixture. Stir quickly with a wooden spoon or rubber spatula until all the ingredients are just moistened. Do not overmix — the batter should still be quite lumpy.
5 Spoon the mixture evenly into the muffin holes. Bake for 20 minutes, or until the muffins are golden and a skewer inserted into the centre comes out clean. Leave the muffins in the tin for a couple of minutes, then gently loosen each muffin with a flat-bladed knife before turning out onto a wire rack to cool slightly. Serve warm.

capsicum and corn muffins

zucchini and carrot muffins

✳

Preparation time: 20 minutes
Cooking time: 20 minutes
Makes 12

250 g (9 oz/2 cups) self-raising flour
1 teaspoon ground cinnamon
½ teaspoon freshly grated nutmeg
2 zucchini (courgettes), grated
2 carrots, grated
60 g (2¼ oz/½ cup) chopped pecans
2 eggs
250 ml (9 fl oz/1 cup) milk
90 g (3¼ oz) butter, melted

1 Preheat the oven to 210°C (425°F/ Gas 6–7). Lightly grease a 12-hole standard muffin tin.
2 Sift the flour, cinnamon, nutmeg and a pinch of salt into a large bowl. Add the

freezing muffins

Muffins are undoubtedly best eaten still warm from the oven on the day they are baked, but they can also be frozen for up to 3 months. Either put them in an airtight container, or wrap each one separately in foil. When you wish to eat them, there is no need to thaw them first — place them straight into a preheated 180°C (350°F/Gas 4) oven for about 10 minutes, until heated through.

zucchini, carrot and pecans and stir until thoroughly combined. Make a well in the centre.

3 In a separate bowl, whisk together the eggs, milk and butter, then add to the flour mixture all at once. Stir quickly with a fork or rubber spatula until all the ingredients are just moistened. Do not overmix — the batter should still be quite lumpy.

4 Spoon the mixture evenly into the muffin holes. Bake for 15–20 minutes, or until the muffins are golden and a skewer inserted into the centre comes out clean. Leave the muffins in the tin for a couple of minutes, then gently loosen each muffin with a flat-bladed knife before turning out onto a wire rack to cool slightly. Serve warm.

spicy vegetable muffins

☀

Preparation time: **20 minutes**
Cooking time: **25 minutes**
Makes **12**

250 g (9 oz/2 cups) self-raising flour
3 teaspoons curry powder
80 g (2¾ oz/½ cup) grated carrot
60 g (2¼ oz/½ cup) grated orange sweet potato
125 g (4½ oz/1 cup) grated cheddar cheese
90 g (3¼ oz) butter, melted
1 egg
185 ml (6 fl oz/¾ cup) milk

1 Preheat the oven to 180°C (350°F/ Gas 4). Lightly grease a 12-hole standard muffin tin, or line the muffin tin with paper cases.
2 Sift the flour, curry powder and some sea salt and freshly ground black pepper into a bowl. Add the carrot, sweet potato and cheese and mix through with your fingertips until the ingredients are evenly combined. Make a well in the centre.

spicy vegetable muffins

3 In a separate bowl, whisk together the butter, egg and milk, then add to the flour mixture all at once. Stir quickly with a wooden spoon until the ingredients are just combined. Do not overmix — the batter should still be slightly lumpy.
4 Spoon the mixture evenly into the muffin holes, filling each hole about three-quarters full. Bake for 20–25 minutes, or until the muffins are golden and a skewer inserted into the centre comes out clean. Leave the muffins in the tin for a couple of minutes, then gently loosen each muffin with a flat-bladed knife before turning out onto a wire rack to cool slightly. Serve warm or at room temperature.

pecans

Pecans are native to the United States and were widely used in American Indian cooking. Now their most renowned use is in that American favourite, pecan pie; they are also often used in stuffing for the Thanksgiving turkey. Their flavour is somewhat similar to that of the walnut, but the pecan is oilier. It is, in fact, one of the oiliest nuts we eat, with an oil content of around 70 per cent.

cheddar cheese

Probably Britain's best-known cheese, cheddar originated in the small Somerset town from which it takes its name. One of cheddar's best qualities is its adaptability: it can be served as a dessert cheese, but also melts well enough to make it good for cooking. Cheddar is available in various strengths, ranging from mild to strong and well matured.

cheese and chive scones

cheese and chive scones

✳

Preparation time: **20 minutes**
Cooking time: **15 minutes**
Makes **9**

250 g (9 oz/2 cups) self-raising flour
30 g (1 oz) butter, chopped
60 g (2¼ oz/½ cup) grated cheddar cheese, plus 3 tablespoons extra, for sprinkling
25 g (1 oz/¼ cup) shredded parmesan cheese
2 tablespoons snipped chives
125 ml (4 fl oz/½ cup) milk

1 Preheat the oven to 210°C (425°F/ Gas 6–7). Brush a baking tray with melted butter or oil.

2 Sift the flour and a pinch of salt into a bowl. Using your fingertips, rub in the butter. Stir in the cheeses and the chives, then make a well in the centre.
3 In another bowl, mix the milk with 125 ml (4 fl oz/½ cup) water, then add almost all of the liquid to the flour mixture. Mix lightly with a flat-bladed knife, using a cutting action, until the mixture forms a soft dough, adding a little more liquid if the dough is too dry.
4 Knead the dough briefly on a lightly floured surface until smooth. Gently press the dough out until 2 cm (¾ inch) thick. Using a floured 5 cm (2 inch) plain round cutter, cut nine rounds from the dough. Place the rounds on the baking tray and sprinkle with the extra cheese.
5 Bake for 12 minutes, or until the cheese is golden. Serve spread with a little butter.

mini onion and parmesan scones

✳

Preparation time: **25 minutes**
Cooking time: **15 minutes**
Makes **24**

30 g (1 oz) butter
1 small onion, finely chopped
250 g (9 oz/2 cups) self-raising flour
50 g (1¾ oz/½ cup) finely shredded parmesan cheese
125 ml (4 oz/½ cup) milk
cayenne pepper, for sprinkling

1 Preheat the oven to 210°C (425°F/ Gas 6–7). Brush a baking tray with melted butter or oil.

2 Melt the butter in a small frying pan over low heat. Add the onion and cook for 2–3 minutes, or until soft. Remove from the heat and cool slightly.

3 Sift the flour and a pinch of salt into a bowl. Add the parmesan and onion and make a well in the centre. In another bowl, mix the milk with 125 ml (4 oz/ ½ cup) water, then add almost all of the liquid to the flour mixture. Mix lightly with a flat-bladed knife, using a cutting action, until the mixture forms a soft dough, adding a little more liquid if the dough is too dry.

4 Knead the dough briefly on a lightly floured surface until smooth. Gently press the dough out until 2 cm (¾ inch) thick. Using a floured 3 cm (1¼ inch) plain round cutter, cut 24 rounds from the dough. Place the rounds on the baking tray and sprinkle lightly with cayenne pepper.

5 Bake for 10–12 minutes, or until golden brown.

NOTE: Handle scone dough with a light touch. Cut the liquid in with a knife, and then take care not to over-knead the dough or your scones will be tough.

potato and olive scones

✳

Preparation time: **25 minutes**
Cooking time: **15 minutes**
Makes **15**

250 g (9 oz) potatoes, chopped
125 ml (4 fl oz/½ cup) milk, plus extra to glaze
250 g (9 oz/2 cups) self-raising flour
30 g (1 oz) butter, chopped
30 g (1 oz/¼ cup) pitted black olives, chopped
3–4 teaspoons chopped rosemary

1 Boil or microwave the potatoes until tender. Drain and leave to cool, then place in a bowl and mash with the milk. Season with freshly ground black pepper and set aside.

2 Meanwhile, preheat the oven to 210°C (425°F/Gas 6–7). Brush a baking tray with melted butter or oil.

3 Sift the flour into a large bowl. Using your fingertips, rub in the butter. Stir in the olives and rosemary, then make a well in the centre. Add the mashed potato and about 100 ml (3½ fl oz) water. Mix lightly with a flat-bladed knife, using a cutting action, until the mixture forms a soft dough, adding a little more liquid if the dough is too dry.

4 Knead the dough briefly on a lightly floured surface until smooth. Gently press the dough out until 2 cm (¾ inch) thick. Using a floured 5 cm (2 inch) plain round cutter, cut 15 rounds from the dough. Place the rounds on the baking tray and brush the tops with extra milk.

5 Bake for 10–15 minutes, or until golden brown.

potato and olive scones

rosemary

An emblem of remembrance, rosemary's Latin name — *Rosmarinus officinalis* — translates rather poetically as 'dew of the sea', and the herb's strong aroma and piney taste are indeed reminiscent of the dry Mediterranean hillsides. Rosemary should be used sparingly and with discretion, as its distinctive flavour can easily overpower dishes.

sauces, dressings & condiments

Designed to enhance both the taste and presentation of a dish, sauces, dressings and condiments offer opportunities for endless inventions, with variations of old favourites appearing with each new cooking trend. Traditional or innovative, they all have a common purpose: adding a special touch to even the simplest dish.

cheese sauce (mornay)

☀

Preparation time: 10 minutes
Cooking time: 10 minutes
Makes 250 ml (9 fl oz/1 cup)

30 g (1 oz) butter
1 tablespoon plain (all-purpose) flour
350 ml (12 fl oz) milk
60 g (2¼ oz/½ cup) finely grated
   cheddar cheese
¼ teaspoon mustard powder

1 Melt the butter in a small saucepan over medium heat. Add the flour and stir for 1 minute, or until the mixture is golden and bubbling. Remove from the heat.
2 Add the milk very slowly, a little at a time, stirring between each addition until the sauce is completely smooth. When all the milk has been added, return the saucepan to the heat and keep stirring until the mixture boils and thickens.
3 Boil for another 1 minute and remove from the heat. Add the cheese and mustard powder and stir until the cheese has melted and the sauce is smooth. Season to taste and serve.

classic white sauce (béchamel)

☀

Preparation time: 5 minutes + 10 minutes
   infusing time
Cooking time: 15 minutes
Makes 250 ml (9 fl oz/1 cup)

250 ml (9 fl oz/1 cup) milk
1 onion slice
1 bay leaf
6 peppercorns
30 g (1 oz) butter
1 tablespoon plain (all-purpose) flour

1 Combine the milk, onion, bay leaf and peppercorns in a small saucepan. Bring to the boil, then remove from the heat and set aside to infuse for 10 minutes. Strain the milk into a bowl and discard flavourings.
2 Melt the butter in a small saucepan over medium heat. Add the flour and stir for 1 minute, or until the mixture is golden and bubbling. Remove from the heat.
3 Add the milk very slowly, a little at a time, stirring between each addition until the sauce is completely smooth. When all the milk has been added, return the saucepan to the heat and keep stirring until the mixture boils and thickens.
4 Boil for another 1 minute and remove from the heat. Season to taste and serve.

NOTE: Infusing the milk with the onion, bay leaves and peppercorns adds extra flavour. Plain milk may be used, particularly if adding other flavourings. This sauce is best made just before using.

VARIATION: To make a parsley sauce, stir 3 tablespoons finely chopped parsley into the finished sauce. Other fresh herbs, such as chives, dill or tarragon, may be added, or try different combinations of your favourite herbs.

cheese sauce (mornay)

basic hollandaise

✳

Preparation time: **5 minutes**
Cooking time: **10 minutes**
Makes **315 ml (11 fl oz)**

175 g (6 oz) butter
4 egg yolks
1 tablespoon lemon juice
ground white pepper, to taste

1 Melt the butter in a small saucepan. Skim off and discard any froth from the surface, then allow the butter to cool.
2 In another small saucepan, combine the egg yolks and 2 tablespoons water. Using a wire whisk, beat for 30 seconds, or until the mixture is pale and creamy. Place the saucepan over very low heat and continue whisking for 3 minutes, or until the egg yolks are thick and foamy. (Make sure the pan does not get too hot or you'll end up with scrambled eggs.) Remove from the heat.
3 Slowly add the cooled butter to the egg yolk mixture, a little at a time at first, whisking well between each addition. Keep adding the butter in a thin stream, whisking continuously, until all the butter is incorporated. (Try to avoid stirring up the milky white whey in the bottom of the pan, but don't worry if a little gets in.)
4 Stir in the lemon juice. Season to taste with sea salt and ground white pepper and serve.

VARIATION: To make orange hollandaise (also called maltaise), replace the tablespoon lemon juice with 2 tablespoons orange juice. (Strain the juice through a fine sieve to remove any pulp before measuring it.)

NOTE: You can also make the sauce in a food processor. Use the same quantities and blend the egg yolks, water and lemon juice for 10 seconds. Melt the butter and skim off the froth, then, with the motor running, add the melted hot butter to the processor in a thin stream. Transfer to a bowl and season to taste.

microwave hollandaise

Hollandaise sauce can also be whipped up quickly in a microwave. Melt 200 g (7 oz) butter in a microwave-proof bowl for 1 minute. In another microwave-proof bowl, beat 3 egg yolks with 2 tablespoons lemon juice, then add the melted butter, stirring well. Cook on medium heat for 1 minute 20 seconds, or until the sauce is thick, stopping to stir the sauce every 20 seconds.

mustard seeds

There are three types of mustard seeds: black, brown and yellow. Black mustard seeds have the strongest flavour, but because they cannot withstand mechanised harvesting processes, they have largely been replaced in prepared mustards by the milder brown seeds.

french dressing

french dressing

✳

Preparation time: **5 minutes**
Cooking time: **nil**
Makes **125 ml (4 fl oz/½ cup)**

2 tablespoons white wine vinegar
80 ml (2½ fl oz/⅓ cup) light olive oil
1 teaspoon dijon mustard

1 Whisk the ingredients in a small bowl until well combined. Season to taste.
2 Toss through a green salad, or cover and refrigerate for up to 5 days.

VARIATION: To make a herb vinaigrette, use a herb-infused vinegar instead of plain vinegar, or add 1 tablespoon finely chopped herbs.

tomato sauce

✳

Preparation time: **15 minutes**
Cooking time: **20 minutes**
Makes **750 ml (26 fl oz/3 cups)**

1.5 kg (3 lb 5 oz) large ripe
    tomatoes
1 tablespoon olive oil
1 onion, finely chopped
2 garlic cloves, crushed
1 teaspoon dried oregano
2 tablespoons tomato paste
    (concentrated purée)
1 teaspoon sugar

1 Score a cross in the base of the tomatoes. Place in a heatproof bowl and cover with boiling water. Leave for 30 seconds, then transfer to cold water and peel the skin away from the cross. Finely chop the flesh.
2 Heat the oil in a frying pan over medium heat. Add the onion and cook, stirring, for 3 minutes, or until soft. Add the garlic and cook for 1 minute.
3 Stir in the tomato, oregano, tomato paste and sugar. Bring to the boil, then reduce the heat and simmer, uncovered, for 15 minutes, or until the sauce has thickened slightly. Season to taste.

NOTE: This sauce will keep in an airtight container for 2 days in the refrigerator, or can be frozen for up to 2 months. Reheat the sauce in a saucepan or in the microwave. Serve hot over pasta, or use as a pizza sauce.

blue cheese dressing

✳

Preparation time: **5 minutes**
Cooking time: **nil**
Makes 250 ml (9 fl oz/1 cup)

125 g (4 oz/½ cup) whole-egg mayonnaise
60 ml (2 fl oz/¼ cup) thick (double/heavy)
    cream
1 teaspoon white wine vinegar
1 tablespoon finely snipped chives
50 g (1¾ oz) blue cheese

1 Combine the mayonnaise, cream, vinegar and chives in a small bowl.
2 Crumble the blue cheese into the mayonnaise mixture and gently stir it through.
3 Spoon the dressing over steamed asparagus, boiled small potatoes, jacket potatoes or a green salad, or cover and refrigerate for up to 3 days.

thousand island dressing

✳

Preparation time: **10 minutes +**
    2 hours chilling time
Cooking time: **nil**
Makes 350 ml (12 fl oz)

250 g (9 oz/1 cup) whole-egg mayonnaise
2–3 tablespoons chilli sauce
1 pimento, finely chopped, or 50 g
    (1¾ oz/⅓ cup) finely chopped olives
1 tablespoon grated onion
2 tablespoons finely chopped green
    capsicum (pepper)
milk (optional)

1 Combine the mayonnaise, chilli sauce, pimento, onion and capsicum in a bowl. Whisk well to combine; for a thinner consistency, stir in a little milk if desired.
2 Cover and refrigerate for at least 2 hours before using, to allow the flavours to develop. The dressing can be refrigerated for up to 3 days.

aïoli (garlic mayonnaise)

✳

Preparation time: **10 minutes**
Cooking time: **nil**
Makes 250 g (9 oz/1 cup)

2 egg yolks
3 garlic cloves, crushed
4 teaspoons lemon juice
250 ml (9 fl oz/1 cup) light olive oil

1 Combine the egg yolks, garlic and 2 teaspoons of the lemon juice in a bowl. Whisk for 30 seconds, or until light and creamy.
2 Slowly add the oil, about a teaspoon at a time at first, whisking continuously; as the mayonnaise thickens, add the oil in a thin steady stream, whisking all the while.
3 When all the oil has been incorporated, stir in the remaining lemon juice and season to taste.
4 Use immediately, or cover and refrigerate for up to 3 days.

basic mayonnaise

✳

Preparation time: **10 minutes**
Cooking time: **nil**
Makes 250 g (9 oz/1 cup)

2 egg yolks
1 teaspoon dijon mustard
4 teaspoons lemon juice
250 ml (9 fl oz/1 cup) light olive oil

1 Combine the egg yolks, mustard and 2 teaspoons of the lemon juice in a bowl. Whisk for 30 seconds, or until light and creamy.
2 Slowly add the oil, about a teaspoon at a time at first, whisking continuously; as the mayonnaise thickens, add the oil in a thin steady stream, whisking all the while.
3 When all the oil has been incorporated, stir in the remaining lemon juice and season to taste.
4 Use immediately, or cover and refrigerate for up to 3 days.

basic mayonnaise

desserts

Sweet pies, warm sticky puddings, home-made mousses and soufflés — even the very thought sets the tastebuds tingling. And that's nothing compared to the actual sight, aroma and taste of a seductively luscious sweet course presented at the end of a meal (who said anything about being full?). The ideas in this sensational selection are just as thrilling for the cook, too, because they're all from the 'to die for' rather than the 'too hard' recipe basket.

blueberry cheesecake

✹ ✹

Preparation time: 40 minutes +
  several hours chilling time
Cooking time: 50 minutes
Serves 8–10

125 g (4½ oz) unsalted butter
100 g (3½ oz/1 cup) rolled (porridge) oats
100 g (3½ oz) wheatmeal biscuits, finely
  crushed
2 tablespoons soft brown sugar

FILLING
375 g (13 oz/1½ cups) light
  cream cheese
100 g (3½ oz) fresh ricotta cheese
80 g (2¾ oz/⅓ cup) caster (superfine)
  sugar
125 g (4½ oz/½ cup) sour cream
2 eggs
1 tablespoon finely grated orange zest
1 tablespoon plain (all-purpose) flour

TOPPING
250 g (9 oz) fresh blueberries
240 g (8¾ oz/¾ cup) blackberry
  jam
60 ml (2 fl oz/¼ cup) cherry brandy

1 Grease a deep, 20 cm (8 inch) round
spring-form cake tin and line the base
with baking paper.
2 Melt the butter in a saucepan over low
heat. Add the oats and biscuit crumbs and
mix well. Stir in the sugar.
3 Press half the biscuit mixture into
the base of the cake tin, then gradually
press the remainder around the sides,
but not all the way up to the rim, using a
glass to firm it into place. Refrigerate for
10–15 minutes.

4 Preheat the oven to 180ºC (350ºF/
Gas 4). To make the filling, beat the
cream cheese, ricotta, sugar and sour
cream in a bowl until smooth, using
electric beaters. Beat in the eggs, orange
zest and flour until smooth.
5 Place the cake tin on a baking tray to
catch any drips, then pour the filling into
the crust. Bake for 40–45 minutes, or until
the filling has just set. Remove from the
oven and leave to cool.
6 To make the topping, arrange the
blueberries on top of the cheesecake.
Sieve the jam into a small saucepan with
the brandy, stir over medium heat until
smooth, then simmer for 2–3 minutes.
Carefully brush the mixture over
the blueberries.
7 Refrigerate for several hours before
serving, or overnight if convenient.

blueberry cheesecake

chocolate hazelnut soufflé omelette

✹

Preparation time: 20 minutes
Cooking time: 15 minutes
Serves 4

60 g (2¼ oz/½ cup) roughly chopped
  dark chocolate
4 egg yolks
3 tablespoons caster (superfine) sugar
5 egg whites
3 tablespoons finely chopped hazelnuts,
  lightly toasted
30 g (1 oz) unsalted butter
1 tablespoon unsweetened
  cocoa powder
vanilla ice cream, to serve
fresh or frozen berries, to serve

1 Place the chocolate in a small
heatproof bowl over a saucepan of
simmering water, making sure the base
of the bowl doesn't touch the water. Stir
until the chocolate has melted, then allow
to cool slightly.
2 Using electric beaters, whisk the egg
  yolks and sugar in a bowl for 1 minute,

or until thick. Add the melted chocolate and beat well.

3 Place the egg whites in a clean, dry bowl and add a pinch of salt. Using electric beaters, whisk until stiff peaks form. Fold one-third of the egg white through the chocolate mixture at a time, then fold the hazelnuts through.

4 Preheat the grill (broiler) to medium–high. Melt the butter in a frying pan over low heat. When the butter is foaming, pour in the chocolate mixture. Swirl the pan until the mixture evenly covers the base. Cook for 1–2 minutes, or until the mixture has set halfway through and bubbles have formed on top. Place under the grill and cook until golden.

5 Cut into 4 wedges and sift the cocoa powder over the top. Serve with vanilla ice cream and fresh or frozen berries.

NOTE: To toast the hazelnuts, fry them in a dry frying pan over medium heat for 2–3 minutes, or until golden, tossing often so they don't burn.

rich chocolate self-saucing pudding

☀

Preparation time: **20 minutes**
Cooking time: **50 minutes**
Serves **6**

185 g (6 oz/1½ cups) self-raising flour
30 g (1 oz/¼ cup) unsweetened
   cocoa powder
170 g (5¾ oz/¾ cup) caster
   (superfine) sugar
90 g (3¼ oz) butter, melted
185 ml (6 fl oz/¾ cup) milk
2 eggs, lightly beaten

CHOCOLATE SAUCE
375 ml (13 fl oz/1½ cups) milk
185 g (6½ oz/1¼ cups) chopped dark
   chocolate

1 Preheat the oven to 180°C (350°F/ Gas 4). Grease a deep, 2.25 litre

(79 fl oz/9 cup) baking dish.

2 Sift the flour and cocoa into a large bowl, add the sugar and make a well in the centre. In another bowl, whisk together the butter, milk and eggs.

3 Using a wooden spoon, stir the butter mixture into the dry ingredients until just combined and smooth. Pour the batter into the baking dish.

4 To make the chocolate sauce, place the milk, chocolate and 250 ml (9 fl oz/

1 cup) water in a small saucepan over low heat and stir until melted and smooth. Slowly pour over the pudding mixture.

5 Bake for 45–50 minutes, or until the pudding is firm to the touch. Serve warm.

NOTE: This pudding is delicious served with cream or ice cream and fresh fruit.

chocolate

The Aztec Indians of Mexico used the beans of the cacao tree to make a special drink. The Spanish explorer Cortez brought these beans to Europe in 1528. For a long time, the Spanish tried to keep the existence of chocolate a secret, and were so successful that Dutch and English pirates would throw the precious beans overboard, unaware of their value. London's first chocolate shop opened in 1657, but high customs duty kept chocolate a luxury for the rich until the 19th century.

vanilla almond biscotti with geranium cream

✳ ✳

Preparation time: 1 hour + 2 hours
    standing time + overnight chilling time
Cooking time: 1 hour
Serves 6–8

125 g (4½ oz/¾ cup) blanched almonds
3 egg whites
90 g (3 oz/¾ cup) plain (all-purpose)
    flour
selection of seasonal fruits, to serve

GERANIUM CREAM
115 g (4 oz/½ cup) caster (superfine) sugar,
    plus 2 tablespoons extra

1 vanilla bean, split in half
3 rose-scented geranium leaves
250 ml (9 fl oz/1 cup) cream
125 ml (4 fl oz/½ cup) thick (double/heavy)
    cream

1 Flavour the sugar for the geranium cream, by placing each measure of sugar in a separate screw-top jar. Add the vanilla bean to the 115 g sugar, and the geranium leaves to the 2 tablespoons sugar. Seal each jar and shake for 10 seconds, then set aside for at least 2 hours to allow the flavours to develop.
2 Meanwhile, preheat the oven to 180°C (350°F/Gas 4). Grease a 26 x 8 x 4.5 cm (10 x 3 x 2 inch) loaf (bar) tin, then line the base and sides with baking paper. Spread the blanched almonds on a baking tray and bake for 4 minutes, or until

lightly golden. Remove from the oven and leave to cool.
3 Place the egg whites in a clean, dry bowl. Using electric beaters, beat until stiff peaks form. Gradually add the vanilla-scented sugar, beating constantly until the mixture is thick and glossy and the sugar has dissolved.
4 Transfer the mixture to a large bowl. Sift the flour over the top and add the almonds. Using a metal spoon, gently fold the ingredients together. Spread the batter into the loaf tin and smooth the surface. Bake for 25 minutes, then remove from the oven and allow to cool completely in the tin. Turn the loaf out, wrap in foil and refrigerate overnight.
5 Preheat the oven to 160°C (315°F/Gas 2–3). Grease two baking trays. Cut

scented geraniums

Geraniums are wonderful in both the kitchen and the garden. There are up to 50 different scented varieties in a multitude of colours and textures. Their leaves can be used in teas, biscuits, muffins and cakes and are great in finger bowls — just lightly crush the lemon-scented leaves in water.

the biscotti loaf into 5 mm (¼ inch) slices. Arrange the slices on the baking trays and bake for 30 minutes, or until lightly golden and crisp.

6 Meanwhile, make the geranium cream. Using electric beaters, beat the geranium-flavoured sugar in a bowl with the cream until firm peaks form. Put the thick cream in a separate bowl, then fold in the geranium cream using a metal spoon.

7 Serve the biscotti with the geranium cream and seasonal fruit.

NOTE: This dessert can be served on individual plates, but would make an attractive platter for a party or buffet. The biscotti are also delicious served plain, as an accompaniment to coffee. As a variation, other nuts can be used instead of almonds. Roasted hazelnuts or pistachios are particularly delicious. The vanilla and geranium sugars can be prepared up to 2 weeks in advance; the biscotti will keep for up to 2 weeks in an airtight container. The geranium cream is best prepared on the day of serving.

peach charlottes with melba sauce

✳ ✳

Preparation time: 30 minutes +
    20 minutes infusing time
Cooking time: 40 minutes
Serves 4

220 g (7¾ oz/1 cup) sugar
6 peaches, unpeeled
80 ml (2½ fl oz/⅓ cup) peach liqueur
2 loaves brioche
100 g (3½ oz) butter, melted
160 g (5½ oz/½ cup) apricot jam,
    warmed and sieved
fresh berries, to serve

MELBA SAUCE
300 g (10½ oz) fresh or thawed
    frozen raspberries
2 tablespoons icing (confectioners')
    sugar, approximately

1 Put the sugar and 1 litre (35 fl oz/ 4 cups) water in a large heavy-based saucepan over medium heat. Stir until the sugar has completely dissolved. Bring to the boil, then reduce the heat slightly and add the whole peaches. Cover and simmer for 20 minutes.

2 Drain the peaches and leave to cool. Peel off the skins, slice the flesh thickly and place in a bowl. Sprinkle with the liqueur and set aside to infuse for 20 minutes.

3 Preheat the oven to 180°C (350°F/ Gas 4). Grease four 250 ml (9 fl oz/1 cup) ovenproof ramekins or dariole moulds.

4 Cut the brioche into 1 cm (½ inch) thick slices and remove the crusts. With a scone-cutter, cut out rounds to fit the tops and bases of each ramekin. Cut the remaining slices into fingers 2 cm (¾ inch) wide and trim them to fit the height of the ramekins.

5 Dip the first round into the melted butter and place in the base of one of the ramekins. Dip the brioche fingers into the melted butter and press around the side

of the ramekin, overlapping slightly. Line all the ramekins with the brioche in the same way.

6 Fill the lined ramekins evenly with peach slices, then top each with the last round of brioche, dipped in melted butter. Press to seal. Put the ramekins on a baking tray and bake for 20 minutes.

7 Meanwhile, make the melba sauce. Put the berries in a food processor and add the icing sugar (you may need a little more, depending on the sweetness of the berries). Transfer to a food processor and blend until smooth, then push the berries through a fine sieve to remove the seeds.

8 Turn the peach charlottes out onto serving plates. Brush with the warmed jam and drizzle some melba sauce around them. Scatter some berries around and serve.

NOTE: The peaches can be cooked, the ramekins lined with brioche and the sauce made up to 6 hours ahead. Refrigerate the charlottes, then fill and bake them close to serving time.

summer fruits

Fresh flowers everywhere, long balmy days, the first swim of the year, plus the promise of rich, ripe stone fruit and berries just around the corner — what better time is there than summer?

raspberry fool (pictured)

In a bowl, whisk 310 ml (10¾ fl oz/1¼ cups) cream, using electric beaters, until soft peaks form. Add 40 g (1½ oz/⅓ cup) sifted icing (confectioners') sugar and whisk until just combined. Lightly crush 250 g (9 oz) fresh raspberries with a fork. Fold the berries through the cream and refrigerate for up to 2 hours. Serve in dessert glasses with brandy snaps or wafers.

mango ice cream

In a small saucepan, heat 310 ml (10¾ fl oz/1¼ cups) cream until it just comes to the boil, then remove from the heat. Whisk 4 egg yolks in a heatproof bowl with 170 g (6 oz/¾ cup) caster (superfine) sugar until thick and pale. Gradually add the hot cream to the egg mixture, whisking constantly. Pour the mixture back into the saucepan and stir over very low heat for 5 minutes, or until the mixture thickens slightly — be careful not to let it boil or it will curdle. Pour the mixture into a clean bowl and set aside to cool, stirring occasionally. Purée the flesh of two large mangoes in a blender and stir into the cooled custard. Pour into a shallow metal tray, then cover and freeze until firm. Transfer to a bowl, then beat with electric beaters until smooth. Return to the tray and freeze once more until firm.

nectarine tarts

Preheat the oven to 200ºC (400ºF/Gas 6) and grease a baking tray. Cut a sheet of thawed frozen puff pastry into four squares, brush each with melted butter and dust with icing (confectioners') sugar. Arrange thick nectarine slices diagonally across the pastry, then fold two corners over and seal in the centre. Brush the pastry parcels again with melted butter and place on the baking tray. Bake for 20 minutes, or until the pastry is golden. Dust with more icing sugar, and serve warm with thick (double/heavy) cream.

fresh fruit with butterscotch mascarpone

Combine 60 g (2¼ oz) butter, 95 g (3¼ oz/½ cup) soft brown sugar and 250 ml (9 fl oz/1 cup) cream in a small saucepan over low heat. Stir until the mixture is melted and smooth, then bring to the boil. Reduce the heat and simmer for about 3 minutes. Drizzle the butterscotch over serving bowls containing a selection of seasonal fruits and mascarpone. Serve immediately.

cherry gratin

Remove the stalks and stones from 500 g (1 lb 2 oz) cherries, then arrange the cherries in a shallow baking tin. Combine 125 ml (4 fl oz/½ cup) cream and 125 ml (4 fl oz/½ cup) thick (double/heavy) cream in a saucepan and gently heat the mixture until it just comes to the boil. In a heatproof bowl, whisk 2 egg yolks with 2 tablespoons caster (superfine) sugar until thick and pale. Gradually pour in the hot cream, whisking until combined. Pour the mixture back into the saucepan and stir over very low heat for 5 minutes, or until it thickens — make sure it doesn't boil. Allow to cool slightly, then pour over the cherries. (The gratin can be refrigerated for up to 4 hours at this stage.) To serve, evenly sprinkle 2 tablespoons soft brown sugar over the surface and cook under a hot grill (broiler) until the top is browned and just bubbling. Sprinkle with icing (confectioners') sugar just before serving.

hot passionfruit soufflés

sticky date pudding

✷

Preparation time: **35 minutes**
Cooking time: **55 minutes**
Serves **6–8**

200 g (7 oz) dates, pitted and chopped
1 teaspoon bicarbonate of soda
   (baking soda)
100 g (3½ oz) butter
145 g (5½ oz/⅔ cup) caster (superfine)
   sugar
2 eggs, lightly beaten
1 teaspoon natural vanilla extract
185 g (6 oz/1½ cups) self-raising flour
cream, to serve
fresh raspberries, to serve

SAUCE
185 g (6½ oz/1 cup) soft brown sugar
125 ml (4 fl oz/½ cup) cream
100 g (3½ oz) butter

1 Preheat the oven to 180ºC (350ºF/Gas 4).
Grease a 20 cm (8 inch) square cake tin
and line the base with baking paper.
2 Put the dates and 250 ml (9 fl oz/
1 cup) water in a small saucepan and
bring to the boil. Remove from the heat,
stir in the bicarbonate of soda and set
aside to cool.
3 Using electric beaters, beat the butter
and sugar in a small bowl until light and
creamy. Add the eggs gradually, beating
thoroughly after each addition. Add the
vanilla and beat until combined, then
transfer to a large bowl.
4 Using a metal spoon, fold in the flour
and the dates with their liquid and stir
until just combined. Pour into the cake tin
and bake for 50 minutes, or until a skewer
inserted into centre of the pudding comes
out clean. Leave in the tin for 10 minutes
before turning out.
5 Meanwhile, make the sauce. Combine
the sugar, cream and butter in a small
saucepan over medium–low heat. Stir
until the butter has melted and the
sugar has dissolved. Bring to the boil,
then reduce the heat and simmer for
2 minutes.

hot passionfruit soufflés

✷ ✷

Preparation time: **20 minutes**
Cooking time: **25 minutes**
Serves **4**

caster (superfine) sugar, for sprinkling
2 egg yolks
125 g (4 oz/½ cup) passionfruit pulp
   (about 6 passionfruit)
2 tablespoons lemon juice
90 g (3¼ oz/¾ cup) icing (confectioners')
   sugar, plus extra sifted icing sugar,
   to serve
6 egg whites

1 Preheat the oven to 210ºC (425ºF/
Gas 6–7). Insert a collar of baking paper
into four small ramekins, to come about
3 cm (1¼ inches) above the side. Tie
securely with string. Lightly grease the
base and side of the ramekins (including
the paper) and sprinkle with caster sugar,
shaking out the excess.
2 Put the egg yolks, passionfruit pulp,
lemon juice and half the icing sugar in a
large bowl and whisk to combine.
3 Place the egg whites in a clean, dry
bowl. Using electric beaters, whisk until
soft peaks form. Gradually add the
remaining icing sugar, whisking well
after each addition.
4 Using a large metal spoon, fold the
egg white mixture in batches through the
passionfruit mixture, then spoon into the
ramekins. Using a flat-bladed knife, cut
through the mixture in a circular motion
2 cm (¾ inch) from the edge.
5 Place the ramekins on a large baking
tray and bake for 20–25 minutes, or until
the soufflés have risen and are cooked
through.
6 Cut the collars from the ramekins and
serve the soufflés immediately, sprinkled
with sifted icing sugar.

6 Cut the pudding into wedges and place on serving plates. Pour the hot sauce over and serve with cream and raspberries, if desired.

apple pie

✳ ✳

Preparation time: 40 minutes
 + 20 minutes chilling time
Cooking time: 45 minutes
Serves 6

155 g (5 oz/1¼ cups) plain
 (all-purpose) flour
30 g (1 oz/¼ cup) icing
 (confectioners') sugar
90 g (3¼ oz) butter, chopped
2 egg yolks, lightly beaten
1 tablespoon iced water
custard, to serve

FILLING
50 g (1¾ oz) butter
45 g (1¾ oz/¼ cup) soft brown
 sugar
1 teaspoon ground cinnamon
1 teaspoon mixed spice
12 cooking apples, peeled and cut
 into 8 slices each
1 egg white
1 teaspoon caster (superfine) sugar

1 Sift the flour and sugar into a large bowl. Using your fingertips, rub in the butter until the mixture is fine and crumbly. Add the egg yolks and mix with a flat-bladed knife, using a cutting action, until the mixture forms a firm dough, adding the iced water if necessary. Turn out onto a lightly floured work surface and press together until smooth.

2 Brush the rim of a 23 cm (9 inch) pie dish with melted butter. On a sheet of baking paper, roll the pastry out to form a 25 cm (10 inch) round. Cut strips 1 cm (½ inch) wide from the pastry edge and use these to cover the rim of the dish. Cover the dish and the remaining pastry with plastic wrap and refrigerate for 20 minutes.

3 Meanwhile, make the filling. Melt the butter in a large non-stick frying pan over medium heat. Add the brown sugar and spices and stir until the sugar has dissolved, then add the apple and toss to coat. Cover and cook for 10 minutes, or until the apple is soft but still holds its shape, turning the apple occasionally. Remove the lid and cook for another 5 minutes, or until the liquid has reduced. Remove from the heat and leave to cool.

4 Preheat the oven to 190ºC (375ºF/Gas 5). Place the apple and any pan juices in the pie dish. Gently place the pastry over the fruit, pressing it lightly onto the rim of the pie dish. Trim the edges, pinch together to seal, then decorate with the pastry trimmings. Brush with the egg white and sprinkle with the caster sugar.

5 Bake for 30 minutes, or until golden. Serve warm, with custard.

apples

When a recipe calls for apples, choose a variety that will maintain its shape and flavour during cooking. Tart apples with a high percentage of acidic tannin cope best with sautéeing, poaching or baking, while dessert apples, which have a sweet taste and are wonderful raw, tend to lose their shape and become very watery when baked. The ever-versatile granny smith apple is ideal for cooking as it remains firm, and is also tasty enough to eat raw.

fast caramel, nut and banana parfait

Place 100 g (3½ oz) butter, 95 g (3¼ oz/½ cup) soft brown sugar, 2 tablespoons golden syrup or maple syrup, 60 g (2¼ oz/¼ cup) sour cream and 250 ml (9 fl oz/1 cup) cream in a saucepan over low heat and whisk until the sugar has dissolved. Simmer gently, without stirring, for 5 minutes, ensuring the mixture doesn't boil over. Remove from the heat. When the bubbles have subsided, stir in 160 g (5½ oz/½ cup) condensed milk and allow to cool slightly. Layer sliced banana, scoops of vanilla ice cream, crushed pecans and the warm caramel sauce in dessert glasses. Drizzle a little melted chocolate or chocolate liqueur over each parfait if desired. Serves 4–6.

fast caramel, nut and banana parfait

marinated figs with raspberry sauce

❋

Preparation time: **20 minutes +**
  2 hours marinating time
Cooking time: **10 minutes**
Serves **4**

6 figs, halved
310 ml (10¾ fl oz/1¼ cups) dessert wine
1 cinnamon stick
1 tablespoon soft brown sugar
300 g (10½ oz) fresh raspberries, plus extra,
  to garnish
55 g (2 oz/¼ cup) caster (superfine) sugar
1 teaspoon lemon juice
110 g (3¾ oz/½ cup) mascarpone cheese

1 Place the figs in a glass or ceramic bowl. Combine the wine, cinnamon and brown sugar in a small saucepan over low heat and stir until the sugar has dissolved. Pour over the figs, cover and leave to marinate for 2 hours.
2 Blend the raspberries and caster sugar in a food processor. Push the mixture through a fine sieve to remove the seeds, then stir in the lemon juice. Set aside.
3 Heat the grill (broiler) to medium–high. Drain the figs, reserving the marinade, then strain the marinade. Grill (broil) the figs for 5 minutes, or until golden.
4 Pour a little raspberry sauce onto each dessert plate. Arrange three fig halves on each plate and drizzle with the marinade. Serve with a dollop of the mascarpone.

citrus delicious

❋

Preparation time: **25 minutes**
Cooking time: **1 hour**
Serves **4**

60 g (2 oz/½ cup) self-raising flour
230 g (8 oz/1 cup) caster (superfine)
  sugar
2 teaspoons finely grated orange zest
80 ml (2½ fl oz/⅓ cup) orange juice
125 ml (4 fl oz/½ cup) lemon juice
125 g (4½ oz) butter, melted
250 ml (9 fl oz/1 cup) milk
3 eggs, separated

1 Preheat the oven to 180ºC (350ºF/Gas 4). Lightly grease a 1.5 litre (52 fl oz/6 cup) ovenproof dish.
2 Sift the flour into a large bowl. Add the sugar and stir until combined. In another bowl, lightly whisk together the orange zest, orange and lemon juice, butter, milk and egg yolks until smooth. Add to the flour mixture and stir to combine.
3 Place the egg whites in a clean, dry bowl. Using electric beaters, whisk until stiff peaks form. Gently fold the egg white into the flour mixture using a metal spoon.

4 Pour the batter into the ovenproof dish. Place the dish in a deep baking dish and pour enough hot water into the baking dish to come halfway up the side. Bake for 1 hour, or until the pudding is firm in the centre.

5 Remove the dish from the water bath. Serve hot.

meringue stacks

✹ ✹

Preparation time: 25 minutes
Cooking time: 40 minutes
Serves 6

4 egg whites
230 g (8½ oz/1 cup) caster (superfine) sugar
500 g (1 lb 2 oz) strawberries, hulled
310 ml (10¾ fl oz/1¼ cups) cream, whipped

1 Preheat the oven to 150ºC (300ºF/Gas 2). Grease two 32 x 28 cm (13 x 11 inch) baking trays. Cut two sheets of non-stick baking paper large enough to line the trays. Using an 8 cm (3 inch) round cutter as a guide, mark 12 circles on the paper and place on the trays, pencil side down.

2 Place the egg whites in a clean, dry bowl. Using electric beaters, whisk until soft peaks form. Gradually add the sugar, whisking constantly until the mixture is thick and glossy and all the sugar has dissolved.

3 Spread the meringue mixture into rounds on the baking trays, using the pencil marks as a guide. Bake for 40 minutes, then turn the oven off, open the door slightly and leave the meringues to cool in oven.

4 Place half the strawberries in a food processor and blend until completely liquid. Slice the other strawberries and fold them through the whipped cream.

5 Sandwich two meringue rounds together with the cream mixture and place on each serving plate. Drizzle some strawberry sauce around the meringues and serve.

meringues

Apparently, Napoleon so loved these airy concoctions of whipped egg whites and sugar that he named them after the small Swiss town of Meringen where they were served to him. Because of their high sugar content, it is important to use a very low oven setting when cooking meringues so they don't burn, but instead slowly dry out. For perfect meringues, bake for the specified time, then turn off the oven, prop the oven door open with a wooden spoon, and leave the meringues inside the oven until the oven is completely cold.

NOTE: The meringues can be made up to 2 days in advance and stored in an airtight container. The strawberry sauce can be made up to a day ahead, and the strawberry cream mixture up to 2 hours; store the sauce and cream, covered, in the refrigerator. After assembling, serve immediately. If you prefer a sweeter sauce, a little caster (superfine) sugar can be added. The meringues can also be garnished with strawberry leaves for serving.

pumpkin pie

✳ ✳

Preparation time: 20 minutes +
  20 minutes chilling time
Cooking time: 1 hour 10 minutes
Serves 8

150 g (5½ oz/1 cup) plain (all-purpose) flour
100 g (3½ oz) unsalted butter, chilled
  and cubed
2 teaspoons caster (superfine) sugar
80 ml (2½ fl oz/⅓ cup) chilled water
1 egg yolk, lightly beaten with
  1 tablespoon milk, to glaze

ice cream or whipped cream,
  to serve (optional)

FILLING
500 g (1 lb 2 oz) seeded and peeled
  pumpkin (winter squash), chopped
  into small chunks
2 eggs, lightly beaten
140 g (5 oz/¾ cup) soft brown sugar
80 ml (2½ fl oz/⅓ cup) pouring (whipping)
  cream
1 tablespoon sweet sherry
1 teaspoon ground cinnamon
½ teaspoon freshly grated nutmeg
½ teaspoon ground ginger

1 To make the pastry, sift the flour into a large bowl. Using your fingertips, rub in the butter until the mixture resembles fine breadcrumbs. Stir in the sugar. Make a well in the centre, add almost all the water and mix with a flat-bladed knife, using a cutting action, until the mixture comes together in beads. Add the remaining water if the dough is too dry.
2 Lightly grease a 23 cm (9 inch) round pie dish. Gather the dough together and roll out between two sheets of baking paper until it is large enough to cover the base and side of the pie dish. Line the dish with the pastry, trim the excess and crimp the edges. Roll out the pastry trimmings to 2 mm (1⁄16 inch) thick and use them to create leaf-shaped decorations for the top of the pie. Refrigerate the pastry-lined dish and the leaf shapes for 20 minutes.
3 Preheat the oven to 180ºC (350ºF/ Gas 4). Cut a sheet of baking paper to cover the pastry-lined dish. Place over the pastry, then spread a layer of baking beads or uncooked rice over the paper. Place the pastry leaves on a baking tray lined with baking paper, then brush with the combined egg yolk and milk. Bake the pastry shell for 10 minutes, then remove the paper and beads. Bake for another 10 minutes, or until lightly golden. Meanwhile, bake the pastry leaves for 10–15 minutes, or until lightly golden. Remove the pie dish and pastry leaves from the oven and leave to cool.
4 To make the filling, steam or boil the pumpkin for 10 minutes, or until just tender. Drain, mash and set aside to cool. Whisk the eggs and sugar in a large bowl until the sugar has dissolved. Add the cooled, mashed pumpkin and remaining filling ingredients and mix until thoroughly combined.
5 Pour the filling into the pastry shell, smooth the surface with the back of a spoon, then bake for 40 minutes, or until the filling has set. If the pastry edges begin to brown too much during cooking, cover the edges with foil.
6 Allow to cool to room temperature, then decorate with the pastry leaves. Serve with ice cream or whipped cream.

mini toffee puffs with liqueur cream

✹ ✹

Preparation time: **30 minutes**
Cooking time: **30 minutes**
Serves **4–6**

30 g (1 oz) butter
30 g (1 oz/¼ cup) plain (all-purpose) flour
1 egg, lightly beaten

LIQUEUR CREAM
125 ml (4 fl oz/½ cup) cream
1 tablespoon Grand Marnier

TOFFEE
230 g (8 oz/1 cup) caster (superfine) sugar

1 Preheat the oven to 220ºC (425ºF/Gas 7). Line a baking tray with baking paper.
2 Combine the butter and 60 ml (2 fl oz/¼ cup) water in a small saucepan over low heat. Stir until the butter has melted and the mixture just comes to the boil. Remove from the heat and add the flour. Using a wooden spoon, beat until smooth. Return to the heat and beat until the mixture thickens and comes away from the side of the pan. Remove from the heat and leave to cool slightly.
3 Transfer the mixture to a small bowl. Gradually add the egg, using electric beaters to beat the mixture until thick and glossy.
4 Drop teaspoons of the mixture about 4 cm (1½ inches) apart on the baking tray. Bake for 10 minutes, then turn the oven down to 180ºC (350ºF/Gas 4) and bake for a further 5–10 minutes, or until golden and well puffed. Pierce the side of each puff to release the steam. Turn off the oven, return the puffs to the oven to dry them out, then allow to cool.
5 Meanwhile, make the liqueur cream. Using electric beaters, beat the cream until soft peaks form. Add the Grand Marnier and beat until just combined. Place in a piping (icing) bag fitted with a small plain nozzle, then pipe into the puffs.

6 To make the toffee, combine the sugar and 80 ml (2½ fl oz/ ⅓ cup) water in a small saucepan over low heat. Stir until the sugar has dissolved, brushing down the inside of the pan occasionally. Bring to the boil, reduce the heat and simmer until golden. Spoon the toffee over the puffs and allow to set.

NOTE: The puffs can be made up to 6 hours in advance; store in an airtight container. Fill and coat with the toffee within 1 hour of serving.

chocolate rum mousse

✹ ✹

Preparation time: **20 minutes +**
  2 hours chilling time
Cooking time: **5 minutes**
Serves **4**

250 g (9 oz/1⅔ cups) chopped dark
  chocolate
3 eggs
55 g (2 oz/¼ cup) caster (superfine) sugar
250 ml (9 fl oz/1 cup) cream
2 teaspoons dark rum

1 Place the chocolate in a small heatproof bowl over a saucepan of simmering water, making sure the base of the bowl doesn't touch the water. Stir until the chocolate has melted, then allow to cool slightly.
2 Using electric beaters, whisk the eggs and sugar in a small bowl for 5 minutes, or until thick, pale and increased in volume. Transfer the mixture to a large bowl.
3 In another small bowl, lightly whip the cream.
4 Using a metal spoon, fold the melted chocolate and the rum into the egg mixture. Leave to cool, then fold in the cream until just combined.
5 Spoon into four 250 ml (9 fl oz/1 cup) ramekins or dessert glasses. Refrigerate for 2 hours, or until set.

cooking with chocolate

When chocolate is called for in a recipe, buy a good-quality 'cooking chocolate'. Compound chocolate, which has extra vegetable fats added, sets much more quickly than cooking chocolate and is best when used for making things such as chocolate decorations.

choc-chip tofu ice cream

✳

Preparation time: 20 minutes + overnight freezing time
Cooking time: nil
Serves 4

500 g (1 lb 2 oz) silken tofu
60 ml (2 fl oz/¼ cup) maple syrup
2 tablespoons honey
60 ml (2 fl oz/¼ cup) macadamia nut oil
250 ml (9 fl oz/1 cup) soy milk
250 ml (9 fl oz/1 cup) thickened cream
220 g (7¾ oz/1¾ cups) macadamia nuts, roasted and roughly chopped
125 g (4½ oz/¾ cup) chopped dark chocolate

1 Soak the tofu in hot water for 2 minutes, then plunge it into iced water for 2 minutes. Drain, then place in a food processor with the maple syrup, honey and oil. Blend until smooth. With the motor running, gradually add the soy milk and cream and process until thick and creamy.
2 Transfer the mixture to a large freezer container or metal tin. Fold the nuts and chocolate through. Cover with a lid or foil and place in the freezer.
3 Gently stir the ice cream when it is starting to freeze around the edges. Repeat the process, partially freezing and stirring twice more, then allow to freeze thoroughly before serving.

fast silken tofu with berries and maple syrup

Drain and cut 500 g (1 lb 2 oz) silken tofu into bite-sized pieces. Divide among four bowls. Top with fresh mulberries, blueberries and strawberries. Drizzle with maple syrup and serve with almond biscotti. Serves 4.

NOTE: Make sure you use silken tofu, which is very soft, rather than firm tofu for this recipe. Silken tofu has a pleasant, creamy texture.

pavlova roll with raspberry coulis

✳ ✳

Preparation time: 25 minutes + chilling time
Cooking time: 15 minutes
Serves 8–10

4 egg whites
230 g (8½ oz/1 cup) caster (superfine) sugar
1 teaspoon cornflour (cornstarch)
2 teaspoons lemon juice or white vinegar
55 g (2 oz/¼ cup) chopped fresh berries
170 ml (5½ fl oz/⅔ cup) whipped cream

RASPBERRY COULIS
2 tablespoons brandy
250 g (9 oz) fresh raspberries
1 tablespoon icing (confectioners') sugar

1 Preheat the oven to 180ºC (350ºF/ Gas 4). Brush a 25 x 30 cm (10 x 12 inch) Swiss roll (jelly roll) tin with oil and line with baking paper, extending the paper up two sides.
2 Place the egg whites in a clean, dry bowl. Using electric beaters, beat until stiff peaks form. Gradually add 170 g (6 oz/¾ cup) of the sugar and beat until thick and glossy. Combine another 1 tablespoon of the sugar with the cornflour, then fold into the egg white with the lemon juice.
3 Spoon the mixture into the roll tin and smooth the surface. Bake for 12–15 minutes, or until the pavlova is springy.
4 Place a large sheet of baking paper on top of a tea towel (dish towel) and generously sprinkle with the remaining sugar. Turn the pavlova onto the baking paper, peel off the tin lining paper and leave for 3 minutes. Roll up the pavlova from the long side using the tea towel to assist, then leave to cool.
5 Fold the berries into the whipped cream. Unroll the pavlova, fill with the cream mixture and re-roll without the tea towel and baking paper. Transfer to a plate and refrigerate until cold.
6 Meanwhile, make the raspberry coulis. Put the brandy, raspberries and icing sugar in a food processor and blend until well combined.
7 Slice the pavlova roll and serve with the raspberry coulis.

NOTE: If you prefer, a thick fruit purée may be used to fill the roll.

free-form blueberry pie

✳

Preparation time: 20 minutes + 10 minutes chilling time
Cooking time: 35 minutes
Serves 4

185 g (6½ oz/1½ cups) plain (all-purpose) flour
90 g (3¼ oz/¾ cup) icing (confectioners') sugar, plus extra, for dusting
125 g (4½ oz) chilled unsalted butter, chopped
60 ml (2 fl oz/¼ cup) lemon juice
500 g (1 lb 2 oz) fresh blueberries
1 teaspoon finely grated lemon zest
½ teaspoon ground cinnamon
1 egg white, lightly beaten
whipped cream or ice cream, to serve

1 Preheat the oven to 180ºC (350ºF/ Gas 4).
2 Sift the flour and 60 g (2¼ oz/½ cup) of the icing sugar into a bowl. Using your fingertips, rub in the butter until the mixture resembles fine breadcrumbs. Make a well in the centre and add almost all the lemon juice. Mix together with a

flat-bladed knife, using a cutting action, until the mixture comes together in beads. Add the remaining lemon juice if the dough is too dry.

3 Gently gather the dough together and lift onto a sheet of baking paper. Roll out to a circle about 30 cm (12 inches) in diameter. Cover with plastic wrap and refrigerate for 10 minutes.

4 Put the blueberries in a bowl and sprinkle them with the remaining icing sugar, lemon zest and cinnamon. Gently toss together.

5 Place the pastry (still on the baking paper) on a baking tray. Lightly brush the pastry centre with the egg white. Pile the blueberry mixture on the pastry in a 20 cm (8 inch) circle. Fold the pastry edges over the filling, leaving the centre uncovered.

6 Bake for 30–35 minutes. Dust with icing sugar and serve warm, with whipped cream or ice cream.

free-form blueberry pie

blueberries

The blueberry is a small, dark, purplish-blue berry collected from an evergreen shrub, with North America producing 75 per cent of the world's entire crop. The wild berry is generally considered superior in flavour to the larger, sweeter, cultivated fruit — an opinion obviously shared by Alaskan voles, small rodents whose teeth are stained blue throughout the entire berry season.

cakes, pastries & sweet muffins

Remember the creamy sponges and sweet-smelling scones that came out of the oven on rainy afternoons when you were a child? Baking is a family tradition that deserves to be kept alive and well, even in these fast-paced times. A selection of favourites old and new, the recipes in this chapter are sure to delight.

nutmeg

Because nutmeg loses its flavour so quickly, ideally you should buy whole nutmegs and grate them as required. Nutmeg graters are available from department stores and specialty kitchen shops. Nutmeg is used in both sweet and savoury dishes, and most commonly those based on cream, milk or eggs. Freshly grated nutmeg is an essential topping for a traditional eggnog.

nutmeg date cake

✳

Preparation time: **25 minutes**
Cooking time: **1 hour**
Serves **8–10**

370 g (13 oz/2 cups) soft brown sugar,
   plus 2 tablespoons extra
250 g (9 oz/2 cups) plain
   (all-purpose) flour
2 teaspoons baking powder
125 g (4½ oz) unsalted butter,
   chilled and chopped
1 teaspoon bicarbonate of soda
   (baking soda)
185 ml (6 fl oz/¾ cup) milk
2 eggs, beaten
1½ teaspoons freshly grated nutmeg
375 g (13 oz) dried dates,
   roughly chopped
icing (confectioners') sugar, for dusting
whipped cream, to serve

1 Preheat the oven to 180°C (350°F/ Gas 4). Lightly grease a 22 cm (8½ inch) spring-form cake tin and line the base with baking paper.
2 Put the brown sugar, flour and baking powder in a food processor and blend for 10 seconds. Add the butter and blend for a further 10 seconds, or until the mixture resembles fine crumbs. Press half the mixture into the base of the cake tin, leaving the remaining mixture in the food processor.
3 In a bowl, dissolve the bicarbonate of soda in the milk. Whisk in the eggs and nutmeg, then pour the mixture into the remaining flour and sugar mixture and process for a further 10 seconds.
4 Pour the batter into the cake tin and arrange half the dates over the top. Bake for 55 minutes, then remove from the oven and leave to cool in the tin for 10 minutes. Remove the cake from the tin and cool on a wire rack.
5 Arrange the remaining dates on top of the cake, sprinkle with the extra brown sugar and place under a very hot grill (broiler) for 1 minute, or until the sugar begins to melt.
6 Allow the cake to cool. Dust the top with icing sugar and serve with whipped cream.

fast chocolate fudge cookies

✳

Preparation time: **20 minutes**
Cooking time: **15 minutes**
Makes **30**

90 g (3¼ oz/¾ cup) plain (all-purpose)
   flour
60 g (2¼ oz/½ cup) self-raising flour
125 g (4½ oz/1 cup) chopped walnuts
90 g (3¼ oz/½ cup) chocolate chips
125 g (4½ oz) unsalted butter, melted
200 g (7 oz) dark chocolate, melted
2 tablespoons golden syrup or honey
2 eggs, beaten

nutmeg date cake

1 Preheat the oven to 180ºC (350ºF/ Gas 4). Lightly grease a baking tray.
2 Sift the flours into a large bowl. Stir in the walnuts and chocolate chips, then make a well in the centre. Add the remaining ingredients and stir until combined.
3 Drop level tablespoons of the batter onto the baking tray, about 4 cm (1½ inches) apart to allow for spreading.
4 Bake for 12 minutes. Transfer to a wire rack to cool.

pineapple and banana cake

❋

Preparation time: **40 minutes**
Cooking time: **1 hour**
Serves **8–10**

2 bananas
130 g (4¾ oz/½ cup) drained tinned crushed pineapple
285 g (10¼ oz/1¼ cups) caster (superfine) sugar
200 g (6½ oz/1⅔ cups) self-raising flour
2 teaspoons ground cinnamon
170 ml (5½ fl oz/⅔ cup) vegetable oil
60 ml (2 fl oz/¼ cup) unsweetened pineapple juice
2 eggs
1 small mango, thinly sliced
glacé pineapple, to decorate (optional)

ICING
250 g (9 oz/1 cup) cream cheese
185 g (6½ oz/1½ cups) icing (confectioners') sugar

1 Preheat the oven to 180ºC (350ºF/ Gas 4). Grease a 23 cm (9 inch) round cake tin and line the base and side with baking paper.
2 Mash the bananas in a large bowl, then stir in the pineapple and sugar. Sift the flour and cinnamon over the top and stir to combine, using a wooden spoon.
3 In a separate bowl, whisk together the oil, pineapple juice and eggs, then

fresh pineapple

When buying pineapple, look for fruit that is fully ripe. A ripe pineapple should generally be pale yellow, have no soft patches, and you should be able to pull the central leaves easily from the top. It will also smell quite sweet. An unripe fruit that has no fragrance and is dark green will be extremely tart, so let it ripen at room temperature for a few days. Small pineapples often have more flavour than the larger specimens.

add to the banana mixture. Stir until the ingredients are combined and the mixture is smooth.
4 Pour the batter into the cake tin, smooth the surface and bake for 1 hour, or until a skewer inserted into the centre of cake comes out clean. Remove from the oven and leave to cool in the tin for 10 minutes, then turn onto a wire rack to cool.
5 To make the icing, put the cream cheese and icing sugar in a bowl and beat using electric beaters until light and fluffy.
6 Using a serrated knife, cut the cake in half horizontally. Spread one-third of the icing over the bottom layer of the cake and arrange the mango slices over the icing. Replace the top cake layer, then cover the top of the cake with the remaining icing. Decorate with pieces of glacé pineapple, if desired.

NOTE: This cake will keep for up to 4 days in an airtight container. Refrigerate during hot weather. Tinned mango, thinly sliced pineapple or papaya may be used in the filling.

flourless chocolate fruit and nut cake

✳

Preparation time: 40 minutes
Cooking time: 1 hour
Serves 8–10

5 egg whites
170 g (6 oz/¾ cup) caster (superfine) sugar
100 g (3½ oz) glacé apricots, chopped
100 g (3½ oz) glacé figs, chopped
80 g (2¾ oz) glacé ginger, chopped
250 g (9 oz/1⅔ cups) blanched almonds, finely chopped
250 g (9 oz/1⅔ cups) chopped dark chocolate
60 g (2¼ oz) dark chocolate, melted
375 ml (13 fl oz/1½ cups) whipping cream
chocolate leaves, to decorate (optional)

1　Preheat the oven to 150ºC (300ºF/ Gas 2). Lightly grease a deep 24 cm (9½ inch) round spring-form cake tin and line the base and side with baking paper.
2　Whisk the egg whites in a bowl using electric beaters until soft peaks form. Gradually add the sugar, whisking well after each addition. Whisk until the sugar has dissolved and the mixture is thick and glossy.
3　Using a metal spoon, fold in the glacé fruits and ginger, almonds, and the chopped and melted chocolate. Stir until just combined.
4　Spread the batter into the cake tin and bake for 1 hour, or until a skewer inserted into the centre of cake comes out clean. Remove from the oven and leave to cool in the tin for 10 minutes. Remove the cake from the tin and cool on a wire rack.
5　Whip the cream in a bowl using electric beaters until stiff peaks form. Using a piping (icing) bag fitted with a plain nozzle, pipe swirls of cream on top of the cake. Decorate with chocolate leaves, if desired.

peanut choc-chip muffins

✳

Preparation time: 15 minutes
Cooking time: 25 minutes
Makes 12

250 g (9 oz/2 cups) self-raising flour
75 g (2¾ oz/⅓ cup) raw sugar
260 g (9¼ oz/1½ cups) dark chocolate chips
1 egg
250 g (9 oz/1 cup) crunchy peanut butter
2 tablespoons strawberry jam
60 g (2¼ oz) unsalted butter, melted
250 ml (9 fl oz/1 cup) milk
icing (confectioners') sugar, for dusting

1　Preheat the oven to 180ºC (350ºF/ Gas 4). Lightly grease a 12-hole standard muffin tin, or line the muffin tin with paper cases.
2　Sift the flour into a large bowl. Stir in the sugar and chocolate chips and make a well in the centre.
3　In a separate bowl, combine the egg, peanut butter, jam, butter and milk. Add to the flour mixture all at once and stir quickly with a fork or rubber spatula until just combined. Do not overmix — the batter should still be slightly lumpy.
4　Spoon the mixture evenly into the muffin holes, filling each hole about three-quarters full. Bake for 20–25 minutes, or until the muffins are golden and a skewer inserted into the centre comes out clean. Leave the muffins in the tin for a couple of minutes, then gently loosen each muffin with a flat-bladed knife before turning out onto a wire rack to cool slightly.
5　Dust with icing sugar and serve warm or at room temperature.

chocolate leaves

Choose a selection of non-toxic leaves (rose or ivy are good) with prominent veins on the underside. Don't pick furry leaves, as the fibres stick to the chocolate and leave it with a dull finish. Melt a little chocolate and paint it generously over the underside of the leaf with a fine brush. Leave to set, then peel away the leaf. If the coating of chocolate is too thin, it will break. Alternatively, use a leaf-shaped cutter to create leaves like those pictured.

sticky almond cake

✳

Preparation time: 30 minutes
Cooking time: 50 minutes
Serves 8–10

4 eggs
170 g (6 oz/¾ cup) caster (superfine) sugar
2 teaspoons finely grated orange zest
90 g (3¼ oz) butter, melted
60 ml (2 fl oz/¼ cup) cream
90 g (3 oz/¾ cup) self-raising flour, sifted

ALMOND TOPPING
180 g (6½ oz/2 cups) flaked almonds
90 g (3¼ oz) butter
80 g (2¾ oz/⅓ cup) caster (superfine) sugar
60 ml (2 fl oz/¼ cup) cream
2 tablespoons honey
½ teaspoon mixed (pumpkin pie) spice

1　Preheat the oven to 180ºC (350ºF/ Gas 4). Grease a deep 23 cm (9 inch) round spring-form cake tin and line the base and side with baking paper.
2　Beat the eggs and sugar in a large bowl using electric beaters until thick and pale. Using a metal spoon, fold in the orange zest, butter and cream. Fold the sifted flour through.
3　Pour batter into the cake tin and bake 40 minutes, or until firm in the centre.
4　Combine all the almond topping ingredients in a saucepan and stir over medium heat until the mixture comes to the boil. Spread the topping over the cake and bake a further 10 minutes, or until the topping is golden.
5　Remove from the oven and leave to cool in the tin for 10 minutes, before transferring to a serving plate.

flourless chocolate fruit and nut cake

strawberries

Strawberries as we know them today are, in fact, a hybrid variety. They were developed by crossing the American Virginian strawberries, which were large in size but lacking in flavour, with Chilean fruit that had a particularly intense flavour. With this cross the modern berry was born and since then hundreds of new varieties have appeared. When you choose strawberries, don't be seduced by the biggest and brightest — those with the most intense perfume have the best flavour.

orange berry sponge

orange berry sponge

❋ ❋ ❋

Preparation time: 1 hour
Cooking time: 45 minutes
Serves 8–10

60 g (2 oz/½ cup) plain (all-purpose) flour
30 g (1 oz/¼ cup) cornflour (cornstarch)
1 teaspoon baking powder
60 ml (2 fl oz/¼ cup) milk
50 g (1¾ oz) butter
170 g (6 oz/¾ cup) caster (superfine) sugar
3 eggs
3 egg yolks
1 teaspoon finely grated orange zest

FILLING
375 ml (13 fl oz/1½ cups) cream
3–4 teaspoons icing (confectioners') sugar
1–2 tablespoons Grand Marnier
250 g (9 oz) strawberries, hulled and sliced
250 g (9 oz) fresh blueberries
2 tablespoons flaked almonds, toasted
icing (confectioners') sugar, for dusting

1   Preheat the oven to 180°C (350°F/
Gas 4). Brush a 30 x 20 cm (12 x 8 inch)
shallow cake tin with melted butter or oil.
Line the base and sides with baking paper,
extending the paper 3 cm (1¼ inches)
over each edge. Sift the flours and
baking powder twice onto a sheet of
baking paper.
2   In a saucepan, stir the milk and butter
over medium heat until the butter has
melted. (Take care not to boil the mixture,
but keep it hot.)
3   Place the sugar, eggs, egg yolks
and orange zest in a large heatproof
bowl. Stand the bowl over a saucepan
of simmering water, ensuring the base
of the bowl does not touch the water.
Using electric beaters, whisk the mixture
until pale yellow, very thick, glossy and
increased in volume. Remove the bowl
from the heat.
4   Using a metal spoon, gently fold in
one-third of the flour at a time. Fold in
the hot butter mixture and stir until just

smooth. (Do not overmix: it is important
to keep as much volume as possible in the
mixture.) Spoon the mixture into the cake
tin and bake for 25–30 minutes, or until
springy to the touch. Remove from the
oven and leave in the tin to cool.
5   Turn the cake out onto a flat surface.
Using a sharp serrated knife, trim away
any dark patches. Cut the cake into three
even rectangles, each about 10 x 20 cm
(4 x 8 inches) in size.
6   To make the filling, beat the cream
and icing sugar in a bowl using electric
beaters until stiff peaks form. Stir in the
Grand Marnier.
7   Spread one-quarter of the cream
mixture over one layer of cake, then top
with one-third of the berries. Top with
a second layer of cake, pressing down
lightly. Add another layer of the cream
and berries, then top with the third
cake layer. Spread the remaining cream
evenly over the top and sides of the cake.
Decorate with the remaining berries and
toasted flaked almonds. Serve lightly
dusted with icing sugar.

NOTE: Don't use frozen or tinned berries
in this recipe as they are too soggy. If
blueberries are unavailable, substitute any
berry in season, such as blackberries, or
omit the second berry variety entirely if
you prefer.

chocolate carrot slice

❋

Preparation time: 20 minutes
Cooking time: 30 minutes
Makes 32

125 g (4½ oz/1 cup) self-raising flour
1 teaspoon ground cinnamon

170 g (6 oz/¾ cup) caster (superfine) sugar
80 g (2¾ oz/½ cup) finely grated carrot
185 g (6½ oz/1 cup) mixed dried fruit
90 g (3¼ oz/½ cup) chocolate chips
30 g (1 oz/⅓ cup) desiccated coconut
2 eggs, beaten
90 g (3¼ oz) unsalted butter, melted
40 g (1½ oz/⅓ cup) chopped walnuts

CREAM CHEESE FROSTING
125 g (4½ oz/½ cup) cream cheese
30 g (1 oz) unsalted butter
185 g (6½ oz/1½ cups) icing
   (confectioners') sugar, sifted

1   Preheat the oven to 180°C (350°F/
Gas 4). Lightly grease a shallow 23 cm
(9 inch) square cake tin and line the base
and sides with baking paper.
2   Sift the flour and cinnamon into a large
bowl. Add the sugar, carrot, mixed fruit,
chocolate chips and coconut and stir until
just combined. Add the beaten eggs and
butter and stir until combined.
3   Spread the mixture evenly into the
cake tin and smooth the surface. Bake for
30 minutes, or until golden. Remove from
the oven and allow to cool in the tin, then
turn out onto a flat surface.
4   To make the cream cheese frosting, beat
the cream cheese and butter in a small
bowl using electric beaters until smooth.
Add the icing sugar and beat for 2 minutes,
or until light and fluffy. Add 1 teaspoon
water and beat until well combined.
5   Spread the frosting over the slice using
a flat-bladed knife, then sprinkle with the
walnuts. Cut into 16 squares, then cut
each square into two triangles.

NOTE: The topping may also be sprinkled
with grated chocolate, if desired. This
slice can be frozen in an airtight container
for up to 2 months.

cream cheese

Cream cheese is made from whole milk, or a
combination of whole milk and cream. It is
lovely as a spread, but also very useful as a base
for dips and icings (frostings). To add a subtle
flavour, press scented leaves or herbs into the
cream cheese and wrap in plastic overnight.
The cheese will be lightly perfumed; discard the
leaves before using.

icings & frostings

Sweet or piquant, cooked or uncooked, toppings like these help convert an unadorned home-made muffin or a simple sweet slice into a sensational treat.

easy butter cream

Using electric beaters, beat 80 g (2¾ oz) soft butter in a bowl with 60 g (2¼ oz/½ cup) icing (confectioners') sugar. Flavourings can be added if you wish, such as 2 teaspoons finely grated orange zest, 60 g (2¼ oz) melted and cooled chocolate, or a few drops of your favourite flavoured extract and some complementary food colouring.

chocolate icing

In a bowl, combine 30 g (1 oz) melted butter, 2 tablespoons hot water and 2 tablespoons sifted unsweetened cocoa powder. Stir to a smooth paste, then add 125 g (4½ oz/1 cup) sifted icing (confectioners') sugar and stir until well combined and quite smooth.

honey mock cream

Using electric beaters, beat 125 g (4½ oz) butter in a bowl with 80 g (2¾ oz/⅓ cup) caster (superfine) sugar and 2 tablespoons honey until light and creamy. Pour cold water onto the mixture, then swirl it around and pour it off. Beat again for 2 minutes, then swirl more water over the mixture and pour it off again. Repeat this process four more times, until the mixture is white and creamy and the sugar has completely dissolved. This cream is a delicious topping for spiced cakes or cupcakes.

citrus glacé icing

In a small heatproof bowl, combine 125 g (4½ oz/1 cup) sifted icing (confectioners') sugar, 10 g (¼ oz) unsalted butter and 1 teaspoon finely grated citrus zest. Stir in sufficient citrus juice (about 1–2 tablespoons) to make a firm paste. Stand the bowl over a saucepan of simmering water, ensuring the base of the bowl does not touch the water. Stir until the icing is smooth and glossy, then remove from the heat. Spread onto cakes or biscuits using a hot, wet knife, as the icing will set very quickly. The zest and juice from oranges, lemons or limes can be used.

simple citrus glacé icing

Make a deliciously simple glacé icing by combining 155 g (5½ oz/1¼ cups) sifted icing (confectioners') sugar, 30 g (1 oz) softened butter, a little finely grated citrus zest and enough hot water to mix to a thick, smooth paste. This mixture is easy to work with as it doesn't set quickly.

cream cheese frosting

Chop 185 g (6½ oz) cream cheese into small cubes and place in a bowl. Using electric beaters, beat until smooth. Add 40 g (1½ oz/⅓ cup) sifted icing (confectioners') sugar and a few teaspoons of lemon juice and beat until well combined. Add a little more juice to taste, but don't make the frosting too runny. This is an excellent topping for carrot or banana cakes.

chocolate ganache

Combine 100 g (3½ oz/¾ cup) chopped dark chocolate, 60 g (2¼ oz) unsalted butter and 1 tablespoon of cream in a heatproof bowl. Stand bowl over a saucepan of simmering water, ensuring the base of the bowl does not touch the water. Stir the mixture until melted and smooth. This mixture can be cooled slightly and poured while still liquid over a very smooth cake. (If the top surface is rough, turn the cake upside down and use the base as the top.) Ganache can also be cooled until it is spreadable, or cooled and then beaten to make a lighter, fluffier topping.

coffee liqueur gateau

☀ ☀ ☀

Preparation time: 1 hour + 1 hour chilling time
Cooking time: 50 minutes
Serves 8–10

125 g (4½ oz/¾ cup) Brazil nuts
100 g (3½ oz/⅔ cup) blanched almonds
80 g (2¾ oz/⅔ cup) hazelnuts
2 tablespoons plain (all-purpose) flour
170 g (6 oz/¾ cup) caster (superfine) sugar
7 egg whites
60 ml (2 fl oz/¼ cup) Tia Maria or Kahlua
small chocolate melts (buttons), to decorate
sifted icing (confectioners') sugar, for
    dusting

COFFEE CREAM
200 g (7 oz) butter
150 g (5½ oz) dark chocolate, melted
2–3 teaspoons icing (confectioners') sugar
3–4 teaspoons instant coffee granules,
    dissolved in 2 teaspoons warm water

1 Preheat the oven to 180ºC (350ºF/Gas 4).
Brush a deep 20 cm (8 inch) round cake
tin with melted butter or oil, then line the
base and side with baking paper.
2 Spread all the nuts on a baking tray
and bake for 5–10 minutes, or until
golden. Rub the nuts vigorously in a clean
tea towel (dish towel) to remove the
hazelnut skins. Grind the nuts finely in
a food processor, then transfer to a large
bowl. Add the flour and ½ cup (125g/
4½ oz) of the sugar and mix well.
3 Using electric beaters, beat the egg
whites in a large bowl until soft peaks
form. Gradually add the remaining sugar,
beating until thick and glossy. Using a
metal spoon, fold the nut mixture into the
egg white mixture one-third at a time.
4 Spoon the batter into the cake tin
and smooth the surface. Bake for
35–40 minutes, or until springy to the
touch. Remove from the oven and leave
the cake in the tin to cool completely.
5 To make the coffee cream, beat the
butter in a small bowl using electric
beaters until light and creamy. Gradually
pour in the melted chocolate, beating

chocolate melts

Small chocolate melts (buttons) can be made at
home using 150 g (5½ oz) of melted chocolate.
Line two trays with baking paper. Gently melt
the chocolate, then place in a small paper piping
(icing) bag. Seal the end of the bag, then snip off
the tip. Pipe small chocolate buttons onto the
baking trays, then tap the trays lightly on the
bench to flatten the buttons. Allow the chocolate
to set, then peel off the paper and use the
buttons to decorate cakes.

until well combined. Add the icing sugar and combined coffee and beat until smooth.

6 To assemble the gateau, turn the cake onto a flat surface. Using a sharp serrated knife, carefully cut it horizontally into three layers. Use the top layer of the cake as the base of the gateau; brush with half the liqueur, then spread with one-fifth of the coffee cream. Place a second cake layer on top. Brush with the remaining liqueur and spread with one-quarter of the remaining coffee cream. Top with the final cake layer, then spread the remaining coffee cream over the top and sides.

7 Decorate the top with chocolate buttons, then dust with icing sugar. Refrigerate for 1 hour, or until firm.

banana cake

✳

Preparation time: 20 minutes
Cooking time: 1 hour
Serves 8

125 g (4½ oz) unsalted butter, softened
115 g (4 oz/½ cup) caster (superfine) sugar
2 eggs, lightly beaten
1 teaspoon natural vanilla extract
4 very ripe bananas, mashed
1 teaspoon bicarbonate of soda (baking soda)
125 ml (4 fl oz/½ cup) milk
250 g (9 oz/2 cups) self-raising flour
½ teaspoon ground mixed (pumpkin pie) spice
15 g (½ oz/¼ cup) flaked coconut, toasted

BUTTER FROSTING
125 g (4½ oz) unsalted butter, softened
90 g (3¼ oz/¾ cup) icing (confectioners') sugar
1 tablespoon lemon juice

1 Preheat the oven to 180°C (350°F/ Gas 4). Lightly grease a 20 cm (8 inch) round cake tin and line the base with baking paper.

2 Cream the butter and sugar in a small bowl using electric beaters until light and creamy. Add the egg gradually, beating thoroughly after each addition. Add the vanilla and banana and beat until combined. Transfer to a large bowl.

3 Dissolve the bicarbonate of soda in the milk. Sift the flour and mixed spice into a bowl. Using a metal spoon, gently fold the sifted flour, alternating with the milk, into the banana mixture. Stir until all the ingredients are just combined and the mixture is smooth.

4 Spoon the batter into the cake tin and smooth the surface. Bake for 1 hour, or until a skewer inserted into the centre of the cake comes out clean. Remove from the oven and leave to cool in the tin for 10 minutes, before turning out onto a wire rack to cool completely.

5 To make the butter frosting, beat the butter, icing sugar and lemon juice in a bowl using electric beaters until smooth and creamy.

6 Spread the frosting over the cooled cake using a flat-bladed knife. Serve sprinkled with the coconut.

blanching almonds

Some recipes call for blanched almonds, which simply refers to almonds with the skins removed. These are available in packets already blanched, or you can blanch them yourself. Cover the almonds with boiling water and leave for 30 seconds, then drain and remove the skins by rubbing the nuts between your fingers or in a tea towel (dish towel).

storing muffins

Muffins are best eaten on the day they are made. However, they may be frozen for up to 3 months. Allow the muffins to cool completely, then seal them in an airtight freezer bag. When you wish to use them, thaw the muffins at room temperature, then either serve them as they are, or warm them briefly in a moderate oven.

strawberry and passionfruit muffins

strawberry and passionfruit muffins

✳

Preparation time: 20 minutes
Cooking time: 15 minutes
Makes 12

215 g (7¾ oz/1¾ cups) self-raising flour
1 teaspoon baking powder
½ teaspoon bicarbonate of soda (baking soda)
55 g (2 oz/¼ cup) caster (superfine) sugar
175 g (6 oz/1 cup) chopped strawberries
125 ml (4 fl oz/½ cup) tinned (or fresh) passionfruit pulp
1 egg
185 ml (6 fl oz/¾ cup) milk
60 g (2¼ oz) unsalted butter, melted
whipped cream, to serve (optional)
fresh strawberry halves, to serve (optional)
icing (confectioners') sugar, for dusting (optional)

1 Preheat the oven to 210ºC (425ºF/ Gas 6–7). Lightly grease a 12-hole standard muffin tin, or line the muffin tin with paper cases.
2 Sift the flour, baking powder, bicarbonate of soda, sugar and a pinch of salt into a bowl. Add the strawberries and stir to combine, then make a well in the centre.
3 In a separate bowl, whisk together the passionfruit pulp, egg, milk and butter, then add to the flour mixture all at once. Stir quickly with a fork until just combined. Do not overbeat — the batter should still be slightly lumpy.
4 Spoon the mixture evenly into the muffin holes, filling each hole about three-quarters full. Bake for 10–15 minutes, or until the muffins are golden and a skewer inserted into the centre comes out clean. Leave the muffins in the tin for a couple of minutes, then gently loosen each muffin with a flat-bladed knife before turning out onto a wire rack to cool.
5 If desired, serve the muffins topped with whipped cream and fresh strawberry halves, sprinkled with icing sugar.

double chocolate muffins

✳

Preparation time: 15 minutes
Cooking time: 15 minutes
Makes 6

250 g (9 oz/2 cups) plain (all-purpose) flour
2½ teaspoons baking powder

30 g (1 oz/¼ cup) unsweetened cocoa
    powder
2 tablespoons caster (superfine) sugar
170 g (6 oz/1 cup) dark chocolate chips
1 egg
125 g (4½ oz/½ cup) sour cream
185 ml (6 fl oz/¾ cup) milk
90 g (3¼ oz) unsalted butter, melted

1 Preheat the oven to 180°C (350°F/
Gas 4). Lightly grease a 6-hole large
muffin tin.
2 Sift the flour, baking powder and
cocoa into a large bowl. Stir in the sugar
and chocolate chips, then make a well in
the centre.
3 In a separate bowl, whisk together the
egg, sour cream, milk and butter, then
add to the flour mixture all at once. Stir
quickly with a fork or rubber spatula until
just combined. Do not overbeat — the
batter should still be slightly lumpy.
4 Spoon the mixture evenly into the
muffin holes, filling each hole about three-
quarters full. Bake for 12–15 minutes, or
until firm. Leave the muffins in the tin for
a couple of minutes, then gently loosen
each muffin with a flat-bladed knife
before turning out onto a wire rack to
cool slightly. Serve warm.

blueberry muffins

✳

Preparation time: **20 minutes**
Cooking time: **25 minutes**
Makes **12**

310 g (11 oz/2½ cups) self-raising flour
300 g (10½ oz) fresh blueberries
115 g (4 oz/½ cup) castor (superfine)
    sugar
375 ml (13 fl oz/1½ cups) milk
2 eggs
1 teaspoon natural vanilla extract
150 g (5½ oz) unsalted butter, melted

1 Preheat the oven to 200°C (400°F/
Gas 6). Lightly grease a 12-hole standard
muffin tin, or line the muffin tin with
paper cases.

muffin tins

The muffins below were made
in American-style non-stick
muffin tins, sold in department
stores or large supermarkets.
The trays generally come with
6 or 12 muffin holes, and the
holes range through three sizes:
mini, standard and large. Our
recipes use the standard size,
unless otherwise indicated.
Even though the tins are 'non-
stick', it is advisable to lightly
grease the base of the holes,
or line them with muffin cases,
as the sugar content of some
muffins can cause them to stick.

blueberry muffins

2 Sift the flour into a bowl. Stir in the
blueberries and sugar, then make a well
in the centre.
3 In a separate bowl, whisk together the
milk, eggs and vanilla, then add to the
flour mixture all at once. Fold quickly
with a metal spoon until just combined.
Do not overmix — the batter should still
be slightly lumpy.
4 Spoon the mixture evenly into the
muffin holes, filling each hole about three-
quarters full. Bake for 20–25 minutes, or
until the muffins are golden and a skewer

inserted into the centre comes out clean.
Leave the muffins in the tin for a couple
of minutes, then gently loosen each
muffin with a flat-bladed knife before
turning out onto a wire rack to cool.
Serve warm or at room temperature.

NOTE: If fresh blueberries are not in
season, frozen ones can be used. Add
them while they are still frozen to avoid
streaking the batter.

apple strudel

apple strudel

✵

Preparation time: 20 minutes
Cooking time: 30 minutes
Makes 2

30 g (1 oz) unsalted butter
4 granny smith apples, peeled, cored
    and thinly sliced
2 tablespoons orange juice
1 tablespoon honey
55 g (2 oz/¼ cup) sugar
60 g (2¼ oz/½ cup) sultanas (golden
    raisins)
2 sheets ready-rolled puff pastry, thawed
25 g (1 oz/¼ cup) ground almonds
1 egg, lightly beaten
2 tablespoons soft brown sugar
1 teaspoon ground cinnamon

1   Preheat the oven to 220ºC (425ºF/
Gas 7). Grease two baking trays.
2   Melt the butter in a saucepan over
medium heat. Add the apple and cook for
2 minutes, or until lightly golden. Add the
orange juice, honey, sugar and sultanas.
Stir over medium heat until the sugar
has dissolved and the apple is just tender.
Transfer the mixture to a bowl and leave
until completely cooled.
3   Place one sheet of pastry on a flat
surface. Fold it in half, then make small
cuts in the folded edge of the pastry at
2 cm (¾ inch) intervals. Open out the
pastry and sprinkle with half the ground
almonds. Drain off all the liquid from
the apple mixture, then place half the
mixture in the centre of the pastry. Brush
the edges with some beaten egg, then fold
together, pressing firmly to seal. Place on
one of the baking trays, seam side down.
Repeat with the remaining pastry sheet
and apple mixture.
4   Brush the strudels with the remaining
egg. Combine the brown sugar and
cinnamon and sprinkle over the top. Bake
for 20–25 minutes, or until the pastry is
golden and crisp.
5   Serve hot with cream or ice cream, or
at room temperature.

NOTE: Many types of fresh or tinned fruit,
such as pears, cherries or apricots, can be
used to make strudel. Just make sure the
fruit is well drained before using, or the
pastry base will become soggy.

scones

✵

Preparation time: 20 minutes
Cooking time: 15 minutes
Makes 12

250 g (8 oz/2 cups) self-raising flour
30 g (1 oz) butter, chopped
125 ml (4 fl oz/½ cup) milk, plus extra,
    for glazing
jam and whipped cream, to serve

1   Preheat the oven to 210ºC (425ºF/
Gas 6–7). Brush a baking tray with melted
butter or oil.
2   Sift the flour and a pinch of salt into
a bowl. Using your fingertips, rub in the
butter, then make a well in the centre.
3   In another bowl, mix the milk with
80 ml (2½ fl oz/⅓ cup) water, then
add almost all of the liquid to the flour
mixture. Mix lightly with a flat-bladed
knife, using a cutting action, until the
mixture forms a soft dough, adding
more liquid if the dough is too dry.
4   Knead the dough briefly on a
lightly floured surface until smooth.
Gently press the dough out until 1.5 cm
(⅝ inch) thick.
5   Using a floured 5 cm (2 inch) plain
round cutter, cut 12 rounds from the
dough. Place the rounds on the baking
tray and brush the tops with extra milk.
6   Bake for 10–12 minutes, or until
golden brown. Serve with jam and
whipped cream.

NOTE: Use a light touch when kneading
scones or they will turn out heavy and
tough — the dough needs very little
handling. It is usual to add a pinch of salt
to the mixture, even when making sweet
scones, to enhance the flavour.

baking hints

The secret to light, tender pastries,
cakes and biscuits (cookies) is all in
the handling of the mixture. It is the
protein (gluten) in the flour which,
if overhandled, causes the finished
product to be tough and heavy.
When a cake recipe says to 'fold' in
the flour, use a large metal spoon
or rubber spatula, and mix until the
flour is just combined. In a pastry or
biscuit recipe, use a butter knife to
'cut' liquid into the dry ingredients,
then gather the dough together,
using only your fingertips.

fast lemon shortbreads

✵

Preparation time: 10 minutes
Cooking time: 15 minutes
Makes 20

125 g (4½ oz/1 cup) plain (all-purpose) flour
1 tablespoon rice flour
100 g (3½ oz) unsalted butter, chilled and
    chopped
½ teaspoon finely grated lemon zest
1 tablespoon lemon juice

1   Preheat the oven to 180ºC (350ºF/
Gas 4). Line a baking tray with
baking paper.
2   Put the flours, butter and lemon zest in
a food processor. Add the lemon juice and
process until combined.
3   Gently gather the dough into a ball,
then roll out on a lightly floured surface
to a thickness of 1 mm (¾ inch). Cut
out the desired shapes and place on the
baking tray.
4   Bake for 10–12 minutes, or until pale
golden. Transfer to a wire rack to cool.

little lemon tarts

chocolate éclairs

✹ ✹

Preparation time: **30 minutes**
Cooking time: **40 minutes**
Makes **18**

125 g (4½ oz) unsalted butter
125 g (4½ oz/1 cup) plain (all-purpose)
     flour, sifted
4 eggs, lightly beaten
300 ml (10½ fl oz) whipped cream
150 g (5½ oz/1 cup) chopped dark chocolate

1 Preheat the oven to 210ºC (425ºF/
Gas 6–7). Grease two baking trays.
2 Combine the butter and 250 ml (9 fl oz/
1 cup) water in a large heavy-based
saucepan. Stir over medium heat until the
butter has melted. Increase the heat, bring
to the boil, then remove from the heat.
3 Add the flour to the saucepan all at
once and quickly beat into the liquid with
a wooden spoon. Return to the heat and
continue beating until the mixture leaves
the side of the pan and forms a ball.
Transfer to a large bowl and cool slightly.
4 Beat the mixture to release any
remaining heat. Add the egg gradually,
3 teaspoons at a time. Beat thoroughly
after each addition until all the egg has
been added and the mixture is glossy —
a wooden spoon should stand upright
in it. If the mixture is too runny, the
egg has been added too quickly; if this
happens, beat for several more minutes,
or until thickened.
5 Spoon the mixture into a piping
(icing) bag fitted with a 1.5 cm (⅝ inch)
plain nozzle. Sprinkle the baking trays
lightly with water. Pipe 15 cm (6 inch)
lengths onto the trays, leaving room for
expansion. Bake for 10–15 minutes.
6 Turn the oven down to 180ºC (350ºF/
Gas 4). Bake the éclairs for a further
15 minutes, or until golden and firm.
Transfer to a wire rack to cool. Split each
éclair, removing any uncooked dough. Fill
the puffs with cream.
7 Place the chocolate in a small
heatproof bowl over a saucepan of
simmering water, making sure the base

little lemon tarts

✹ ✹

Preparation time: **40 minutes +**
     10 minutes chilling time
Cooking time: **15 minutes**
Makes **24**

250 g (9 oz/2 cups) plain (all-purpose)
     flour
125 g (4½ oz) unsalted butter, chopped
2 teaspoons caster (superfine) sugar
1 teaspoon finely grated lemon zest
1 egg yolk
2–3 tablespoons iced water
strips of candied lemon peel,
     to garnish (optional)

FILLING
125 g (4½ oz/½ cup) cream cheese,
     softened
115 g (4 oz/½ cup) caster (superfine)
     sugar
2 egg yolks
2 tablespoons lemon juice
160 g (5¾ oz/½ cup) sweetened
     condensed milk

1 Preheat the oven to 180ºC (350ºF/
Gas 4). Grease two round-based, 12-cup
shallow patty pans or mini muffin tins.

2 Sift the flour and a pinch of salt into
a bowl. Using your fingertips, rub in the
butter. Add the sugar, lemon zest, egg yolk
and 2 tablespoons of the iced water. Mix
lightly with a flat-bladed knife, using a
cutting action, until the mixture forms a
soft dough, adding more iced water if the
dough is too dry. Gather into a ball and
gently knead on a lightly floured surface
until smooth. Cover in plastic wrap and
chill for 10 minutes.
3 To make the filling, beat the cream
cheese, sugar and egg yolks in a bowl
using electric beaters until smooth
and thickened. Add the lemon juice
and condensed milk and beat until
well combined.
4 Roll the dough out between two sheets
of baking paper to a 3 mm (⅛ inch)
thickness. Using a 7 cm (2¾ inch) fluted
round cutter, cut 24 rounds from the
pastry. Gently press each round into the
patty pans, then lightly prick each three
times with a fork. Bake for 10 minutes,
or until just starting to turn golden.
5 Remove from the oven and spoon
2 teaspoons of the filling into each case.
Bake for a further 5 minutes, or until the
filling has set. Allow to cool slightly before
removing from the pans. Garnish with
strips of candied lemon peel, if desired.

of the bowl doesn't touch the water. Stir until the chocolate has melted, then allow to cool slightly. Spread the chocolate over the éclairs.

chocolate wheat biscuits

✳

Preparation time: 20 minutes
Cooking time: 25 minutes
Makes 25

125 g (4½ oz) butter
95 g (3¼ oz/½ cup) soft brown sugar
60 ml (2 fl oz/¼ cup) milk
225 g (8 oz/1½ cups) wholemeal (whole-wheat) plain (all-purpose) flour
40 g (1½ oz/⅓ cup) self-raising flour
30 g (1 oz/⅓ cup) desiccated coconut
200 g (7 oz) dark chocolate

1 Preheat the oven to 180ºC (350ºF/ Gas 4). Grease two baking trays and line with baking paper.
2 Beat the butter and sugar in a bowl using electric beaters until light and creamy. Add the milk and beat until combined.
3 Sift the flours and add to the butter mixture with the coconut. Mix lightly with a flat-bladed knife, using a cutting action, until the mixture forms a soft dough. Gather into a ball.
4 Roll the dough out between two sheets of baking paper to a 5 mm (¼ inch) thickness. Using a 5 cm (2 inch) round cutter, cut 25 rounds from the dough. Place on the baking trays and bake for 15–20 minutes, or until golden. Remove from the oven and leave on the trays for 5 minutes, then transfer to a wire rack to cool.
5 Place the chocolate in a small heatproof bowl over a saucepan of simmering water, making sure the base of the bowl doesn't touch the water. Stir until the chocolate has melted, then allow to cool slightly. Spread evenly over the tops of the biscuits and allow to set.

coffee kisses

✳

Preparation time: 40 minutes
Cooking time: 10 minutes
Makes 30

375 g (13 oz/3 cups) self-raising flour
160 g (5¾ oz) unsalted butter, chopped
115 g (4 oz/½ cup) caster (superfine) sugar
1 egg, lightly beaten
1 tablespoon instant coffee granules, dissolved in 1–2 tablespoons water
100 g (3½ oz) white chocolate, melted
chocolate-coated coffee beans, to decorate (optional)

COFFEE BUTTERCREAM
80 g (2¾ oz) unsalted butter
125 g (4½ oz/1 cup) icing (confectioners') sugar, sifted
2 teaspoons instant coffee granules, dissolved in 2 teaspoons water

1 Preheat the oven to 180ºC (350ºF/ Gas 4). Grease two baking trays and line with baking paper.

2 Sift the flour into a bowl. Using your fingertips, rub in the butter until the mixture resembles fine breadcrumbs.
3 In a separate bowl, whisk together the sugar, egg and coffee. Add to the flour mixture all at once and mix lightly with a flat-bladed knife, using a cutting action, until the mixture forms a soft dough. Gather into a ball and gently knead on a lightly floured surface until smooth.
4 Roll the dough out between two sheets of baking paper to a 5 mm (¼ inch) thickness. Using a 5 cm (2 inch) fluted biscuit (cookie) cutter, cut into 60 rounds. Place on the baking trays and bake for 10 minutes, or until lightly golden. Transfer to a wire rack to cool.
5 To make the coffee buttercream, beat the butter and icing sugar in a bowl using electric beaters until light and creamy. Add the coffee and beat until mixed through.
6 Spoon the coffee buttercream into a piping (icing) bag fitted with a fluted nozzle and pipe onto half the biscuits. Top with another biscuit, then sandwich together. Pipe the melted chocolate over and top with a coffee bean, if desired.

coffee kisses

lemon and lime biscuits

Preparation time: 40 minutes + 1 hour chilling time
Cooking time: 15 minutes
Makes 30

150 g (5½ oz) unsalted butter, softened
170 g (6 oz/¾ cup) caster (superfine) sugar
1 egg, lightly beaten
1 tablespoon lime juice
2 teaspoons finely grated lime zest
2 teaspoons finely grated lemon zest
125 g (4½ oz/1 cup) plain (all-purpose) flour
60 g (2¼ oz/½ cup) self-raising flour
60 g (2¼ oz) marzipan, grated

LIME ICING
125 g (4½ oz/1 cup) icing (confectioners') sugar, sifted
1 teaspoon finely grated lime zest
1 tablespoon lime juice

1 Beat the butter and sugar in a bowl using electric beaters until light and creamy. Add the egg, lime juice, lime zest and lemon zest, beating until well combined.
2 Transfer the mixture to a large bowl. Using a flat-bladed knife, mix in the flours and marzipan to form a soft dough. Divide the mixture in two.
3 Working with one portion at a time, turn each portion out onto a lightly floured surface and press together until smooth. Form into a log shape about 4 cm (1½ inches) in diameter. Wrap in plastic wrap and refrigerate for 1 hour.
4 Preheat the oven to 180°C (350°F/Gas 4). Line two baking trays with baking paper. Cut the dough into 1 cm (½ inch) slices. Place on the baking trays and bake for 10–15 minutes, or until the biscuits are lightly golden. Remove from the oven and leave on the trays until cool.
5 To make the lime icing, place the icing sugar, lime zest, lime juice and 2 teaspoons water in a small bowl. Beat the mixture until smooth — if the mixture is too thick, add a little extra lime juice or water.
6 Dip the cooled biscuits in the icing. Decorate as desired.

lemon and lime biscuits

melting moments with jam and cream

Preparation time: 15 minutes
Cooking time: 15 minutes
Makes 20

125 g (4½ oz) unsalted butter
115 g (4 oz/½ cup) caster (superfine) sugar
2 egg yolks
1 teaspoon natural vanilla extract
30 g (1 oz/¼ cup) custard powder or instant vanilla pudding mix
90 g (3 oz/¾ cup) plain (all-purpose) flour, sifted
90 g (3⁹ oz/¾ cup) self-raising flour, sifted
160 g (5¾ oz/½ cup) strawberry jam
185 ml (6½ fl oz/¾ cup) thick (double/heavy) cream, whipped

1 Preheat the oven to 180°C (350°F/Gas 4). Line two baking trays with baking paper.
2 Using electric beaters, beat the butter and sugar in a bowl until light and creamy. Add the egg yolks one at a time, beating thoroughly after each addition. Add the vanilla and beat until combined.
3 Transfer the mixture to a large bowl. Using a flat-bladed knife, incorporate the custard powder and sifted flours until just combined. Using your fingertips, gather the mixture into a soft dough.
4 Roll 1 level teaspoonful of the mixture at a time into balls, then arrange about 5 cm (2 inches) apart on the baking trays. Flatten slightly with a fork and bake for 12 minutes, or until golden. Remove from the oven and leave on the trays for 5 minutes, then transfer to a wire rack to cool.
5 Spread half the biscuits with about ¼ teaspoon of the jam. Spoon or pipe the cream over the jam, then sandwich with the remaining biscuits.

continental slice

❋

Preparation time: 30 minutes +
　　6 hours chilling time
Cooking time: 5 minutes
Makes 36

125 g (4½ oz) unsalted butter
115 g (4 oz/½ cup) caster (superfine) sugar
30 g (1 oz/¼ cup) unsweetened cocoa
　　powder
250 g (9 oz) shredded wheat biscuits,
　　crushed
65 g (2½ oz/¾ cup) desiccated coconut
30 g (1 oz/¼ cup) chopped hazelnuts
60 g (2¼ oz/¼ cup) chopped glacé cherries
1 egg, lightly beaten
1 teaspoon natural vanilla extract

TOPPING
215 g (7¾ oz/1¾ cups) icing
　　(confectioners') sugar
2 tablespoons custard powder or instant
　　vanilla pudding mix
1 tablespoon Grand Marnier
60 g (2¼ oz) unsalted butter
125 g (4½ oz) dark chocolate
60 g (2¼ oz) Copha (white vegetable
　　shortening)

1 Line the base and sides of an 18 x 28 cm
(7 x 11 inch) shallow tin with foil.
2 Combine the butter, sugar and cocoa
powder in a small saucepan. Stir over low
heat until the butter has melted and the
mixture is well combined. Cook, stirring,
for 1 minute, then remove from the heat
and leave to cool slightly.
3 In a large bowl, combine the biscuit
crumbs, coconut, hazelnuts and cherries.
Make a well in the centre, then add the
butter mixture, egg and vanilla all at once
and stir well. Press the mixture firmly into
the foil-lined tin with the back of a spoon.
Refrigerate for 1 hour, or until firm.
4 To make the topping, combine the
icing sugar with the custard powder, and
mix the Grand Marnier with 1 tablespoon
hot water. Beat the butter in a bowl using
electric beaters until creamy. Gradually
add the sugar mixture, alternating with

fresh eggs

When buying eggs, look for those that are
less than 2 weeks old — they must be fresh
if you want good flavour. A fresh egg will lie
horizontally on the bottom of a glass of water. If
it stands upright it is old, and if it actually rises
it is stale. (This test determines the amount of
air in the rounded end of the egg.) Eggs should
be stored with the pointed end downwards, and
will keep longest in the refrigerator. Eggs at room
temperature will give more volume when beaten,
while cold eggs are easier to separate as the yolk
is less likely to break. Some people prefer brown
eggs as they look more 'wholesome', but they
have no more nutritional value than white ones.

the Grand Marnier mixture. Beat until
light and creamy, then spread evenly over
the biscuit base. Refrigerate for 1 hour,
or until set.
5 Place the chocolate and Copha in a
heatproof bowl over a saucepan of
simmering water, making sure the base of
the bowl doesn't touch the water. Stir until
the chocolate has melted and the mixture
is smooth. Spread evenly over the slice
and refrigerate for 4 hours, or until firm.
6 Cut the slice into squares to serve.

index

Page numbers in *italics* indicate
photographs. Page numbers in **bold**
refer to margin notes.